RAISING YOUR
Teenager

5 Crucial Skills for Moms and Dads

Dr. Roger McIntire

Copyright 2010 by Roger W. McIntire

All rights reserved under International and Pan-American Copyright Conventions. No part of this book may be reproduced, stored in a retrieval system or transmitted in any form or by any means, electronic, mechanical, photocopying, recording or otherwise, without express written permission of the publisher, except for brief quotations or critical reviews.

LCCN: 2010927898

Publisher's Cataloging-in-Publication Dataa

McIntire, Roger.
    Raising your teenager : 5 crucial skills for moms and dads / by Roger McIntire.
    p. cm.
    Includes index.
    ISBN-13: 978-0-615-35670-9
    ISBN-10: 0-615-35670-2

    1. Parent and teenager. 2. Parenting. 3. Child rearing.   I. Title.

HQ799.15.M35 2010   649'.125
                              QBI10-600042

Edited by Lorien Haavik and Eileen Haavik
Cover and interior design by Deborah Perdue of Illumination Graphics
Photographs courtesy of www.dreamstime.com and www.istockphoto.com

Printed in the United States of America
ISBN 978-0-615-35670-9

Summit Crossroads Press
410-290-7058
info@parentsuccess.com
www.parentsuccess.com

All names in the parent-child examples and not connected with published research are fictitious and do not refer to any person living or dead.

Parentsuccess.com -
resources, tips and online bookstore for parents, grandparents and their kids.

About the Author

Roger McIntire is Professor Emeritus of Psychology at the University of Maryland. He has worked with families and served as consultant and teacher of teachers in preschools, grade schools, high schools and colleges since the 1960s. He is the father of three children, now adults. Dr. McIntire's scientific publications, over 100 in all, address infant vocalizations, eating problems, strategies for teachers, high school motivation, and college retention.

Since the 1990's, Dr. McIntire has been the Corresponding Editor for parent-visitors to the *Cambridge Center for Behavioral Studies* website, behavior.com. His column, *Raising Good Kids in Tough Times*, appears regularly in the *Martinsburg Journal*, and other regional newspapers and websites.

Dr. McIntire's books include:

• *Teenagers and Parents: 10 Steps for a Better Relationship*, Summit Crossroads Press, 1991, Revised 5th Edition: 2000. Also published in Croatian, German, Indonesian, Korean, Latvian, Polish, Portuguese, and Slovenian.

• *Raising Good Kids in Tough Times: 7 Crucial Habits for Parent Success*, Summit Crossroads Press, 1999. Also published in Korean and Thai.

• *College Keys: Getting In, Doing Well, and Avoiding the 4 Big Mistakes*, Summit Crossroads Press, 1998.

• *Enjoy Successful Parenting: Practical Strategies for Parents of Children 2-12*, Summit Crossroads Press, 1995, Revised Edition.

> Dr. McIntire invites questions and comments on his blog, **www.rogermcintire.wordpress.com**. An archive of his tips for parents is at **www.parentsuccess.com**, which also offers resources and an online bookstore for parents, grandparents and their children.

TABLE OF CONTENTS

Preface: The Five Skills of Parenthood iii
Skill 1: *Knowing How to Talk With Your Teenager* 1
    Chapter 1: **Finding their wavelength** 3
        1. "Can we talk?"
        2. Why do teenagers take everything so personally?
        3. How much explanation is too much?
        4. Why don't they listen?
        5. What's the right thing to say?

    Chapter 2: **One-ups, put-downs and shortcut parenting** 15
        1. Where does shortcut parenting lead?
        2. Winners, losers and friends
        3. Parenting shortcuts often come up short
        4. A boy or girl with "an attitude"
        5. Too busy for mealtime talk?

    Chapter 3: **When serious topics come up** 25
        1. When serious topics get short shrift
        2. What is your teen's biggest concern?
        3. What to say about sex
        4. Fears during the teen years
        5. Worry warts
        6. What do you say about evil and terrorists?

    Chapter 4: **Loving and liking your kids** 39
        1. "Do you like me?"
        2. Two stories about too much feedback: Ben and Alex
        3. At the morning send-off, *give* a nice day
        4. Is your son or daughter still waiting for Dad?
        5. What makes up a father's rating?

6. How are you at compliments?
7. Who is to blame when the talking is over?
8. Watch your example

Skill 2: *Knowing the Family "Games"* 57

   Chapter 5: Spotting manipulative games 59
1. "Referees are fun"
2. "Let's make my problem your problem"
3. "Do I give you a 'nagging feeling?'"
4. The "hurry up" strategy
5. Let's build a parent's bill of rights
6. Blackmail at home
7. The aftermath of the lying game

   Chapter 6: Priorities in parent games 73
1. The priorities of the games are changing
2. "Testing, testing, are you still my friend?"
3. Siblings, pecking order and genetics
4. The most important games have life-long effects
5. The game of "You're responsible for my bad behavior"

   Chapter 7: Feeding snacks to the tiger 83
1. "Do what I say or I'll have a fit!"
2. Why is he so stubborn?
3. Parents can be enablers feeding the tiger
4. The moody teenager
5. Early bites of parent abuse

   Chapter 8: Family dynamics 93
1. Stay at home, now or later?
2. Preventing Mom abuse
3. Learning about your parents
4. Aunts and uncles chiming in

Chapter 9: Punishment: before 2 it's abuse; after 18 it's hopeless 101
      1. Should you "get tough?"
      2. Punishment alternatives
      3. Parent power and its limitations
      4. Mind your model for safety

Chapter 10: Negotiating 111
      1. When do they become deserving?
      2. Rewards, punishments and threats
      3. Magic, diet and strange behavior
      4. Our expectations of boys and girls
      5. The gender gap
      6. What's your discipline style?
      7. When parents disagree

Skill 3: *Steering Through the Minefield of Bad Habits* 129
    Chapter 11: The early basics 131
      1. Why are the basics so much trouble?
      2. Basic number 1: What, when and how to eat
      3. Meal time should be family time
      4. Even teenagers don't know what's good for them
      5. Basics 2 and 3: Bedtime and toilet training problems still hanging on
      6. Other basics they need to know
      7. Allowing practice
      8. Emergency basics

Chapter 12: Their privacy, your responsibility 147
      1. "I know what's good for me, just leave me alone"
      2. Computer companions, game addiction: "Why do you spoil my fun?"
      3. Bad movies: "All the other kids are going, why can't I?"
      4. The video obsession

Chapter 13: Setting limits 159
    1. Couch potato tubby: "I'm tired, can't I just watch my show?"
    2. Weight gain causes other early problems
    3. Thumb and finger exercise is not enough
    4. Rhythmic habits: "Quit bugging me, I can't help it"
    5. Is a Linus-comforter an obsession even if he's a teenager?
    6. Sports fanatics: "Coach says I have to go, will you drive me?"

Chapter 14: Meds, drugs and diets 171
    1. Medications: "I didn't get my pill today, can I help it?"
    2. Drugs and other troubles after school
    3 ADHD, Ritalin and diet
    4. Birth circumstances and health
    5. Depression in teenagers

Chapter 15: Sad, bad habits 183
    1. The SAD behaviors: sex, alcohol, and drugs
    2. Ten to 20-year-olds back on the bottle
    3. When should your teen start smoking?
    4. When can you relax and count on his common sense?
    5. Bad language habits: "Oh, come on, Mom, 'screw' is just a word"

Chapter 16: Other dangerous temptations 195
    1. Are the kids ready to try risky behaviors?
    2. When should dating start?
    3. Pregnancy: What about the father?
    4. Thinking is not dangerous to your health
    5. Sex and curiosity
    6. Who points the way through the dangerous temptations?

Skill 4: *Teaching School Strategies* 207

Chapter 17: School adjustment and separation shock 209
1. What can you teach your teenager about getting along at school?
2. Risk-takers have to feel safe
3. Separation shock: The first day back at school
4. Give your middle schooler extra help
5. Should students be paid?
6. "Mom, I can't go to school today."
7. How can you keep them motivated?

Chapter 18: "Who am I at school?" 225
1. Who is "gifted?"
2. Mixed blessings
3. Which teenagers are at risk for trouble?
4. Bullies, victims and hiding out in school
5. Magical thinking and mental habits
6. Yearning to be told

Chapter 19: How to do better on tests 237
1. Students who "have trouble with tests"
2. Practice counts at home, your teenager's attitude counts at school
3. How can your teenager make the grade?

Chapter 20: Keeping their attitude on target 245
1. Support the creative projects
2. The gender difference at school
3. Why do boys do better later on?
4. Time, teachers and tutors
5. Making the most of a school conference
6. How can you help their school measure up?
7. Taking school seriously

Chapter 21: Building character 257
       1. How do you pass along character?
       2. The subject that never came up
       3. It's easier to lead a camel than to push him
       4. Deflating peer pressure
       5. Resistance to peer pressure and LMS

Skill 5: *Coaching about Time, Money and Happiness* 267

Chapter 22: Spending time 269
       1. Teaching priorities
       2. Before we go on about the kids' time, have you prepared their future?
       3. Big projects and time management
       4. Summer games and looking ahead
       5. Gifts of time

Chapter 23: Spending money 279
       1. Teaching about money
       2. Home rules about money
       3. Money arguments
       4. More about money matters

Chapter 24: Pursuing happiness 285
       1. "I bet you can't make me happy"
       2. Picking a partner
       3. Growing up mid-season
       4. Happiness revisited

Chapter 25: Now that high school is ending 293
       1. When will it be over?
       2. Use allowances wisely
       3. Graduation, what's the big deal?

Chapter 26: Planning college or something else 301
    1. What do you want to do five years from Tuesday?
    2. College visits this summer?
    3. Financing college
    4. College Applications
    5. The market
    6. College is going to be a SNAP
    7. Tricks to college
    8. Raising the next generation—up

Epilogue: Start a parent group to keep ahead of their age 313

Subject Index 317

DEDICATION

To my wife, Eileen and her daughter, Lorien, two professional editors who helped me correct many stumbles in this manuscript; to my daughters, Pamela, Jennifer and Donna, whose lifestyle makes their father proud, and to my late wife, Carol, whose life is the example they so often follow.

PREFACE

The Five Skills of Parenthood

Most parents hope to raise bright, perfect children with presidential potential and without baggy clothes, black lipstick or metal piercings in unlikely, sometimes embarrassing, places. Yet daily family life can be complicated and parents find themselves facing a myriad of unanticipated problems. Arguments about the kids rank second only to money problems as a cause of marital strife and divorce.

I have answered over 600 emails from troubled parents in the last ten years while editor for the parenting section of behavior.org, the website that represents the *Cambridge Center for Behavioral Studies*. Letters from parent-readers of my column, *Raising Good Kids in Tough Times*, have also provided another treasure of insights, advice and comments since the 1990s.

This book describes five skills in 140 brief discussions that will help parents deal with their teen's adjustment and yet still maintain cooperation and a pleasant family atmosphere.

The letters and emails range from complaints about young teens who go into total snits in the mall to those who skip school and cause their parents many evenings of grief. From parents with a teen a little older, the complaints are about teens with drugs or alcohol problems, or teens with the social skills of a deranged badger. The list goes on.

Most parents have theorized about the origins of these problems. Here are some quotes from my readers and website visitors. From the believers in sibling influence: "Roy followed his big brother around even before he could walk! He has copied him ever since." Others believe in the birth order theory: "She's a third child so you have to expect she will be less aggressive and more artistic." The genetic explanation is also popular: "Knowing her father, it's easy to see where she gets her attitude!" And the critical experience theory is also common: "Ever since he got lost in the mall when he was three, Evan has never been comfortable with strangers."

All of these theories—about siblings, birth order, genetics, and early experiences—provide some understanding, but such past influences cannot be changed. Mom's or Dad's best opportunity to influence their teenager, really their only opportunity, is confined to the here-and-now—the present family interactions.

Dads may hold back on their emotions when trying to keep their teenager on the right path, especially when positive reactions such as compliments and praise are in order. It may be that we Dads set our standards too high or we may think that compliments will indicate weakness. Afraid we will lose our thunder, we leave the positive stuff, too often, to Mom.

It's hard for a teenager to measure up and be good enough if Dad holds back too much. One father told me that by age 15, he had taught himself to play the clarinet so well that he entered a school recital. He won an award. When he told his Dad, his Dad said, "Well, the clarinet is easy for you."

The same discounting attitude surfaced when a working mom told me that when she was in high school and announced her junior-year grades, all A's and one B in math, her father snapped, "Why didn't you ask for help? You know I've always been good in math." This daughter, even though she is now grown up and a mother on her own, still feels she will never be quite good enough in her father's eyes.

Many counselors believe that parents who hold back too much have a lasting negative influence on their children. Dr. Gloria Wright counsels corporate administrators who often suffer from depression. At a recent workshop she said that the root of the problem was often an unfulfilled need for acceptance from Dad. She noted that every man longs for the day when his father says, "You're the son I hoped you would be." Some of the audience had to leave the room to pull themselves together because, evidently, they had never heard that praise from Dad.

Daughters have had the same feelings I'm sure, and Mom's acceptance is just as important as Dad's. But Dads may hold back on the gushier stuff when it's needed most. Often called upon to be the heavies—*Wait 'till your father gets home!*—Dads may miss their opportunities to give deserved praise and admiration.

Questions and solutions raised in this book come from both parents and their teens who were my clients, regular readers of my column or website visitors. Common questions from the kids have been quoted by parents writing in, "Can we talk?" "Can I quit school?" "What birth control is best?" "I want a sister. You have more eggs don't you?" Parental questions range from, "How can I deal with her tantrums?" to "What about his computer addiction and her interest in alcohol, drugs and sex?"

The struggle to grow up is a confusion of emotions—a desire to break free from parental control is mixed with a desire for parental admiration and support. Of course, teenagers want to be on their own and different from their parents. And conversely, parents want their children to stay close to their example and be more like them. The compromise is in a gradually changing mixture of granting greater independence and decreasing control.

For tips about a particular problem, go directly to the index at the end of this book. Then, to bring all five skills together, start again and follow the chapters as they describe the necessary practice. Also, consider starting a parent discussion group in your church or PTA as described in the epilogue on page 313.

The five skills are:

Skill 1: Knowing How to Talk with Your Teenager. Parents and their teenager have talking styles that can create misunderstandings. A good start here and the whole week will go better.

Skill 2: Knowing the Family "Games." Strategies and maneuvers in family negotiations can go unrecognized, but parents who are aware of these games can smooth the family airways.

Skill 3: Steering Through the Minefield of Bad Habits. From bad movies, violent computer games and gutter language to sex, alcohol and drugs, identifying early signs of bad habits can help parents steer clear of trouble.

Skill 4: Teaching School Strategies. School can be the largest part of happiness in the teenage years. Any help that a parent can give will last a lifetime.

Skill 5: Coaching about Time, Money and Happiness. Habits and attitudes in using time, handling money and searching for happiness require important parenting guideposts.

As you apply these skills, don't worry that your teenager is not always listening—worry that he or she is always watching.

SKILL 1

Knowing How to Talk with Your Teenager

Parents build a reputation with their children and teens. A teenager learns to predict Mom's and Dad's opinions and reactions. Everybody in the family quickly learns what's coming up. Parents, worried because there is so much for their teen to learn and so much to correct, are likely to think, "I have to get in my objections to their mistakes when I can."

Sorting out bad and good behavior. Most of us parents can list the bad behaviors right away: Don't hit your brother. Don't make a mess. Don't yell. Don't forget your homework. Don't be so grumpy. Don't sit on the cat.

Good behaviors can also be listed, but the specifics are more difficult: Stay away from drugs. Show a better attitude. Stay out of trouble in school. When should "Staying away from drugs, showing a better attitude, and avoiding

> **Bad behaviors have their obvious moments, but good behaviors are often vague and ongoing and more difficult to highlight.**

trouble" be complimented? Bad behaviors have their obvious moments, but good behaviors are often vague and ongoing and are, therefore, more difficult to highlight.

Since we have a very good idea of what bad behavior is when we see it, and only a vague idea of what good behavior is, what is likely to attract our attention as we scan the present family scene? In the family routine, assigning blame can turn out to be the most common interaction.

Once "what's wrong" dominates the talking, the talking becomes a struggle (She takes things so personally!) and the kids are always ready to reciprocate a negative attitude, "He just wants to argue."

Family conversation would be safer and more pleasant if we could avoid always singling out the mistakes and assigning blame. This chapter begins with basic verbal habits that build a friendly atmosphere into conversations between you and your teenager.

CHAPTER 1
◆
Problems with finding their wavelength

1. "Can we talk?"

A right answer here and the rest of the day will be easier. Teenagers are not always straightforward with this crucial question, but they are always knocking at the window of your attention.

It's not easy to turn off the TV or interrupt your work when you hear, "Can we talk?" Yet your full attention is important.

At the beginning, your attitude is signaled by your behavior and posture. Remember that difficult teacher who never looked at you when you had a question? She or he always seemed distracted, looked away, and showed poor, tired posture. As you formed your question, your attention lagged, no doubt, and your confidence drained away. The listening habit requires facing up to your conversational partner, not "in their face" but looking at them and sitting up to show an attentive attitude.

The next part of listening requires an understanding of a fundamental difference between parents and teens in conversation. Teens, first of all, want to know, "What does this

Your attitude is signaled by your physical reaction.

> We parents thought the topic was the most important part.

conversation say about ME?" We parents thought the topic was the most important part! So at the beginning of conversation, parents need to put the blames, faults, and "quick-fixes" on hold while protecting a teen's always-fragile self-confidence. It's a risky moment for your teenager because of his or her vulnerability and possible embarrassment. Instead of saying, "You should be more..." and "Don't be so..." keep the conversation open by saying, "What did they say after that?" and "Then what happened?"

Talking about "it" instead of "you." Even offering a solution with the best intentions may be viewed as an opinion of your son or daughter's incompetence that implies, "You don't know, be quiet and let me tell you." A teen can become defensive before his real topic has even surfaced. So avoid the solutions and personal criticism by getting into the "It" instead of the "You" habit.

Conversation does not make a good competitive sport. Constant maneuvering to be a winner only makes someone else into a loser and turns the attention to the score instead of the topic. Not every tennis ball that is served needs to be returned; not every mistake must be noted and corrected. Without the competitive feeling, parents can set a less frantic pace.

> Conversation does not make a good competitive sport.

So mind your body language; conversation is more than what is said and heard. Slow down, avoid instant criticism, blame and accusations, and try the "it" instead of the "you" method. Often when a teen says, "You just don't understand!" he really means, "You're blaming me as a person; I want to start with something else." Good listening allows information to flow to you; poor listening only produces a game with an irrelevant score. That's why the first requirement of tolerance and acceptance is needed in the earliest part of each conversation.

Family arguments can become almost a way of life. It is a contagious habit started by a teen's confrontational habit or a parent's "fix-it" agenda.

 **Mind your body language.** We parents lean toward wanting perfection and the kids always seem to fall far short of that. Yet many parents feel that time with their son or daughter is in short supply and they'd better get their complaints and corrections in while they can. This can lead to frequent arguments.

Teenager: "This terrorism business is awful."

Mom: "Well, you just have to learn to live with it. The world is dangerous."

An argument has already started just because Mom is in a hurry. Of course Mom didn't mean that terrorism is not awful, she just moved on (too quickly) to giving advice (You just have to learn…) and missed the opportunity to agree with her daughter.

Mom is next in line for a "Yes, but…," an exchange leading to a louder argument because her pace is too fast. Now the focus has changed to winning the argument. Mom will make her points and her daughter will struggle to stay even. Distracted now by the argument, there will be little help with anxieties about terrorism. Sons and daughters in this situation just copy their mother's argumentative style of conversation and look for mistakes to correct. Once again, a simple conversation has become a competition.

Develop and use the following habits to avoid an argumentative style with your teenager:

Habit 1: Deliberately slow your talking pace. The high speed of your chatter may leave little time for agreement and companionship. Make time because even a smart-mouth teenager lacks your skills for putting thoughts into words quickly.

Habit 2: Keep frequent eye contact and an attentive posture that shows you are listening.

Habit 3: Confirm you are listening by occasionally repeating, without opinion, what your teenager said.

> **Mom didn't mean that terrorism is not awful, she just moved on (too quickly) to give advice.**

Habit 4: Avoid too many fix-it solutions given too quickly. They make you sound superior and encourage defensive arguments.

A parent's first question in a conversation can often be a signal for a teenager's attitude. Instead of a question, "Did you leave all of this stuff out of the refrigerator?" try a statement instead, "These things will spoil out here; help me put it all back."

Even "What did you do in school today?" can produce an argument if it demands more memory and creativity than your son or daughter can muster late in the day. Specific and neutral questions may be less threatening such as, "Did you have music class (art class, basketball) today?"

> Make time because even a smart-mouth teenager lacks your skills for putting thoughts into words quickly.

Some questions, reserved only for children, should be avoided altogether because they are traps that are bound to produce argument: "Why don't you do as well in math as your brother?" Better: "Let's go over your math homework together." And "Why don't you turn off the TV and get to your homework?" can be more constructive and less critical by saying, "I'm here to help with your homework until supper, after that you're on your own."

Teenagers will often say you don't have an influence, but you do. Even when they say they are not listening, they are. Most teenagers need a lot of attention and time to talk as well as time to listen. If the argument routine soaks up the family air time, who will they turn to for those important conversations?

2. Why do teenagers take everything so personally?

Productive conversation with a teenager is hard to come by. Many parents find their son or daughter an elusive prey not easily cornered or impressed.

This resistant attitude has a history, of course. When Mom says, "We need to talk," she is not likely to be introducing, "I really like the clever way you answered our neighbor." Teens and preteens learn the signals early.

Slow your talking pace. We adults are not so continuously personal and goal-oriented with each other, but with our kids we don't get many chances and we almost always have a point. If we get more than a sound-bite moment for a complaint, we're likely to go on to complaint number two. In the rushed schedule we all have these days, it's easy to send the message, "And while I'm thinking about you, another thing I don't like is …"

The hard fact is that it takes time to do more than list complaints and give instructions.

We adults are very good talkers. We have decades of practice translating thoughts, feelings, and reactions quickly into words. Teenagers, even ones with snappy comebacks, are less practiced and, in fast conversation, they often lose out. So first of all, deliberately slow your pace so they can go slow, too. Moments of silence are not bad; they allow the conversation to be two-way.

Watch your signals: folding your arms, getting louder, and turning away all have their messages. Avoid the "Always-the-Critic" habit and make sure your "liking" shows through. Many parents have told me, "As far as my own parents are concerned, they loved me but I'm not sure they liked me." Let this not be said by your children.

Here are some cautions for parents I have learned.

Caution 1. Children and teens look first for what the conversation says about them personally. Since we parents thought the subject was the important part, we conclude, "He always takes things too personally." Keep the subject on a third person basis as much as possible as you would with an adult. Use "it" and "what" instead of "you."

Caution 2. Avoid the "quick fix" temptation. The most important subject may not have come up yet. "Why don't you…" "You should try…" "Don't be so…" all have the potential of closing a conversation too soon. They also indicate a superior position and may be offensive. If you tell me you had trouble getting to work, and I

> **M**ost kids need a lot of time to talk as well as time to listen.

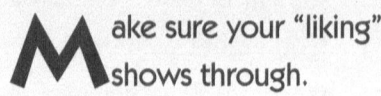

Make sure your "liking" shows through. tell you to try another route and start earlier, you might think, "What nerve! I just wanted to gripe about the traffic and you turned it into a driving lesson!" A real conversation stopper.

Caution 3. Use reflective statements occasionally. Often a teen's first remarks are only an expression of feelings and are short on facts. A reflective reaction is sympathetic and says you're listening.

Teenage son: "What a crummy math teacher."

Mom: "Hard to get that stuff the first time." Mom sides with her son by not falling into an argument ("You shouldn't talk about your teachers that way"). She just agrees with the feeling by reflecting, in other words, her son's unhappiness with math, but she says nothing new while waiting for more information.

> The most important subject may not have come up yet.

3. How much explanation is too much?

Repeated arguments about limits are a challenge to both the kids and parents. The teen nags for permission and the parent has to explain once again, "why not." Repeated explanations and reminders may serve as a source of entertainment for a bored teenager, and they may also encourage a son or daughter to look for loopholes.

Mark: "Mom, why do you care if I stay at Maureen's all afternoon?"
Mom: "I already told you why, Mark."
Mark: "We're not going to do anything, her parents come home at six anyway."
Mom: "No."
Mark: "You don't trust me."
Mom: "It's not about trust. It's too much free time and too much temptation."

> Often a teen's first remarks are only an expression of feelings and are short on facts.

The next day it starts all over again: "Mom, Maureen wants me to come over. I won't stay long. I promise to come back by four. Can I go?"

What events maintain Mark's nagging? The topic always brings disagreement and reprimands, but he continues to bring it up. If Mom and Dad haven't agreed ahead of time on the answers and change the reasons they give Mark from time to time, they may occasionally disagree with each other and lose confidence in their decisions. The inconsistency encourages Mark to keep trying because one day he thinks he might hit the right combination of attitudes and get to go. He probably will.

Mom and Dad need to pinpoint their agreement with honest reasons for the decision.

Mom: "Your father and I have decided you can't be over at Maureen's when her parents are not there. We think it's too much temptation. Right, David?"

Dad: "Right."

> Repeated explanations and reminders may serve as a source of entertainment for a bored teenager.

Now will Mark stop nagging? Probably not, but the amount of nagging will decrease, and arguments will get shorter because the situation is now clear and fair, at least Mark's parents think so, and it gives them confidence. For Mark, although it's still not what he wants, the rule is concrete and detailed—not much room for loopholes.

How much explanation do you need? When you learn to drive a car, you don't need to know how the pistons, cams, and ignition systems work. As long as the accelerator, brake, steering wheel, and ignition key work consistently, you can learn very well. Learning becomes a nightmare if the car (or the instructor) is inconsistent, balking when cranky, difficult to shift, and forgiving one day but a perfectionist the next.

Teenagers learn from a reliable set of rules in the same way. Consistency is enough. Understanding why parents are anxious about a boy's afternoon plans may help, but repeated explanations will not.

In the early years of psychology, E. R. Guthrie and G. P. Horton conducted

> Consistency is enough. Understanding why parents are anxious may help, but repeated explanations will not.

a study concerning insight without understanding. A cat was placed in a problem box. As most cat owners know, cats enjoy exploring small spaces, but it is not in a cat's nature to be content in a confined place. A pole in the center of the box could open the door if the cat pushed it. The cat tried various escape methods, mewing and scratching the door at first, and then as it wiggled around, it bumped the pole and gained its freedom. This was not an insight any more than a child's first use of a doorknob is an insight. Nevertheless, a certain accident did produce a good result, and when the cat was put in the box again, it was a little faster getting out.

History does not tell us how many scratches Guthrie and Horton suffered, but they did put the cat into the box several times. The cat escaped faster and faster by rubbing the pole in the way a cat rubs a person's leg, releasing the latch (and snapping a picture of itself each time). The pictures showed that the cat didn't learn anything about latches, springs or hinges. Mechanical engineering is above the mind of a cat. It didn't face the pole thoughtfully, grab it or scratch it. The cat only learned the necessary: stand here, rub yourself against the pole, leave.

Children and teenagers do the same. From rattles and noisy toys, to spoons, doorknobs, computers and TV remotes, to pleasing Dad and Mom, their skills develop and race far ahead of their understanding. So it's best to be brief and conservative with explanations of rules—especially when a teenager seems to be enjoying the argument.

4. Why don't they listen?

I occasionally visit chapters of Club Mom. This national organization helps moms get together to support each other and get advice from other moms who have "been there."

One evening the concern was that kids don't seem to listen to what their parents say. The length of time the kids pay attention is about normal (two microseconds) but the reaction ("Huh?") and the effect ("What?") makes Mom weary after two (or six) repeats.

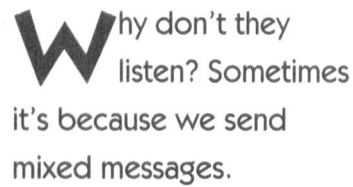

Why don't they listen? Sometimes it's because we send mixed messages.

"Teresa, I'm not going to tell you again. Get your shoes. The school bus will be here any minute."

"OK, just a second." Teresa is still staring at her video game—no attention deficit here!

"Teresa, the bus is coming, get your shoes," Mom yells from the kitchen.

"Just one more zap and I win."

"Teresa!" Mom is now screaming as a flash of yellow passes by the window.

"OK!" Teresa grabs her shoes and backpack and hobbles out the door. One sock hits a puddle so she hops while she covers it with a shoe.

"Teresa, your lunch money!" Teresa reverses course, snatches the coins from Mom and goes stumbling down the driveway with shoestrings trailing in the mud. Mom has lived through another send-off hassle.

Avoid mixed messages. Why don't they listen? Sometimes it's because we send mixed messages. "Teresa, get your shoes on" is said while distracted by TV and filling lunch bags.

"Where are they?" she may say while the shoes lay under her chair.

Later, "Don't poke your sister," is said while distracted by kitchen routine. Mom's gaze and attention is on lunches and Teresa sneaks another poke at her sister.

Teresa has a natural sound barrier to challenges that threaten her freedom to do exactly what she wants, and it is not penetrated by glancing remarks from a distracted Mom. She requires a touch on the arm until she looks at her Mom, and then Mom should deliver the message with a firm voice—eye contact, tone of voice, and facial expression all working together to help Teresa sort out the important remarks from the din of noise coming in.

Little extras also make a difference. "Can I have a knife to fix the electric outlet?" This query requires a conscious change in Dad's expression to let his budding scientist know the request is out of the question. If only the audio works (No!) but the video is out of sync, then, to a teenage mind, it may seem there is, again, a loophole.

Experienced adults use these cues, and their common sense, to extract the true importance and meaning of comments at work and at home. But common sense and experience are in short supply for 10-to 20-year-olds. So for these moments of discipline, make sure your teen gets the message. Keep your shoulder tapping, eye contact, posture, tone of voice, and facial expression in synch and deliberate when it's important.

Develop a habit of facial expression that will break through the haze of misunderstanding sometimes deliberately created by the kids. Just raising the volume will not necessarily improve communication and it makes your own day less enjoyable.

> **Keep your shoulder tapping, eye contact, posture, tone of voice, and facial expression in synch and deliberate.**

Try helping your spouse or other relatives who may deal with your children to use these cues to get the messages across—the whole house could become a little quieter.

5. What's the right thing to say?

Talking to your son or daughter, or even with nieces and nephews of the extended family, can challenge an adult's conversational skills. The usual questions so easily handled by adults, "How are you doing?" "What's new?" seem to tax the creativity of a shy young mind. If the pace is too quick, a teen can be terrified of making an embarrassing flub.

If you're not used to talking to other teenagers or just trying to get your own to be a little more friendly, realize they may have hidden fears.

Remember those holiday conversations you had with aunts and uncles? What stress! I still remember the dread of being told, "Go say 'Hello' to your grandpa."

"Hello, Grandpa."

"Well, Merry Christmas, Roger. How's school going?"

"Oh, it's OK." (Twisting the truth a little to avoid possible embarrassment.)

"Are you keeping up with your piano lessons?"

"Well, I kinda stopped after school started this year."

Pause. "Sorry to hear that. Are you going to start again?"

Pause. "Ah, well, yeah, I might." (Twisting the truth a lot.)

Pause. "Are you getting along with your brother?"

Pause. "We get along OK." (Crushing the truth beyond recognition.)

"Well, be good."

"OK. 'bye." Ah, relief, another anxious task over.

Later I felt guilty when Mom reminded me of what I should have said when all I was doing was trying to survive the conversation. "Did you tell grandpa about your school project? Did you mention the book he sent you? Did you tell him about the tractor you saw that's just like his?"

No, no, and no, I forgot.

I just wanted to avoid giving my eavesdropping brother something to humiliate me with the rest of the day. Escaping without embarrassment was as high as I aspired.

A teens' greatest fear is likely to be embarrassment. They are easily embarrassed by a minefield of questions.

Crowded family get-togethers are not good times for teaching potentially embarrassing lessons but they are good times for a teen to talk and for adults to listen. Here are some ways to bridge the generation gap and still help a son, daughter or relative with the stressful moments of conversation.

Conversation strategy 1. General questions (How's school?) are often difficult for the kids because they demand the most memory and creativity. These qualities are not likely to be available to a socially stressed teenager. Specific questions can produce an easier conversation: "What was that tune you were playing when we came in, it sounded familiar" or "Do you have Mrs. Anderson for history class?"

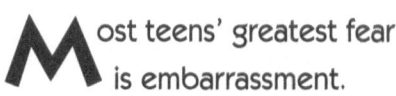

Most teens' greatest fear is embarrassment.

Conversation strategy 2. Beware of questions that invade the sacred ground of fears and inadequacies such as: "Do you have many friends in school? Are you doing better in school now?" Stay close to known strengths, especially at the beginning: "You're doing really well in math this year."

Conversation strategy 3. Often questions about a third thing, not you, not me, are better than items that may be too close to home. "You're in the new middle school now, pretty different from your old school I guess," is much more comfortable than, "How are you doing at the new school? Do you have lots of friends?" These questions tempt teens to stretch the truth and then keep the conversation short lest they be discovered.

Conversation strategy 4. Questions with loopholes are better than the blunt kind. "Playing a lot of soccer these days?" or, "Do you like games better than the practice?" would be better than, "Do you go to all your soccer practices?"

Conversation strategy 5. Compliments are always welcome, as long as they don't draw too much attention to the self-conscious teenager. "Nice shirt, I like it," is about the shirt and is better than, "That shirt looks good on you, you're really filling out," which is about the person, not the shirt.

Conversation strategy 6. Avoid pointed conversations in situations too public. Talks that might go well in private might be too threatening with the whole family at the dinner table.

The best strategy is to admire any reported progress and leave plenty of time for a teen seeking the right things to say.

> Beware of questions that invade the sacred ground of fear and inadequacies.

Strong opinions and outright criticism are off the mark in these short and infrequent contacts. Leave the heavy stuff for longer and less crowded situations.

CHAPTER 2

One-ups, put-downs and shortcut parenting

Put-downs and one-ups can disrupt and even stop useful family conversation. They give too much attention to winners and losers. Then parents have a tough time getting any information about the temptations and troubles the kids are facing.

1. Where does shortcut parenting lead?

Both parents and teenagers have verbal habits and attitudes that can turn an otherwise valuable conversation into an argument.

Put-downs are tempting parenting shortcuts to get the point across, but they are too vague and personal. For example, vague complaints are sometimes triggered by a particular infraction, "Only ignorant people use that language." Of course he knows you're talking about a particular (usually four-letter) word, but, for impact, this objection is expressed as an insult of the whole person.

Better to avoid the general put-down and focus on the present mistake. "Don't say that word in our family; it's rude, abusive and as an adjective to "car" it doesn't even make sense. It sounds as if you don't know enough language to express yourself."

I agree this is still a put-down but, focused on the behavior with some extra explanation, it is more constructive. This will not immediately take care of the problem, but at least he may search for other words next time. When he finds them, let him know you are impressed.

One-upmanship is also a bad habit. It usually comes near the end of a conversation when we decide to declare ourselves the winner. We often like to see starts and ends where only a continuing process of change exists. For example, as parents we hope to persuade our children to avoid bad habits at the very beginning. No smoking, no drugs, no alcohol.

Conclusions on the end of these conversations are better left off. "So I don't ever want to hear that you…" is better replaced by a reason, "Once those brain cells are gone, they don't re-grow."

These discussions will continue beyond the age of 20. The best help will be your reasoning against the bad habits and your example. Statistically, smoking kids come from smoking families. Alcohol abuse breeds alcohol abuse—regardless of Mom's and Dad's rationalizations or excuses for their own behavior. Teens copy better than they listen.

> One-upmanship is also a bad habit. It usually comes near the end of a conversation when we decide to declare ourselves the winner.

"You can't quit school. You won't get anywhere without an education."

"They don't teach anything I need to know."

Now Mom could remain inflexible, stay with put-downs and disagree, saying her son needs to learn the basics and also he doesn't know what needs to be learned.

She could also go with a one-up. "Your father wouldn't have the job he has today if he had quit, and I wouldn't be teaching without my extra schooling."

A better approach might be to look for agreement. Certainly there's more to learn since we were in school. Maybe he is right about what he needs to know and it's time to ask the school for a better menu. Just working out what needs to be learned may help him start learning it, whether the school decides to teach it or not.

2. Winners, losers and friends

All candidates for public office know it's dangerous to admit they are not perfect, right, efficient, and the best. But candidate strategies are not productive in family conversation.

> **Teens copy better than they listen.**

Parents can easily slip into office-candidate modes with their own children, but unlike political campaigns where only the candidates are judged, at home everyone is in for the long haul and everyone is a player on stage. This makes a big difference.

How to keep the conversation going. Conversation should not be a game. Games have an end and winners are declared. For every winner, we must also declare a loser. If parents play to win, the games will be short because parents have more practice putting everything into words. Sooner or later Mom and Dad won't find anyone who wants to play.

"How was school?"

"Same old thing."

Mom has a choice right away. She could say, "Come on, something must have happened." Mom's score is up one, daughter's is down one. Or Mom could leave the score at zero saying, "Gets pretty dull in the middle of the year."

"Yeah, everybody's going nuts having to stay inside all day—even for soccer practice."

Now Mom could say something else agreeable and understanding, "This weather has certainly been awful." Or she could play to win, "Well, at least you get more time to get your homework done." Daughter's alarm goes off. Her defenses are activated, here comes Mom's topic and criticism.

Parents can easily slip into this efficiency mode. Mom might say, "I don't have all day to blabber; she needs to spend more time on her work, so I have to steer her in the right direction when I have the chance." This is a parenting style reserved for speaking to children,

> **At home everyone is in for the long haul and everyone is a player on stage.**

of course. We know the conversation will end soon, and we want to wrap it up with our point.

Better to forget about the ending and let most conversations explore situations without conclusions. Neither side wants instructions or advice anyway.

The real disadvantage to adversarial games is that losers quickly become non-risk takers. Then creativity goes down and conversations increasingly become defensive and short. Sometimes both sides end up just attacking and defending.

> **Take your time with reactions as you would with an adult.**

Often parents suspect that these confrontations have become a habit and an entertainment. They are inefficient encounters for a teen looking for the satisfaction of dominating at least in a conversation at home.

You don't have to be drawn into these tennis-game conversations. It isn't necessary to return every argument with a retort. Take your time with reactions as you would with an adult. Avoid the personal comments as much as possible and encourage your offspring to think (and talk) like an adult.

With the time-limit ignored and the score left at zero, future talks will be frequent, more productive and probably more interesting.

3. Parenting shortcuts often come up short

Shortcuts in parenting can make us feel we are protecting and disciplining our kids when we are actually giving no specific help or instructions at all.

"You need to try a little harder to be nice at these family gatherings."

"Your manners were terrible, and you should be nicer to your cousins."

"You had better shape up and make an effort, Jeff."

Mom's well-intended advice to Jeff is little help. Trying harder, showing better manners, being nicer, shaping up and making an effort are not specific. They could strike a teenager as magical ideas.

> **You don't have to be drawn into these tennis-game conversations.**

These general directions leave enough loopholes to allow Jeff to avoid any new effort and still have room to defend himself later. The old adage, "It's easier to get forgiveness than permission," applies to much of the teenage years if rules are vague and general.

> Sometimes we engage in magic to avoid direct confrontation and sometimes because we have no answers.

Catch 'em being good. Better to be specific and say, "When your aunt asks you about school, stop and answer her." Better yet, "Stop and tell her about your science project." The specific suggestion is no longer magical, and if Jeff takes the advice, he can be more pleasant next time.

Sometimes we engage in magic to avoid direct confrontation and sometimes because we have no answers. We only know we want things to be better. Mom may think, "He knows what I mean. I don't have to spell it out for him." Vague criticism makes it easy for her but confusing for a teen.

"Jeff, you had better start acting right."

"What did I do?"

"You're always fighting with your sister."

"She starts it."

"Well, you'd better learn to get along."

Not much information in this exchange. What is "acting right?" What strategy should he learn to "get along" besides the one he has already learned—blame the problems on his sister?

Better to quit this game of teen-parent dodge ball and be specific, "Jeff, when your sister calls you names, tell her you won't talk to her when she does that and then leave." Will this advice solve the problem? Probably not, but a specific plan gives Jeff a little more control and Mom a way to be truly helpful.

Separating sister and brother is sometimes necessary but doesn't teach much. It just satisfies Mom with a temporary stop to the arguing, and her guilt is relieved because she has "done something" about the problem.

Often it's our definitions, or lack of them, that get us into trouble. "OK, you can ride your motorbike out on the road, but be careful." What does "be careful" mean? Go slow? The whole idea of getting on the road is to go faster. These two are going to have another argument about the motor bike. Mom should be specific or refuse to let him use the road.

To make real progress, Mom will need to identify actions of her son that will directly contribute to a better adjustment. Usually this requires coming up with specific and clear alternatives to bad behavior.

The best advice you can give your teenagers is not spoken but shown. Your example is the best control you have in arguments. If you lower your voice they will lower theirs, and you'll have a better chance to get your suggestions across to them.

> **Often, it's our definitions, or lack of them, that get us into trouble.**

4. A boy or girl with "an attitude"

The Southern Regional Education Board studied 40,000 typical high school students, not stars and not low performers, in 2002. While 84 percent of girls said it was important to continue schooling after high school, only 67 percent of boys agreed.

Many parents, teachers, and counselors believe girls are more socially skilled at an earlier age because of time spent on regular chores with Mom. Girls attract encouraging support, acceptance, and admiration for the chores they do at home and then for the schoolwork as well.

On the other hand, boys may get fewer requests and put up greater resistance when asked. They may still want to be competent and admired for it, yet they seem to ignore their chances and shun the gushier praise.

Parents shouldn't be misled by a son's bland reaction. To prove he is not easily influenced, a boy will often fend off practice and the praise that should go with it. He may seem to be trying hard NOT to be happy.

A son's lack of enthusiasm may lead his parents to conclude that compliments and admiration won't work with him so they should lay off the positive approach. This is a bad mistake.

Practical and active projects can inspire boys. Projects in home improvement, cooking, financial management, small business management, mortgages, stock markets, computer management, applied science, and tracking diet and exercise all encourage boys as well as girls to be proud of their abilities right now. Even abstract subjects can include practical projects.

College applications won't ask about these "non-academic" skills, but schoolwork should help your son or daughter with concerns now, at their present age. "Someday you'll need this," is not enough. They need a good answer to, "What good is this (homework, project, learning, work) now?"

The girl advantage. At the end of the 1990s, 133 women earned bachelor's degrees per 100 men. In 2010, 142 women will finish college for every 100 men.

Is this a school problem or a home problem? Or both?

Parents tend to cave in to flack from boys while resisting any flack from girls. Insistence on girls doing their chores and homework develops their skills and their enthusiasm for work done successfully. Boys may receive less encouragement from exasperated parents or because boys dodge the work altogether and, as a result, fall further behind in the experience department.

Another source of the gender difference may come from the trend to single-parent families. The U.S. Census says one-third of our children are raised in single-parent households, up from only one in 10 in 1960. These children are five times more likely to be raised by single Moms than single Dads. Girls will have a same-sex role model while the boys may be looking to teachers, relatives, and media for guidance part of the time. Whatever the sources of influence, the differences between boys and girls in school are worrisome.

> In 2010, 142 women will finish college for every 100 men. Is this a school problem or a home problem? Or both?

By 11th grade, 44 percent of girls had become proficient readers but only 28 percent of boys made the cut in a 2004 study. Only 41 percent of boys said they "often" tried to do their best work in school, compared with 67 percent of the girls.

> **P**arents tend to cave in to flack from boys while resisting any flack from girls.

Girls and boys need any encouragement we can give, and the most useful encouragement will be time—time with homework, time for talking over career plans and time for looking into the prospects after high school graduation. Don't be discouraged by a teenager's apparent lack of enthusiasm for these topics. Kids often feel obligated to act independent (I don't need any homework help) and competent (I know all about those college programs).

It's a parenting pitfall to become discouraged by the apparently indifferent attitude of a teen and leave him or her short on attention.

When your school asks for volunteers for field trips or away games, encourage Dad to take up the opportunity. It will give him a chance to learn more about his children, and it will set a standard for students who need the male example.

In those conversations at home, remember that often a teenager's number one fear is embarrassment. Avoid beginning with a question you know they can't answer, "How are you going to learn if you don't pay attention?" Start with information they might want to know, "Here's a flyer about that golf scholarship in Virginia. What do you think? Maybe we should drive down and take a look."

5. Too busy for mealtime talk?

Mealtimes can provide a snapshot of general family happiness, but many families have given up the tradition. Breakfast is either nonexistent or taken on the run in the morning rush. Lunch takes place at either school or work. Shawna eats by herself in the evening, in front of the TV, and her big sister snacks and sends text messages to friends. Dad and Mom eat supper while watching the news. Little time is left for serious talk.

> **D**on't be discouraged by a teenager's lack of enthusiasm for these topics. Kids often feel obligated to act independent.

Without mealtime practice, parents and kids forget how to talk to each other. Family conversation is reduced to sound bites. Parents try to get in their points and the kids mimic the latest patter from TV sitcoms where zingers have been memorized in advance. Big mistakes can result.

Joey at 13 years old can talk at a breakneck speed if he thinks talking fast and acting impatient will get an "OK" when a slower pace might produce a "no."

Joey: "Dad, Ross is getting a ride with his family to the school football game tonight. Can I go?"

Dad, still looking at his e-mails: "Ah, what did your mother say?"

Joey: "She said it's up to you."

Dad, still looking at his computer: "OK, as long as you are with them."

With more mealtime practice Dad might have recognized Joey's devious use of "family" and said, "Who did you say was going?"

> Without mealtime practice, parents and kids forget how to talk to each other.

Joey might have said (still in the rapid fire mode) "Ross and some of his family." And then with a very painful face, "Dad, he's waiting on the phone."

Dad, knowing Joey's impatience, might have said, "Let's talk it over. Do you mean Ross's brother is driving?"

Joey would say, "Dad, I don't know who all is going. Anyway, Ross's brother is a good driver, can I go or not?"

A teenager's view is on the short-term, but Dad should have paid attention to more than going to the ballgame. Certainly Joey's idea of what makes Ross's brother a good driver is not enough.

Dad missed all this and while the consequences were serious, they were not tragic. Ross's brother was arrested for driving under the influence, and it caused a family row. Dad said Joey had mislead him, Joey said he hadn't. Little was said about drinking and driving.

Are you too busy for a slow pace? Most of our social skills are learned from our parents' example and cannot be learned at a fast pace. Often violence,

Most of our social skills are learned from our parents' example and cannot be learned at a fast pace.

tantrums and general aggression in teenagers are habits learned to fill in the gaps where reasonable slow-paced discussion and practice have been left out because we don't have time.

One mother told me she was too busy to sit down with the kids at supper. "They've got to learn to shift for themselves," she said. What choices will they make in learning to "shift for themselves?"

Sit down with the kids for at least one meal every day—deliberately use a slow pace, no newspaper, no TV, no distractions. This is a great time for family stories. Avoid starting remarks with "you," don't try to steer the conversation, don't try to "win" and, oh yes, don't expect any changes in the first month.

CHAPTER 3

When serious topics come up

Discussing issues and new ideas are part of the "brain exercise" all teens need. On sensitive topics, parents may be tempted to "tell" their teen what to do instead of discussing it. With their long experience in the verbal skills of conversation, parents can usually "win" if that becomes the goal. When this happens creativity goes down and the kids duck any conversation that seems risky.

1. When serious topics get short shrift

When every childish remark is evaluated, and every conversation is treated as a game of ping pong where each return requires yet another return until someone wins, parents will often "win," and the kids will harden their defensive style. They'll take fewer chances in talks with Mom or Dad, and the exploration stage will be shorter next time. If you are always "telling," you have no time for listening.

The volley of blames and "Yes, buts" directs the conversation away from the ideas and toward the person. "Why would you think that? That shows that you are to blame (wrong or off-base)." In half-hour TV sit-com's, put-downs can be entertaining, but in life-long family relationships, positive support should be the main ingredient.

Family conversation where honesty, risk-taking, and creativity are encouraged requires a moratorium on who is right or wrong. For discussions

If you are always "telling," you have no time for listening.

of character and personal or religious values, put the score card and your conclusions aside so that all aspects of the topic can be brought up.

Recognize good points in a conversation: "Good point!" "That's right!" "I never thought of that!" Avoid blaming and name-calling your teen for wrong or misguided remarks. That only cuts the conversation short and makes your teenager eager to leave.

Avoid criticisms that are likely to be taken personally and internalized by your teen-child. "What (internal personal flaw) makes you so inconsiderate, so negative? Why don't you pay more attention to what you're saying? What were you thinking of?"

"Inside blame" is a dangerous parental habit because your teen is viewed as "having" a nearly unchangeable character. Outside blame is better but may still be offensive because it can imply the teen is a doltish sheep following the influence of others: "Where did you get that idea?" "Who told you that nonsense?" Instead, try to keep the "you" out of it: "That's a different point of view." "What would your teacher think of that?"

Stay on the lookout to give credit for remarks that show growth, common sense, and maturity.

Megan: "Gary said marijuana and stuff like that are no different than the stuff in the drugstore."

Dad: "Well, they're more dangerous than that."

Megan: "Sure. Why does he think they're illegal anyway? My gym teacher says all those drugs are dangerous."

Here's a crucial moment for Dad. What kind of credit should he give Megan for her common sense position?

If he gives the credit to Megan's teacher for driving her to the right conclusion, he doesn't give credit to Megan at all: "You should listen to your teacher, he's right!"

But he shouldn't take the credit for himself either by saying, "Well, isn't that what I've been telling you all along?"

Dad should give the credit directly to Megan for getting it right: "Your teacher is right. And you're right to sort that out—you're smart about things like that."

Stay close to your kids. Be willing to discuss ideas without blame and criticism, it builds a good relationship, and even though there may be no conclusion, it's still good "brain exercise" and sets the stage for more.

2. What is your teen's biggest concern?

Both adults and teenagers would list family, security, and friends near the top of concerns. But most teens and preteens would also include being liked, viewed as competent, and seen as "cool."

Knowing the kids' priorities can be an advantage in parenting especially when a son or daughter is facing a hard job:

Anthony: "These new math problems sure are tough, I haven't got one yet."

Mom: "New ones are always confusing, but you've always had a knack for working them out." Mom had a choice here. She could have pointed out that Anthony needs to try harder or she could have said how competent he is when the going gets tough. Emphasizing Anthony's competence was a good choice.

> "Inside blame" is a dangerous parental habit because your teen is viewed as "having" a nearly unchangeable character.

Parents should look for chances to bolster their teen's self-respect, likable characteristics, and competency. This helps establish a teenager's confidence to resist temptations later on. When counseling teens who experimented with drugs, I often heard this incredible remark, "Well, what did I have to lose?"

"What did you have to lose?" My parent outrage almost kicks in. I barely resist saying, "You've got your whole life ahead of you!" Why doesn't this teenager know what he has to lose? Hasn't anyone told him about his own special abilities? His own great promise? A little more conversation with him, and I get the feeling nobody ever has. Maybe they felt he would become conceited with too many compliments. But that possibility is far less likely and

Hasn't anyone told him about his own special abilities? His own great promise? A little more conversation with him, and I get the feeling nobody has.

less dangerous than creating a teen "with nothing to lose."

Kids who feel they are not liked at home become more vulnerable to wild temptations with peers in an effort to be accepted. With embarrassment as the major fear of teenagedom, the stage is set for "going along with the gang." The dangerous and risky behaviors of sex, alcohol, and drugs, are much more likely when you're down on yourself.

A parent's memories of teen years are usually the same. As kids, we parents were worried about embarrassment and yearning to be liked.

It's easy for teens to lose confidence in themselves. The TV constantly presents people larger than life, "perfect" people who are quick-witted and beautiful. Parents, always hoping for improvement, can undermine their teen's confidence by dwelling on shortcomings.

So a parent's quick fix and advice in conversation with her daughter or son may lack any message about good points. Even when parents feel they have helped, the overall impression may be, "You're still far from perfect."

For the next few weeks, promise yourself that you will find one good thing about your teenager to compliment every day. It can give the kids a new impression of themselves—and their parents. The change is not likely to be immediate, but a teen's self-image is bound to change for the better when the emphasis is on good points.

3. What to say about sex

A parent's first encounter with embarrassing questions about sex is likely to occur during toilet training. By the time your budding teenager is 10 or 14 the questions can get downright difficult. Of course, parents are concerned about what their teen will repeat to others, about what temptations or experimentation might begin, and what consequences, pregnancy or health problems might develop.

When fielding the first questions about where babies come from, keep your answers simple. Anatomical questions should be answered with the correct words. Slang terms may seem easier and the polite language of sex may seem awkward. But crude language is much more likely to be repeated at the worst moment.

When the later discussions come along, include a balanced discussion of baby care to fill in gaps left by pop-culture TV's view of sex. Twenty-seven minute programs keep the focus on the short term. It's a parent's job to broaden and lengthen the view.

The discussions will also set the stage for later relationships, so it's a good time for parental strategy sessions that exemplify the attitude you want your teenager to have.

The topic requires some private discussion between parents.

Dad: "Matt said he wanted to take a shower only once a week. He was sort of kidding, but he didn't buy my answer that he would smell bad."

Mom: "I just said that's ridiculous and told him to go take his shower. I'm not going to have a discussion with a fourteen-year-old when he's just being silly."

Dad: "That's good enough for now, but I hope interest in girls will help us out on this one."

Mom: "He needs good common sense in taking care of himself. If we help him avoid simple-minded ideas such as 'nobody cares what you look like' or, 'social rules serve no purpose,' the moral sense and the common sense have a better chance to take root."

When it comes to conversations about sex, learning the right attitude is more important than a plumbing lesson.

Matt: "Why don't you have more babies? You have more eggs, don't you?"

> Promise yourself that you will find one good thing about your teenager to compliment every day.

Mom could go different ways with this out-of-left-field question. She could go the route of "why in the world would you ask a thing like that! You'd better keep your mind where it belongs!" This approach will assure us that Matt will keep his mind anywhere but where Mom wants it.

Another approach for Mom could keep the long-term considerations in the picture. "Matt, when you have a baby, it's a growing person and you have to be ready to care for it—not just feeding it and making sure it's clean and comfortable, but babies need time for talking and learning, too. You love your dog but sometimes you are too busy to walk him, right?"

> It's a parent's job to broaden and lengthen the view.

"So you don't want another baby because it's too much trouble?"

"You and your sister and your dad and the dog have all my love right now."

4. Fears during the teen years

Whether it's sex, pollution, global warming or impending disaster, the fears in the minds of young teenagers are sometimes hard to take seriously. It's easy for adults to react by correcting their son or daughter:

"Darnell says pollution will make us all sick."

"Donna, where we live there's not that much pollution."

"There's pollution everywhere."

"Yes, but it's much better where we live."

"But Darnell says..."

Every parent has struggled with trying to calm down a scared teenager. There's often a thread of truth in what a teen says, but the notion of probabilities that an adult would consider are hard for a teenager to subtract from the anxiety.

Adolescent fears will usually not yield to common sense: "Larry, we are not going to be hit by a meteor."

"It could happen."

"Well, it could, but the probabilities..." (Larry's face goes blank).

Telling a teenager he's wrong won't reduce his fear. Especially when words like "probabilities" are involved. Better to merely make observations that are calming, "No meteors have landed around here."

"A long time ago they did."

"I guess that's right."

Mom's measured agreement puts Larry in better control of his own thinking about meteors. Often the lack of control has fueled the panic. When a parent denies the thread of truth in a teenager's remarks, the conflict keeps the insecurities high.

> There's often a thread of truth in what a teen says, but the notion of probabilities that an adult would consder are hard for a teenager to subtract from the anxiety.

Irrational fears come in several variations. Fears such as Donna's fear of pollution and Larry's fear of meteors come from suggestions. A little bit of information, until more is added, has become a dangerous thing. The best approach here is to add more information without discouraging your learning teen. Put-downs only risk that the fears will become secret ones.

First of all, keep your head when your teenager is losing his. This includes not only controlling your emotion but also avoiding being drawn into pointless arguments or reprimands such as, "Just calm down and get hold of yourself."

Better to keep your voice low, slow and sympathetic.

Arguments and intense attention can build unwanted habits such as using fears to attract a kind of social confrontation that is entertaining.

Second, remember that emotional fears ordinarily don't yield to logic. Some fears do have a real history such as a frightening dog or bee sting that has planted a fear lasting far beyond what is reasonable. But logic has little to do with fears and telling a child to "snap out of it" won't help.

Irrational fear is just that, and an adolescent will not be talked out of it. Over time, probably months or years, the more common experiences with dogs or bees will mellow the teenager's reaction. Mind your model when you are in the feared situation. Your

> Telling a teenager he's wrong won't reduce his fear.

> **Logic has little to do with fears and telling a child to "snap out of it" won't help.**

reaction is being noted in detail. You are in the lead and your teenager is watching.

Some fears seem to have no basis at all. Panic attacks where breathing is difficult and a teen becomes agitated can arise without any apparent reason. The situation looks suspiciously like a tantrum but without the anger. Like a tantrum, it may be attention-getting, but panic attacks can be real and it's time for a checkup by your family doctor. Such "panic attacks" can be a symptom of asthma or other respiratory problem.

> **Mind your model when you are in the feared situation.**

5. Worry warts

Have you ever felt your worries were out of control? Have you ever "read" three or four pages and realized your mind was elsewhere? Have you found it difficult to listen to a teacher because you were so preoccupied with something else?

In working with behavior, you can easily assess improvement or failure by the person's action. Did he change his actions or not? But there are times when the thoughts are the problem, not the actions.

A student complains, "I keep worrying about the same thing over and over."

A concerned teacher says, "You're not listening to me!"

The counselor asks, "What is distracting you?"

The parent complains, "You always seem to be daydreaming."

Both adults and teens often have repetitious thoughts expressing dread of some threatening future event—a test or a difficult social situation. One way they can relieve these fears is to take action—even if it's just a small action.

This "taking action" strategy allows fears and unanswerable questions to be replaced with small actions. "How will I get into college if I can't pass English?" gives way to writing a list of possible questions and answers coming up on the English test. Practicing a classroom presentation in front of family can ease worries about the class performance.

If worry creeps back in, it could be put off to a "worry time." The student designates a time such as "the 20 minutes I always have to wait for the bus." Then, when worry interferes at other times, the student uses a positive form of procrastinating, "I'll think about that on my worry time."

In addition to taking action and setting a designated worry time, some worries can be reduced by seeing the other person's point of view.

"I just know I won't make a good impression on Kevin," Marie said.

In this case you might ask, "What do you think Kevin is worrying about, Marie?" Maybe he is also worrying about making a good impression on you."

Armed with this view "from the other side," Marie can discover something concrete to do about the worry. Instead of fretting about being liked, she can plan to do some liking of the other person. This strategy relieves worry by providing some control instead of leaving the situation to fate. Most friends and dates will like people who show they like them.

> One way they can relieve these fears is to take action – even if it's just a small action.

Liking your companion means listening well, remembering details, and asking questions. We all need a little proof that we are liked. Did you remember I had a test coming up today? That my brother is coming home from college? That I like pizza with mushrooms?

"I wish he/she would ask me about myself sometimes!" is the common complaint of a boy or girl friend thinking about moving on.

So when worries become a plague, these three habits can help: find little actions to replace big worries, move fears to a worry time, and, in social situations, consider the desire of others to be liked as one guide to successful social solutions.

6. What do you say about evil and terrorists?

Terrorists remind us everyday how evil they can be. As we parents and grandparents try to deal with the war and help our young ones understand terrorists we may fall into our old habit of doing most of the talking.

My first thought of what to say to my grandsons after being horrified by the latest TV images was one of retribution, justice, and punishment. But who should be punished? The most guilty have committed suicide, and the others are dispersed and they are unknown at the moment. My first impulse was off the mark and advocated more evil instead of less.

We may find that one country is more guilty than another because it encourages the terrorists and provides a place for the preparations to be done. Yet innocent people live in those countries as well as the guilty. Most citizens have no idea what their government is up to any more than we know about ours, let alone what one small part of the population is up to. The innocent in those countries are just as precious as the innocent here at home.

> First of all, teens need their chance to express their reactions and ask their questions.

The difference between ourselves and terrorists is that we do have principles concerning the welfare of the innocent and the value of human life. We do not seek a world dominated by any religion chanting decadence and hate. We seek a world of peace for all people.

So how can we help our children as they see and hear about terrorists? First of all, teens need their chance to express their reactions and ask their questions. We're tempted to take a severe and intense tone in these conversations because we feel strongly and want our children to understand how very serious this is. But that attitude can inadvertently intimidate their part of the conversation.

Better to remain calm and focus on the "part truths" of their remarks instead of lecturing, confronting, and correcting errors. Your model is important if they are to continue to tell you their view and be guided to a reasonable approach to this subject.

Nan: "Those people are awful! They should all be killed!"

Mom: "They are awful." (Mom's focus is on the undeniable truth and leaves the rest for later in the talk.)

Nan: "We should hunt down the ones that helped."

Mom: "Yes, and all the ones who are guilty should be punished." (Mom agrees without getting into a frustrating argument about how hard this will be.)

"Mom, why are people so bad?" Here Mom is tempted to say, "You're wrong, only a few people are bad." Mom is exasperated and angry also, and it's easy to find fault with every comment on the topic.

But now her daughter needs close companionship with someone on her side. And Mom hopes Nan will say what's most upsetting, so it's better to stay well clear of disagreement and corrections:

"I guess some people seem to be bad right from the start, but others live in or were brought up in bad situations."

"Will the bad people get us?"

"I don't think so. In our country we try to protect each other. You help your friends at school, and they help you."

In the longer view of the weeks ahead, Mom and Dad should also point out positive events that provide a balance from the continual shocking replays on TV.

At home, parents should show an attitude that sets a thoughtful example for the kids who will create the security of the future. Our children see terrorism as a new threat, but we parents know that terrorism under many names has been around for centuries.

Our grandparents worried about attacks on our shores in the 1940s. Our parents practiced diving under their desks in the '50s. Bombs, biological warfare, and ICBMs hounded us throughout the twentieth century. The new century brings jet planes crashing into skyscrapers and other forms of gruesome attack.

Still the fears of terrorism aren't quite the same for the present generation. Parents of the '50s had more time to help with the anxieties of their children. Stay-at-home parents were more common. The pace of life was slower, and the media was less graphic and a smaller part of a family life.

Today, we are afflicted with "time poverty;" we average 52 hours a week at our jobs. The breadwinner of a single parent family may be even busier. Even with enough money, modern parents often suffer from chronic time poverty.

What can a parent say to a frightened teen or preteen who has become overdosed by media coverage of the newest terrors?

Remember the five rules of good listening skills.

    1. Look at your son or daughter during conversation.

    2. Show encouragement by facing your child and sitting in an attentive position.

    3. Avoid advice and solutions that send the message that you are superior. Use questions instead.

    4. Keep your pace slow so your teen can steer the conversation some of the time.

    5. Refrain from beginning too many comments with "You."

Mom: "You look a little down, you should get out and get some fresh air. Why don't you take a walk?"

Starting with all those "you's" makes Mom seem pushy. A better start might be, "Another warm day. Let's take a walk, it always makes me feel better."

Walks or rides together are great ways to learn more about your teen's worries. Even gaps of silence are acceptable in the car or walking around the block.

Damon: "Did you see those awful people on TV? Why are they always fighting? Do you think they will come over here?"

Mom: "I don't think so. Weren't those people fighting about their own government?" Mom soothes feelings a little and then gives the lead of the conversation back to her son with a question. If she is also looking at her son and showing good attention, she will be able to help with his anxieties instead of risking argument.

Damon: "I guess so, but they would fight with anybody."

Mom: "Don't be so concerned with what they say on TV. Why don't you do your homework reading, then you won't get so upset." Mom has slipped back into her advice mode using "you" again and she implies that Damon is wrong to be upset. Let's give Mom another chance: "Well, at least they are over there, but I know it can be scary."

This conversation will take extra time to help Damon. Good listening doesn't allow for a quick fix. Mom might want to be efficient, taking over and getting to the point, but disturbing and emotional topics require a slower pace.

"Telling" will take less time, but listening will be more help.

CHAPTER 4

Loving and liking your kids

Whatever the children do, parents react in some way—negatively, positively or with indifference. They easily spot the bad behaviors but their reactions to good behaviors are usually vague and non-specific. Yet the most important parental job is to find good points and be sure they know you found them. This responsibility is often overlooked in the daily rush. Without it, support dwindles to accidental recognitions of good performance, and a teen can conclude he's not quite good enough, again.

1. "Do you like me?"

Liking Tyler. When parents lose sight of what they admire and give up on expressing it, the parent-teen relationship deteriorates fast. I heard the following conversation while visiting a family who had asked for help when a new baby joined the first-born, 12-year-old Tyler:

Mom: "Leave the baby alone, Tyler."

Tyler: "I was just going to pat him."

Mom: "I know what you were going to do. Now just stay away, you will wake him!" Mom had a choice here, but she went with her first impulse. She could have said, "I like to pat him too, but it will wake him and he's tired."

She had the same choice later that day when Tyler stumbled against the kitchen table, and a glass of juice fell over. Mom said, "You are so clumsy! Look what you did!" She could have said, "Oh, look what happened! Better pick up the glass and get a paper towel."

Mom's first impulse in both incidents was to identify the fault; she emphasized the mistake and blamed Tyler, the person, "You will wake him; you are clumsy!" If she went with another choice, she could have emphasized a situation that she and Tyler were dealing with together, "It will wake him. Look what happened."

I'm sure it didn't make much difference to Tyler on these two occasions, but when "you" is too frequent in the days and months ahead, Tyler will have a less positive impression of himself and a very different relationship with Mom.

> When "you" is too frequent in the days and months ahead, Tyler will have a less positive impression of himself and a very different relationship with Mom.

Liking Clifton. With Clifton, Mom has a hard time dealing with his frequently disagreeable and angry attitude. When I asked her for examples of Clifton's good behavior, she had trouble getting started but finally came up with common ones such as "doing well in school" and "being nice to his baby brother." I asked her to look for specifics of these during the next week and compliment Clifton when he showed success.

At our next meeting she reported an odd reaction after she said, "I liked the way you helped your brother with getting his toy when he couldn't reach it."

Always ready with a snappy comeback, Clifton said, "What's the matter with you?" And after a third week of Mom looking for opportunities to compliment him, Clifton asked, "Do you like me?"

"Clifton, I love you. Of course, I like you," Mom said.

"Wow," said Clifton, already 12, but just finding out that his Mom not only loves him, she likes him!

Here's a good resolution for parents: Vow to find and highlight a new behavior of your teen each week and tell her or him you like it. Kids often feel obligated to be independent, so don't be discouraged by the apparent lack of enthusiasm your teenager has for your compliment.

Dads seem to have the most trouble with this assignment. Some Dads overlook the good and focus on the vulnerable spots. The kids tend to pull away from their Dads and cover up. But when praise and kind comments about specifics are a habit, the love becomes believable.

Parents and their children should be friends. Not in the sense of enjoying the same music or having friends in common or playing similar roles in the family, but in the sense of enjoying time together, looking and supporting the strengths and successes in each other—teen still imitating parent. Like a searchlight looking for sparkles to highlight.

> "Wow," said Clifton, already 12, but just finding out that his Mom not only loves him, but she likes him!

Some people have another focus. Their search overlooks the good we try to do and zeros in on vulnerable spots. We pull back and risk very little. Because we know what they're looking for, we cover up.

Aim your searchlight carefully. What are you looking for?

2. Two stories about too much feedback: Ben and Alex

Ben. When 14-year-old Ben came into the school counselor's waiting room, he sat on the nearest chair. Mom sat on the opposite side of the seating area. "Sit over here," she said. He moved next to her. "Don't swing your foot like that!" Ben picked up a magazine. "Be careful with that," she said. He turned a page noisily. "Shh, I told you to be careful!"

As it turned out, one of the complaints from both teachers and Mom was that Ben was bossy and constantly critical of others. Ben had picked up Mom's contagious example of low tolerance.

Had Mom ever thought about whether Ben should always sit next to her? She said she had not, but she was afraid he "might do something wrong over there." Some boys might deserve such distrust, but for Ben, Mom had a

> Mom jerked Ben's psychological leash regularly and often.

correction habit with a little reprimand thrown in. Mom jerked Ben's psychological leash regularly and often.

To break the psychological leash, a good rule is, "Don't correct or instruct your child or teen until you are certain a mistake is being made." It's the rule that all adults expect you to apply to them, and your children and teens deserve the same treatment until they prove otherwise. Hesitate before reprimanding, correcting or discouraging a behavior that is not worth the trouble.

The psychological leash is worth breaking for additional reasons. Corrections that are intended as reprimands may become rewards over the years. The leash could replace Ben's responsibility for himself. We all know a boy who does just what he wants and depends on Mom to make all the corrections. And we all know kids who, once away from Mom and off the leash, have no clue and no experience with how to act.

Alex. When Alex was a young child, Mom liked him, even when he got mad. She thought he was so cute, and she couldn't blame him without smiling. Even when he was abusive to her it just showed how smart he was and she let her pride show. But then Alex began growing. He became obstinate and abusive to his younger siblings. What's a mother to do with a difficult child who is, "So cute, but mean sometimes, too."

When Alex was in preschool, not everyone agreed on how cute he was. He became an angry terror, aggressive with other kids and uncooperative with the teacher. "She doesn't always treat me nice," Alex said.

Alex at 14. On home visits, a counseling student observed Mom dealing with sometimes-nasty Alex, now 14. Actually, Alex's behavior seemed more interesting than his mother's because, as the student said, "The behavior was so outrageous, the answer must be there somewhere. Alex argues with his mom all the time, I think he likes being disagreeable."

"What did Mom do?" I asked.

"She talked to him and tried to calm him down."

"Did that work?"

"Not really. It's a running battle."

All parents, at times, suffer from "unconditional positive regard." No matter what Alex did, Mom regarded him positively. She liked him and tried to encourage him. However, if Alex was going to learn what was right and what was not, the signals needed to be separated and clear.

Alex also had a speech problem, and Mom helped him with flash cards with basic sounds represented in pictures for Alex to practice.

"What's this?" Mom would say holding up a picture of an apple.

"A...fal," Alex said, partly because of his disability but also out of laziness.

"Very good," Mom said even though she told

> Alex's Mom thought Alex was so cute, she couldn't blame him without smiling.

us he had responded to the picture with the same mistake for weeks. She said she didn't want to discourage him, but she hoped he would stop making so many mistakes.

We asked Mom to give Alex clearer signals. She learned to frown and just say "No" when Alex was wrong and brighten up and say, "Very good," only when he was right. Finding the right level of satisfaction for when to brighten up and when to frown is not easy. Once learned, it is a challenge to switch yourself on and off abruptly and also remain consistent. To break through Alex's cloud of distractions he needed to hear clear messages about what was unacceptable not only with flash cards, but also in his daily behavior. He was too old for his childish disposition.

Mom practiced reacting more slowly, more consistently and sometimes negatively with a frown and disapproval. To get the right reaction, Alex had to be more careful. As he learned better social habits, Mom became more natural, appropriate in her reactions and more helpful to Alex as he grew up.

"When I was a kid, I think I just didn't know what to do," Alex said.

3. At the morning send-off *give* a nice day

Ask your average parents to name their most difficult time of day, and if they still have school-age teenagers, they will vote overwhelmingly for the morning rush.

This is no surprise to any parent who has replaced the school bus because her adolescent procrastinator missed the yellow one. After Mom finally gets him out of the house and has a moment to relax, he REAPPEARS at the door—"Mom, the bus was gone!"

Notice he didn't say, "I missed the bus," he says IT was gone. Whose fault is this? The bus driver for coming right when she was supposed to?

The best progress on this problem will come from getting the priorities straight. If the most pleasant parts of the morning routine come first, and life's regular drudgeries, like finding your socks, are left until you hear the brakes of the bus, the procrastination will only get worse.

So the enjoyable parts of the morning—breakfast, comics and fooling around—need to follow getting dressed, lunch decisions and last-minute homework. It's too easy for a young mind to procrastinate to the very end if he or she dreads the last task.

> The best progress will come from getting the priorities straight.

Another tempting strategy is to just say, "Well, if you miss the bus you'll suffer the conse-quences." But the consequences will include a more complicated day for Mom or Dad. For the kids, just missing school might be OK. They would suffer in the long run, but teens don't often think more than 10 minutes into the future—that's how we got into this problem in the first place.

The positive consequences have to come in small and frequent amounts during the times when the choices of what to do next are being made.

One mother I know uses stickers for getting each task done in order and on time every morning. Another Mom uses points on the allowance chart—one point for getting dressed by 10 minutes of seven, one for having all the items for school ready at the door by seven o'clock. Then the less crucial activities can proceed without points.

> The consequences have to come in small and frequent amounts.

Many parents I talk to about the morning problem also offer this advice: Pay attention in the morning. A little extra praise for getting the morning tasks done and extra conversation and attention at breakfast will give the day a better, and not so lonely, start. School problems you would ordinarily never hear about often bubble up on school mornings. Don't try to reach conclusions in these brief moments.

A rushed morning conversation is not a good time for arguments either. It is a good time for listening and a positive send-off. If your kids seem unresponsive, it's still best to try out a few days of the new morning schedule before deciding, "They are just not morning people."

4. Is your son or daughter still waiting for Dad?

Dan finished his paper route about six p.m. and then waited at the commuter train station for his dad. Actually, this same wait had been tragically disappointed a year earlier when his dad had died of a heart attack at work, but 13-year-old Dan concentrated on each arriving train car trying to "will" his father to reappear in the doorway. The passengers hurried off from the station, and Dan realized once again he could not wish his father back.

I met Dan on that platform when we moved to Chicago. I was also 13, and my family was waiting for a real estate agent to show us possible places to live.

When the train left, Dan looked down the empty tracks, but he knew no other train would come. Only my parents and I were left on the platform.

As Dan walked by, my dad asked him if he had an extra Tribune in his bag. Dan sold the extra to Dad, and we talked about how long his paper route had become.

When the real estate agent arrived, I stayed with Dan while my family drove around looking at available housing. We started a life-long friendship that day as we drank cherry Cokes and waited for my family to return. I didn't know we were also waiting for another dad.

We were roommates in college before Dan told me why he was at the station that evening.

Too many dads, by choice or circumstances, miss their chance to get off the afternoon commuter train and spend time with their kids. The lesson here: take the time now to be with your kids. The years are crucial but very short.

Single-parent families feel these demands more. A close friend said that when she and her husband separated, she wanted to be sure her son kept a close relationship with his dad. She knew she would always support and remain close to her son, but to be sure her husband would remain dedicated, she agreed that he would have custody and she would be the weekend parent.

> Too many Dads miss their chance to spend time with their kids.

Every day, even with a partner, each parent needs to put aside time to give to the children while they still have it to give.

The early years seem to require the most attention because the needs are obvious. A five-year-old requires lots of help. Once children reach ten, it seems they're starting to care for themselves. But as the children grow into teenagers, the problem areas actually multiply and become more dangerous, harder to evaluate, and harder to control. Sex, drugs, and cars are becoming part of childhood at earlier ages in each new generation.

Dan tried to be an engineer like his dad, but he found another path teaching comparative religions at a local college. Going to work, he used the same station where we met.

He takes every chance to be with his kids. He says we have only seven years from ages 11 to 18 and by 18 most opportunities will have gone by. He's right.

Lafcadio Hearn, journalist and 19th century author of Japanese life and history, said, "No man can possibly know what life means, what the world means, what anything means, until he loves his child. Then the whole universe changes and nothing will ever again seem exactly as it seemed before."

Dan's father kept a diary and Dan was very pleased to find he was mentioned on nearly every page. If you discovered that your parents had such a diary, what would you hope to find there? Would you hope to find the many hours spent with you, listening, supporting, talking, and helping? Or would the family stories be confined to a few pages with criticism, correction, and child-rearing problems?

> Every day, even with a partner, each parent needs to put aside time to give to their children while they still have it to give.

Chances for conversation appear and disappear from one situation to the next. Mom has a tough role switching back and forth from friend to enforcer of rules and back again. It's an imperfect, but necessary, alternating process. What memories and examples of your parenting style and conversation will your teenagers remember, model and pass along to your grandchildren?

A friend told me her Dad had been silent on his 1960s war experiences until her mother died and left them with only each other—daughter and father. Then he told the story of keeping a fishing boat at home for an army buddy who, taken as a prisoner of war, died when his prisoner transfer river boat was bombed. After her Dad returned from the war and heard of his friend's death, he said he sold the fishing boat and traveled a long way to give the money to his buddy's mother. It was a war story of respect for those who serve and also one of honesty and empathy for those left behind.

Another friend told me that when his family farm fell on hard times during the depression of the 30's, his grandfather said he was required to put the farm up for a sheriff's auction to pay off the mortgage and taxes.

The sheriff, in evaluating the farm's holdings before auction day, made remarks such as, "Twenty hogs, more or less. Thirty chickens, more or less." His grandfather realized that the sheriff was telling him, "You can sell some of these for a few extra dollars before the auction; it won't be noticed and it will

> **Mom has a tough role switching back and forth from friend to enforcer of rules and back again. It's an imperfect, but necessary, alternating process.**

be all right." The sheriff's compassion allowed his grandfather to support his family until he had another job.

Some stories just bring warmth and laughter to family gatherings. My Dad always got a laugh telling—again—about the barnyard duck that could peck and bully everyone but Grandma who was so quick she could grab and tumble the duck aside without getting pecked.

Dads often repeat stories about their own parents to help the next generation with the challenges of raising children. A young mother told me that her dad, at 55, had survived a hike to the bottom of the Grand Canyon and back. This stressful two-day hike required weeks of preparation—stretching his endurance until he could stand the steep grades down and up.

> **This opportunity for a Dad and son to celebrate was lost, taken instead as an opportunity to criticize.**

When he returned and described his trip to his father, the only response was, "Maybe you lost some weight." This opportunity for a Dad and son to celebrate was lost, taken instead as an opportunity to criticize. Young Mom made a mental note to do better.

As one parent advised, "Make your face light up now and then when you see the kids; that's really all they want."

Another father told me he had helped his daughter make a dress for her Girl Scout badge. At the award ceremonies, his daughter worried that her dad would be embarrassed to come and say it was he, not her mother, who had given the necessary instruction. But her face lit up when her father arrived and stood with his daughter for the badge.

> **Make your face light up now and then when you see the kids; that's really all they want.**

As a Dad, it's always a good day for a story, an example, some directions, and some praise for the children.

5. What makes up a father's rating?

It's hard for us Dads, but when thinking of how to show appreciation for, let's say, a gift from our son or daughter, we need to gush a little: "What a great idea! I've been thinking about one of those for a long time. Right on target. Thank you!"

> A parent's compliment is a highlight for any child even if he or she doesn't show it.

Holding back can turn a child's longing into frustration and then to teenage cynicism about pleasing Dad. Once that stage is reached, the turn-around will take a real effort: As one father said when his son complained about how long it took to make his very impressive science project: "It's great. People won't ask how long it took. They'll ask who did it."

A parent's compliment is a highlight for any teenager even if he or she doesn't show it. Parents may think they are having little effect, but just remember that kids often feel obligated to act cool and pretend that praise doesn't make a difference. Don't be misled. The reaction may be bland, but the long-term accumulated effects will contribute to a great relationship.

Brent's incidental education. Brent spent two days camping with his father and then a day with him on bring-your-child-to-work day.

The special days didn't include detailed plans, but Brent remembers a lot about them. Those of us who went to work with our fathers have a special place for that memory.

Brent told his teacher about it: "Dad's a dispatcher. He says you have to be careful to get it right and to get along with the other people."

Although it was not a spectacular event, Brent remembers nearly all the details of his day at Dad's work, and the influence of his dad is strong. Brent's father probably did not intend to teach Brent anything specific, but during his time with Brent he was sharing his values and his example.

Brent's mother has an impact also. Possibly in this case her influence will be underestimated because she is with Brent a great deal and the influence is subtle and obscured at times by less pleasant but necessary interactions. Along with the dispositions and attitudes of other adults, teachers and coaches, his parents add to the collection of values Brent encounters that dominate his attitude as he grows up.

How are you handling this important aspect of character-building? Here's a checklist for Dads and Moms:

Character Building Strategy 1. Are you more often the encourager or the critic? It is tempting to react to the mistakes of others and forget to recognize the other person's successes. The father who chooses the role of encourager improves the family atmosphere and has a closer relationship with his kids. The critic builds distance.

Character Building Strategy 2. Are you available to listen or more often in a hurry and distracted? Your reaction sends many messages including how much you value the other person. Chances to be close to a teen are missed when a father is overly talkative about his concerns or silently aloof when his son or daughter has the airways. An available parent will be blessed with available children.

Character Building Strategy 3. Are you more often a model of cooperation or competition? Fathers have experienced a competitive world and want to provide their children with a strong spirit for success. Yet Brent's busy father emphasized cooperation so that Brent would have a social life to enjoy as well as things to possess.

Character Building Strategy 4. Are you more often a man with time available for your kids or a man with other priorities? The priorities of love are best assessed not by words but by how you share your time.

What values do you want to model for your son or daughter? Try keeping a diary for two weeks to note how you spend your time with your tween or teen. What values do you think will come through? How do you model those values? How would the four strategies above measure up in your diary?

What will be on the wish-list of your son when he looks back to your diary years from now? John F. Kennedy, short-changed by his father, I think, often thought of his older brother Joe as a father-model. In his teenage years he wrote: "If the Kennedy children ever amount to anything, it will be due more to Joe's behavior and his constant example than any other factor."

6. How are you at compliments?

No matter how competent Dads may be in other categories, most of us awkwardly fumble incoming compliments, gifts, and praise.

Don't hold back on the thanks just because his reaction is short, mild, or even self-depracating.

So when you express your appreciation to your own children, don't hold back on the thanks just because their reactions are short, mild, or even self-deprecating. Few of us get much practice handling compliments so, like most of us, Dads are also out of practice. The main effect of such appreciation usually hits years later in subtle ways.

Many of us fathers and grandfathers avoid positive reactions and thank you's. We're afraid we'll lose our control and power in family discipline because the positive stuff may be taken as a sign of weakness. But it's the "positive stuff" that has the most influence in the long run. Threats may intimidate a teen who is acting up, but it's the positive messages that tell him when he's doing right. Punishment and reprimands only tell him he is wrong—try again.

Also, showing a model of punishment is bad. The kids will eventually start copying it themselves and as they get bigger, you'll have to look for a new strategy. Better to model a strategy that doesn't depend on the other person being smaller or weaker. Anyway, you can't make a garden just by pulling weeds—you have to nurture something.

We fathers particularly have to watch the example we set. It may not be obvious that your kids are imitating you, but the day will come when they will say, "I can't believe I said that, I sound just like my Dad (or Mom)."

So how should a Dad return the Father's Day compliment? What gesture or comment can he watch for? Father's Day might be a good time to practice the habit of highlighting a few of the skills and progress the kids have made:

"Happy Father's Day, Dad."

"Thanks, Alisha, maybe we could go out for lunch after your soccer game to celebrate. Your Mom told me you were the one who suggested that the team go over to shake hands with the other team after the game last week. That's a good thing to do."

"Oh, that. I just did what our coach had told us to do earlier."

Alisha's response to Dad's compliment is mild, as Dad's would be, but the support will have a good effect in the soccer games to come.

> You can't make a garden just by pulling weeds — you have to nurture something.

Don't be stingy with your compliments. Make sure your kids know they are what you hoped they would be.

7. Who is to blame when the talking is over?

Teenager bashing has been a favorite pastime as far back as history goes. From Socrates of ancient Greece, who complained about disrespectful teenagers, to President Clinton's proposals concerning guns in schools, the kids seem to be the long-standing problem. But when the numbers are considered, you get a different picture.

President Clinton was right to worry about the gun violence in our culture, but he got the age wrong when he singled out murders by "13-year-olds with automatic weapons" as the top priority. Actually FBI reports show that peak gun violence is among 47-year-olds (Clinton's age at the time) who are twice as likely to commit murder as 13-year-olds. In fact, 83 percent of murdered children, 85 percent of murdered adults, and over half the murdered teenagers are killed by adults over 20.

Even respected organizations exaggerate the statistics when bashing teens. The American Medical Association reports "half a million" unmarried teenagers become pregnant each year (the actual number was about 280,000). They also claimed a "30-fold" increase in teenage crime since 1950 but don't mention that since 1985, comprehensive national reports show no increase at all.

Also, overall teenager drug and alcohol use has remained constant or decreased over the last 15 years. For example, the percent of high school seniors who tried cocaine within the last 12 months is down from 12 percent in 1984 to 5 percent in 2000—not good, but better.

For adults, the statistics are grim. Federal crime statistics show federal drug offenders (almost all of them adults) up from 12,000 in the 1980's to 25,000 in 2005.

Of course, supporting programs for teens is money well spent. But when teens are also blamed as the primary cause, it lets us adults off the hook.

Articles about bad teens blame, first of all, teen depravity made worse by rap music, gangs, and lenient courts. Mentioned later on, or not at all, are causes that are too expensive for the well-paid men and women of Congress and state legislatures: poverty, racial injustice, unemployment and bad schools.

In fact, for every act of violence or sexual offense committed by a person under 18, three such crimes are committed by adults against children and teens. Here's the topper: the 1992 report of the National Victims Center found that of 12 million women raped, 62 percent were raped before they were 18. The average age of these girls was 11, but the average age of their attackers was 27! Men over 20 cause nearly 90 percent of the pregnancies among middle school girls and 70 percent of the high school pregnancies. Even if every high school boy abstained from sex as conservatives would like or used a condom as others have proposed, most "teen pregnancies" would still happen, because, most often, it is an adult man who is the abuser. This is not "children having children;" this is adults abusing children.

Another example of teenager bashing is auto accidents. Senator Christopher Dodd (D-Conn.) and John Warner (R-Va.) lamented the 3,600 lives lost in accidents involving teenage drivers in 2005. They called for laws to further restrict these drivers.

After researching their statistics, I gather they meant the 16- to 20-year-olds who make up 8 percent of the drivers but 14 percent of fatal accidents—almost twice as many more than would be expected. That means 86 percent of the accidents are caused by the rest of us. Politicians are often too interested in blaming problems on people who are too young to vote. The senators are right, but they are missing most of the problem.

> **Teens make up 8 percent of the drivers but 14 percent of fatal accidents – almost twice as many more than would be expected.**

At the same time, the Washington, D.C. government imposed an earlier curfew (10 p.m. instead of midnight) for those 16 and younger because of increases in crime. The 10 to 16-age group represents about 7 percent of the population but accounts for 10 percent of the crime, leaving 90 percent of the crime for those of us over 16, according to the Bureau of Justice Statistics. Half of the adult crime is done by the 17- to 25-age group. Also, most crime by the 10- to 16-year-olds is done in the afternoon. Again the restriction on the 16-and-under group is reasonable and very convenient politically, but it misses nearly all of the problem.

Behind these disturbing teen statistics is alcohol consumption. About half the fatal driving accidents among teens involve alcohol, usually purchased by an older adult or the parents themselves.

These statistics are not only about delinquent kids but also about delinquent parents who often say, "The teens are going to do it anyway" as an excuse for setting no limits. This is not true. In fact, less than half of our young teens report any use of alcohol. Among the ones who do drink, 38 percent say their parents are okay with that. So most kids are not "going to do it anyway." Parents should bite the bullet, take the car keys, forbid the drinking and examine their own habits.

As the comic strip character, Pogo so rightly said, "We have met the enemy and he is us."

8. Watch your example

Not that our teenagers don't think independently much of the time, but when living out a regular day, we all follow the leads of others. Teenagers are especially good at

> **Men over 20 cause nearly 90 percent of the pregnancies among junior-high girls and 70 percent of the high school pregnancies.**

copying others—particularly their parents. Specific verbal and behavioral similarities attract a great deal of attention, but the characteristics most likely to be copied by the kids will be dispositions—and not always the best parts.

Parents create a certain atmosphere in family conversation and the kids will pick up the cues and copy the habits. If parents become aggravated, the teenagers will too. Many parents have told me they are surprised how much their children copy them—even when the parents were sure the kids weren't listening or paying attention to what was going on.

The kids may try to hide it, but they always have you on stage. For us parents, presenting a positive model at all times can be a tough responsibility, and most of us will fail, at least occasionally. In all the rush and pressure these days, parents need to be especially careful.

On holidays, what do you remember from your childhood? For me, the gifts I received are hard to remember, even the memories of food and relatives are not clear, but I do remember how it felt.

I remember the predominating atmosphere set by Mom in our home. Even though she was the one doing the secret wrapping after she had done the shopping and before she cooked the large family-day dinner, she was usually cheerful.

As a child, I didn't know I was imitating her attitude, but it was easy since I only had a little shopping and wrapping to do and no kitchen chores at least until clean-up time. She set a good standard. We never met it, but what a precious gift it was.

The importance of a good leader. At 36 I learned to play soccer (not well), and how to enjoy it, from Brian Pillenger—a British professional soccer player who was in town to play for the Washington Diplomats. He joined our neighborhood team as well. He was a good-natured but intense player who kept soccer in its place even though it was his livelihood. "Run when you pass, 'Rolger' (he always rolled my name through his British accent), you're not too old for that, are ya?" he kidded.

He valued the comradeship of the players above the outcome of the game. His example was another gift much appreciated. Because he was a professional, he felt a responsibility to lead the way and that way was toward enjoyment of the game and the players first and then the sport.

A family needs a similar leader to show the importance of consideration and acknowledgement of the value of each person in the family.

SKILL 2

Knowing the Family "Games"

CHAPTER 5

Spotting parent games

"Don't play games with me!" an aggravated parent will say. All kids play some manipulative games, but these parent games can become much less troublesome when parents identify their son or daughter's motivation and adjust their reactions to help solve the problem but not prolong the game.

1. **"Referees are fun"**

"Referees are fun" is the most common game among siblings. Mom, the referee, will interfere only when the siblings are "going too far." She protects them from their extremes and each one appeals to her when they think they have been fouled. Mom stops the game for the moment, the kids may feel successful and they have a chance to reload. Mom also keeps the wounds to a minimum.

"Mom! Todd won't let me watch my program!"

"Todd, let your brother alone, Steven gets to watch his program now."

"It's a dumb program, and we can see the last of it later, I'm turning it to my show!"

"Mom, Todd changed the channel."

"Todd, you come out here and help me and leave Steven alone!"

"Todd pushed me!"

"You two cut that out! Todd, get out here right now! If I have to come in there..."

Mom, the referee, is the third party the kids turn to for judgment calls, penalties, and control of the game. The ref also provides attention and some entertainment. But as all Little League and soccer mothers know, referees are always 50 percent wrong.

> The goal is to get Mom out of the referee role.

Most referees are also tempted to coach: "Todd, why don't you let Steven watch his program and then you can watch yours, and tomorrow at this time you will get to choose." Coaching is usually a more comfortable role for a parent. The resolution here can't be perfect, but the goal is to get Mom out of the referee role. The brothers can stop the game and fix the problem when they want to. But be careful, coaching can become the next new game of "Let's make my problem your problem."

2. "Let's make my problem your problem"

Here's another common kid's game that will develop during the teenage years into "It's your fault because you're my parent(s)." As with many of these games, frankly stating the fair truth may stop the game and allow some real progress.

Jamar: My homework is due tomorrow!"

Mom: "Well, you'd better get at it."

Jamar: "Where's some paper?"

Mom: "In the desk."

Jamar: "I already looked there."

Mom: "Why don't you try upstairs?"

Jamar: "Mom! It's supposed to be down here! Could you go look?"

Mom: "Hold it, Jamar, your homework is your responsibility, don't make your problem my problem."

Many readers have told me of similar games: "Yes, but..," "I gotcha!" "I'm not responsible, you are guilty for my mistakes," and "If you really loved me, you would serve me"—all played, in part, for parental service and attention.

Solutions to games. Good listening skills are important in handling these games. When the conversation starts, look at your son or daughter instead of the TV or newspaper so you don't give the impression that you will miss what's really going on. That will let your teen know that you're not likely to be fooled by some game.

Feeding back what your teenager just said is a good habit during these parent games. Let him know that you heard what he said by repeating it. Avoid suggesting solutions in these games; they only lead to "make-me-happy" or "my-problem-is-yours." Also, suggesting solutions makes you sound superior and tempts your teenager to counter with another complaint just to stay even.

Another form of, "Let's make my problem your problem" is **I'll bet you can't make me happy,** and it pulls parents into their kids' problems when the kids should be taking responsibility for themselves.

Debbie: "Mom, what can I do, I'm bored."

Mom: "Why don't you work on your puzzle?"

Debbie: "I've done everything but the sky part, and that's too hard."

Mom: "OK, how about helping me outside?"

Debbie: "That's just work."

Mom: "Then you might as well get your homework done."

Debbie: "I don't have to do it yet."

Mom: "Well, why don't you..."

> Don't make your problem my problem.

Many parents will recognize this game. As long as no suggestion is right, the adolescent gets some attention that fills the time and that may have been the point of the conversation in the first place.

Parents can't win this game; they just have to quit and let their grumbler get some experience taking control of his own time.

3. "Do I give you a 'nagging feeling'?"

Ashley: "Mom, can I get a tattoo?" Daughter, 15, points to a place near her navel.

Mom: "No, it's too hard to get off."

Ashley: "I don't want to ever get it off. Anyway it's not that hard."

Mom: "No."

Ashley: "It would be so cool and it won't show." She points to a very low place on her stomach.

Mom: "What good is it there if it doesn't show?"

Ashley: "Mom! So I'll have it here." She points to a place a little higher.

Nagging is a replay of the old standard, "I'll Bet You Can't Make Me Happy," with a promise of unending reruns. If Ashley gives up the tattoo idea, the game would be over. As long as Mom is too hurried to recognize the game, Ashley can make the game work for attention and entertainment.

This kind of nagging game requires a straightforward reaction:

"Ashley, no tattoo. It's too permanent and you'll regret it. Take some of your allowance and find something nice to wear at the mall."

Now will Ashley stop nagging? Probably not, but a few encouragements to look for an accessory that is not so permanent, will reduce her dependence on Mom for entertainment. Mom's stream of reasons will only encourage Ashley to continue the game in order to accumulate more rejections.

"Nagging for a loophole" is a variation that depends on Mom's (or Dad's) reaction. On I-95 going toward Florida, a passersby can see this sign for the "South of the Border" amusement area coming up: "Pedro Says: Keep Up the Whining, Kids, They'll Give In!" All parents know this drill very well. It's the nagging that never dies!

Caroline: "But Mom, why can't I ride to school with Nathan?"

Mom: "I already told you why, Caroline."

Caroline: "I know, but can't I, pleeease! Nathan's a good driver."

Mom: "No. He just got his license and driving to school with him is just asking for trouble."

But the next day it starts all over again:

Caroline: "Mom, Nathan wants me to ride with him to the mall, can I go? We're not going near school."

The topic is always disagreeable, so why does Caroline keep bringing it up? The most likely reason for this running battle is that Mom and Dad seem to change their reasons occasionally or they disagree on the reasons. So they lose confidence when Caroline presents new details (mall or school). Caroline keeps trying because she thinks she might hit the right combination of loopholes one day and get to go. Maybe she will.

A moment of contemplation by Mom or discussion with her partner would nail down the reasons and bring confidence.

> Usually the best strategy, dull as it may be, is to stick to your first reason in a matter-of-fact, uninteresting way.

Mom: "Your father and I (or just 'I' if you're doing this solo) have decided you can't ride with other boys to school or on errands without an adult. We think others will get in on it and make trouble whether you're going to school or anywhere else."

Caroline is not going to give up right away. And Mom may be tempted to add another argument to stop the nagging. But usually the best strategy, dull as it may be, is to stick to your first reason in a matter-of-fact, uninteresting way.

Kids keep up the nagging games because of the consequences—either the attention or the debate is entertaining or parents give the impression that changes and loopholes hold out promise.

The next time you think a nagging game is starting, keep your reasons consistent, in the same words and repetitive. Avoid encouraging whining or excessive dependency by keeping the conversation plain vanilla. Don't try to think up zingers in these mild confrontations, they only add to the fun. Look at your teenager to assure him or her that you are paying attention and are not likely to be easily hoodwinked by a "game."

4. The "hurry up" strategy

It's easy to slip out of your adult perspective when dealing with a frantic teen or pre-teen. Everyone is in a hurry, even the kids, and the combination of a hassled rush and a teen's outrageous arguments can lead to raised voices and a decision that will be regretted.

Elena. A parent needs to keep the conversation slow so even a teenager has time to express herself without resorting to defensiveness. But parents can be the ones rushed into mistakes if the kids have learned that picking up the pace has its advantages.

> A parent needs to keep the conversation slow so even a teenager has time to express himself without resorting to defensiveness.

Elena: "Dad, Sofi asked me to go to the movies, can I go?"

Dad: "What movie?"

Elena: "That war flick over at the mall across town. She's waiting on the phone!"

Dad: "Well, I think we should talk about it; Sofi's parents are going?"

Elena: "Dad, I don't know, can I go or not?"

Here's a good place for a "parent pause." Can a 15-year-old girl go off to a movie across town without Dad getting into details?

Staying away from details may be the idea.

Dad: "Tell Sofi you'll call her back."

Elena: "She needs to know now! Can I go or not?"

Dad: "Not. Until we talk."

Elena: "This is ridiculous." She turns back to the phone. "Sofi? I'll call you right back, OK?"

Make time for yourself in moments of demands when the teen advantage is avoiding details. Dad needs a moment to pay attention to his intuition and instincts. Exactly what is missing in Elena's proposal?

Elena: "OK, I'm off the phone. What's bugging you?"

Dad: "Elena, who's going and who's driving?"

Elena: "Dad! I'm 15!"

Dad: "Yes, but Sofi's also 15 and she shouldn't drive without her parents in the car. I need to talk to her parents."

Elena: "Dad, don't make a big thing out of this. I'm not a kid any more."

Dad: "Right. But I still want to call and see if it's all right."

Is this the end of the argument? Probably not, but Dad knows what is reasonable and he's not going to be stampeded into a bad decision just because Elena's friend can't wait. If Elena misses her chance because Sofi is in a hurry and her parents are not there or have no time to talk, maybe it's just as well it doesn't work out. This is not going to be a great family moment, but it's better than an evening of worry or worse.

Dad is just exercising his right to take time to see that his daughter is safe. This is one of the many rights parents need to protect.

5. Let's build a parent's bill of rights

Strategies of parents, whether developed by the parents or suggested by others, often give little consideration to the parents themselves. This is a serious mistake.

Young parents starting out with an infant usually stick to a rule that says: Make whatever sacrifice it takes to solve the current crisis. But as a child grows into her teenage years, the time comes when parents ought to sacrifice less and encourage their teenager to grow up a little instead of letting her continue to abuse her parents.

Child-rearing is a long process, and parents need to be comfortable with it in order to cope with the years to come. Many marriages have broken up over one spouse feeling abused by the kids. Protecting our own rights will help all of us keep up our enthusiasm for the parenting job.

We all have our own idea of what a parent's bill of rights ought to be, and many items would appear on every parent's list.

After one of those frantic rounds when parents are setting limits and negotiating a teen's need for money, entertainment, or expanded curfew time, moms and dads often think, "Wait a minute, I have rights too!"

Parents should not always put off their own desires to meet the needs of their children. Sacrifice is not a good

> Child-rearing is a long process, and parents need to be comfortable with it in order to cope with the years to come.

model for our teens to imitate and defending your own rights will set a good example even for the teen who, at the moment, opposes his parents. Here are my candidates for seven rights for parents.

Parent Right Number 1. Parents have the right to say "no" when demands don't fit their priorities. If Mom is called to be the assistant coach on yet another soccer team, she has the right to think of her time and energy limits and answer, "No."

Parent Right Number 2. Parents also have a right to expect others to come to their defense when they, or others, are abused, whether the abuse was directed at Mom or Dad. "Don't talk to your mother like that!" sends a message to a teen that abuse will not be tolerated as well as giving Mom needed support.

Parent Right Number 3. Parents have the right to make mistakes. It is unfair to hold a person to a standard of perfection—parent or child. When a standard of perfection is not expected, a person feels a greater freedom to go ahead and risk new solutions. Mistakes become evidence of trying something new, not evidence of failure. Both parent and teen will find more solutions if their right to make a mistake is respected.

Parent Right Number 4. Parents have the right to take time with decisions. Children of all ages are inclined to make disturbing emergency announcements: "I'm walking to Bobby's!" "I'm flunking math!" "I'm quitting band!" "I have to work in Ocean City this summer!" Dramatic announcements challenge Mom and Dad's right to think. They deserve that right and should resist the demand with a slow conversational pace. After all, the announcements are, so far, just words, not yet actions.

Parent Right Number 5. Parents have the right to change their minds. To coach a growing child-teen requires flexibility as his capabilities increase and circumstances change. One family I know didn't allow sleep-over friends for a long time because their teenage daughter, Ericka, became sick and impossibly grumpy the day after each sleep-over. But in the next school year, Ericka had matured a little and they let her try again.

Parent Right Number 6. Parents have the right to ask for what they need. As all working folks know, you won't get what you don't ask for. Some parents sacrifice for their teenagers instead of requesting help. Mom wanted assistance unloading and putting away groceries, but instead of asking for it, she thought, "My kids are tired and I can do this for them." However, after she finished the work she felt worn out and her sacrificial attitude had turned to resentment. She might be teaching her children to take advantage of her (by acting tired), and she and they are likely to pay a price for that later on.

Parent Right Number 7. Parents have the right to feel good about themselves. When actions work out, a teenager happily takes credit, like a player on a winning team, and a parent feels proud, as a winning coach. But when things don't work out, parents may blame themselves and their teens are tempted to agree.

Parents can set a good example for their children by adopting the habit of accepting credit as well as blame only for their own actions. A boy will learn to accept responsibility for problems as well as successes if parents don't accept blame when they are not responsible. Guide your son or daughter to connect outcomes with his or her own behavior, and not use past parent behaviors as a scapegoat.

Review your own bill of rights occasionally just to shore up your comfort and update your confidence in the whirlwind of teen-rearing. Attitudes recycle through the family and the benefits of a healthy defense of your rights will encourage family members to be considerate of the rights of others and to protect each other when necessary.

6. Blackmail at home

Blackmail is not the first word that comes to mind in childrearing, but it does come to the minds of most parents during negotiations with teenagers.

"Mom, all my friends are going and if you don't let me, I'm going to have a fit!"

Attitudes recycle through the family.

For permission to go with friends, substitute money, movie, car, or late night out depending on the age of your potential fit-thrower, and you have the makings of blackmail if not downright parent abuse.

The blackmail by the **Do-what-I-say-or-I'll-throw-a-fit** game can be an imitation of parenting discipline with a little extra emotion thrown in. Once a parent is under the influence of this strategy, it's hard to break.

How does parent blackmail become a habit? Often the threat is not carried out for a long time, since parents learn how to make little Ms. (or Mr.) Tyrant happy before the explosion happens. If Mom becomes too sensitive to the prospect of a tantrum, she may agree to Tyrant's demands for weeks at a time, but the family situation will be miserable.

Kids know that a fast pace is to their advantage.

Of course, avoiding the explosion doesn't end the game because there's always another demand and another threat. Mom or Dad may be hesitant to tough it out and risk the explosion because they know how the escalation will go. But giving in also seems wrong because it rewards bad behavior. This common teen-rearing quagmire continues because when the parents give in, both sides win a little. The teenager wins by getting his way, and the parent wins by avoiding the threatened tantrum.

Two parental habits can help parents work their way out of this dilemma, and both require planning. The first is to set limits in advance; the second is to keep the pace of negotiation slow.

Weak limits are often part of the problem and a parent's first reaction to a request may be weak support for the limit. Now a half-hearted refusal may encourage an outburst that Mom or Dad must deal with, possibly by giving in, then the tantrum scores as a success.

This mistake is often produced by the pace of conversation and general hassle. So in addition to a strategy session about limits, parents need to slow the pace during the negotiations so that the limits can be kept consistently in mind. Kids know that a fast pace is to their advantage.

"Mom, I need to know now, let me go or forget it!" You know if you refuse to let him go, he's not going to let you forget it, but you can still remain calm and consistent:

"Mark, you can't go because it would be too late, you know our rule is in by ten."

It won't stop here, but Mom is in control instead of Mark. She knows the limit she wants and will not let the discussion escalate into a shouting match. So the best defense for the blackmailing abuse is consistent limits and answers thought out in advance. No stampeding allowed. Slowing the discussion lowers the pressure and keeps your child from trying to stampede his parent(s) into a bad decision.

> In spite of examples of lying on TV every minute and examples at home every day, we still hope our children won't lie.

The paradox of keeping control while also giving it away creates tough times for parents. Rules and limits need constant review because the children are growing. But rule changes need to be made under calm circumstances. Changes and compromises under threat will only encourage more threats.

7. The aftermath of the lying game

Nothing seems to anger parents more than discovering their teenager is lying. The punishments are likely to be severe, and no excuse will be accepted. In spite of examples of lying on TV every minute and examples at home every day, we still hope our children won't lie.

Of course, we don't mean the fantasies or the magical thinking of flying to never-never land. We don't even include the TV examples of lying in order to "trick" the bad guys. We mean lying to parents and, maybe, teachers.

Why would a child lie? It's a set-up sometimes, because the parent didn't ask a clear question and left loopholes. Mom says, "Have you done all your piano practicing?" What does "all your piano practicing" mean to a young person? Looked at it all? Played it all once? Played it until it was right? Because Mom's question is vague, it opens the door to being devious. A teenager is tempted to say "Yes" to avoid argument. Watch your language and be specific when the stakes are high.

Fear can be a reason for lying. If emotions are likely to skyrocket, lying may seem to be the only way out. So avoid threatening large, scary punishments while the facts are still coming in. Big punishments are hard to reverse and they are hard to use repeatedly. And your fibber is likely to pick up your punishment habit when dealing with friends and siblings and maybe you.

Speaking of habits, mind your model. Adult "little white lies" that smooth social situations can be misinterpreted by the kids as a license to deceive whenever it's convenient.

> **If your twister of the truth does deceive you, keep the consequences on target.**

If your twister of the truth does deceive you, keep the consequences on target. One mother wrote me, "My eight-year-old, Kareem, made a big deal out of having no homework last night. His dad asked him twice and he said, "No" both times. The next morning he said, "Mom, I have to tell you something. I did have homework, but it's not due until Friday." What should Mom do? Should "homework tonight" include that big project due, not tomorrow, but on Friday? If he really wants to watch TV tonight, then is "No" not a lie because Friday is the project deadline?

One starting point on this problem is to stay up-to-date on what's happening with your children. Volunteer at school whenever you can. Ask for specifics about assignments to avoid misunderstandings and to help your child avoid the temptation to lie.

The consequence for lying should not only fit the crime but also fix the problem. For scheming Kareem, perhaps his teacher would agree to sign a note, written by Kareem, stating the homework assignments for that night. If he comes home without the signed note, Mom needs an extra homework assignment that Kareem will have to do in place of one missing from school.

Kareem's deception became a problem because Mom and Dad had no direct information. When the note provides the information, "little white lies" won't work well anymore. A week of this and Kareem had served his "sentence" and he's back on his own to learn to live life without deception.

A recent *Newsweek* poll reports that 42 percent of parents say their most important goal is to raise their child to be a moral person. Eighty percent say they send, or plan to send, their teenager to Sunday school or some other kind of religious education.

While Newsweek didn't ask, I'm sure most parents feel that outside temptations and influences from media, school, and friends are the greatest threat to the success they hope for.

Another poll shows that the fears may be well founded. A national organization called Character Counts (see www.charactercounts.org) reported that of 8,600 high school students surveyed, 71 percent said they cheated on exams in the last 12 months, 78 percent had lied to a teacher, and nearly 20 percent said they had been drunk in school in the past year. Also, 68 percent said they hit someone out of anger in the past year and about half did so more than once.

When parents approve and disapprove of the behaviors of their kids, they also pass along their values. So while a baby knows only what it needs, and a toddler has learned some practical strategies for satisfying those needs, a preteen or teenager also acquires opinions about what is right and wrong through the examples and standards his parents set.

Evidence for the constant influence of hereditary and semi-constant "disposition" and "personality" on a teen are easier to see than the gradual influence of experience. So parents may become pessimistic about their day-to-day influence, but when you think of the many families you know, you can see how strong the parent model is.

Studies of families have often supported theories about the strong role of heredity and inborn dispositions. Since it's harder to evaluate the environmental influences of parents, community, extended family, church, and religion, these factors are often left out.

The theories have at least a thread of truth to them. All parents have recognized a little heredity in the actions of their children but have also watched them learn from experience. While most explanations can help us understand how a child's values develop, the theories and labels say little about how to teach values and character in the day-to-day work of parenting.

"Dad, I didn't do that report this weekend because we went to see Uncle Cliff. Help me think of something to say to my teacher."

"Something to say?"

"You know, some excuse."

"Bob, you mean a lie?"

"Dad! All the kids do it; you even do it."

"That doesn't make it right."

"I'll say we went to the Washington museums; she can't object to that."

> When you think of the many families you know, you can see how strong the parent model is.

"You'll just get in deeper when she asks you what you liked. You become your own worst enemy in these stories. Just say the truth and take your medicine."

One experience won't change Bob very much. But praise from Dad and Mom for being honest, even when the result is extra work from his teacher, will improve Bob's self-respect just a little.

This is only one brick in the foundation of good character. It will take years of conversations. Bob will make continual adjustments to the reactions of his parents as best he can, and his parents will react to Bob's temptations as best they can. Parenting is a tough job, as the statistics show us everyday.

CHAPTER 6

Priorities in parent games

Competition with our children starts with a two-year-old's "no" stage but continues right through the teen years. We parents often hesitate to let our kids do things their own way because it means giving up on perfection and allowing for mistakes. Since both parents and children are somewhat control freaks, the struggle can end in a deadlock of wills.

1. The priorities of the games are changing

Often even praise for doing something the right way (our way) is rejected by our offspring because it is a sign they have knuckled under and Mom (or Dad) has won again.

Parents can feel trapped in a "catch 22" when they see the need for support and encouragement but their praise is worded (and interpreted) as gloating. "See? Didn't I tell you?"

We buy into this destructive game when our impatience takes over, and we fail to use the powerful social tools we have. Our urge to get on with the quick-fix trips us up.

If you recognize this obsession with who's in charge in the negotiations with your teenager, the job can become easier—not easy, but easier. Slowing the pace and withholding reactions to each and every childish comment

> Since both parents and children are somewhat control freaks, the struggle can end in a deadlock of wills.

reduces the risk of sounding superior.

The important principles in these strategies for games are:

Principle 1. Control and responsibility foster self-respect. Don't take that away from your teens.

Principle 2. Slow the pace. A fast pace in conversation is the biggest pitfall of parenting.

Principle 3. Compliments and agreement are more effective than your teenager will admit. Giving time for listening and moments of agreement will not get much attention, but the effort may bring your teen back for more conversations later on.

Jeremy: "Mrs. Brown just doesn't like me. Her class is boring and I think she knows I don't like her."

Mom: "I'm sure she's doing her best. You just have to learn to get along with her."

This response emphasizes Jeremy's lack of control so let's back up and take a more positive tack.

Mom: "I'll bet you could influence her if you wanted to. You know, pay attention, keep your eyes up, and ask questions whenever you can. I bet she would change her mind about you." Whether he takes the suggestion or not, this response suggests that Jeremy has some control.

Other family situations may be harder for parents. An adult should feel comfortable and in control in his or her own home. Your son is becoming an adult and should be acquiring the same privileges.

Giving control to a teen concerning the schedule of homework, music practice, or chores takes some courage because he will make mistakes. But the family is the best place to allow mistakes. It can be the place of the most tolerance and the most helpful advice.

Giving over responsibility to your teenager and allowing the satisfaction of control should not be delayed until your teen can guarantee perfection or until he is out on his own. Perfection will not come without practice and practice before leaving home is the least painful.

As children grow, their priorities change. A shy three-year-old's concern for being near Mommy decreases later on as independence develops. A six-year-old's concern with pleasing his teacher is complicated later on by a concern to be properly "cool" with friends.

Habitual games change to supply new needs. One key to understanding a budding teenager is to recognize that the old concerns for Mom's and Dad's protection have only been covered over, not replaced. Until the "kids" are 20 or 30 they may deny it, but all transitions require holding on to dependence while testing the future. The games are serious.

> The family is the best place to allow mistakes. It can be the place of the most tolerance and the most helpful advice.

2. "Testing, testing, are you still my friend?"

Amy: "Those teachers are so out of it. They said we can't wear earrings in school."

Here is one version of "Testing, testing, are you still my friend?" Mom answers, "No earrings?" Mom doesn't immediately join the opposition with, "They're right," and she doesn't say the teachers are wrong until the whole story is told. Often teenish announcements are long on impact but short on details.

Amy: "Well, no dangling ones. Can they do that?"

Mom is once again put to the test. Is she for her daughter or against her? Her ex-three-year-old who is now 13 wants to be near Mom but also wants independence. The trick here is to accommodate old basic companionship needs without embarrassing a growing would-be independent teenager.

Mom: "I guess they're worried the dangling ones will get caught on something or somebody."

Amy: "That could happen anywhere. You're just taking their side." Testing Mom is not always the first intention of these complaints but it often creeps into the conversation later on.

Now Mom could say that's why earrings are bad and that's why she didn't want Amy to get her ears pierced in the first place, and the school has a responsibility. All good points; all heard before; and all feeding into the accusation: "You always take their side (you're not my friend)."

So to avoid the sticky problems of being both parent and friend and to answer the "Can they do that?" question, Mom just says, "I guess they can," and stops without feeding the argument.

The earrings-at-school problem is one of many games where parents will be tempted to play the opposition. Sometimes that will be necessary. But when you know the outcome is not going to change, why spend your social points by rubbing it in?

3. Siblings, pecking order and genetics.

Jim was four when Steve was born. At first, he was excited by the idea of a new companion, but Steve turned out to be more competition than companion. Now Jim is 12 and Steve is eight.

"Jim teases and hits Steve sometimes and other times he just ignores him. Last week Steve brought home a school drawing and Jim said it was a dumb picture and tore it up. Steve cried and we didn't know what to do. We asked Jim why he tore it up and he said he didn't know, he thought it wasn't important. He said he was sorry, but he always says he is sorry then keeps doing these things.

"They have their moments when they play together and sometimes seem to be each other's best friend. At other times you would think they stay up nights working on ways to torment the other."

How parents react is important here, especially in encouraging good behavior, avoiding comparisons, and, most of all, modeling for the boys.

Jim: "You always side with him, you don't know what names he called me!"

Mom: "I'm not siding with anyone! But Steve is younger and you shouldn't be so touchy when he tries to make you mad."

Steve: "I didn't say anything! You always blame me! He just hit me."

Mom: "OK, you (grabs Steve's arm) are coming out with me! And you (she glares at Jim) better learn to keep your hands to yourself!"

Siblings Without Rivalry: How to help your children live together so you can live too by Adele Faber and Elaine Mazlish offers good advice concerning sibling complaints. They advise parents to avoid disagreeing with the child or teen in a way that denies the person's right to feel aggravated. For example, responding to, "Mom, Steve said I sound stupid" with "Just ignore him" tells your teenager to change his feelings—good advice, but not an easy thing to do. A sympathetic remark would be, "A comment like that could make you mad!" Or, Mom could respond with an understanding of the complainer's gripe, "That hurt your feelings. I bet you wish he would be more of a friend."

> "Just ignore him" tells your teenager to change his feelings – good advice, but not an easy thing to do. A sympathetic remark would be, "A comment like that could make you mad!"

Negative comparisons between siblings fuel the sibling conflict. Faber and Mazlish suggest focusing on the behavior of one sibling without using another for contrast. For example, instead of saying, "Even the baby isn't that messy with her food," a better response might be, "There's a little milk dripping down the front of your shirt." Likewise, instead of, "You're always late. Why can't you be on time like your brother?," the focus can be sharpened to, "Your music teacher has been waiting ten minutes and the lesson will have to go later now."

Parents often underestimate the power of their example, and if they set the right example, they may see no immediate change. Little moments where Mom or Dad show tolerance and patience while a teenager works out how to say something, clean up a spill, or correct a mistake, will have an effect on how the kids react to each other, trying to grow up.

> The closer you look at child-rearing studies, the more you realize the nature-nurture question does not have a simple answer.

Parents often see the same tendencies and dispositions continued in their children as they grow. It seems to prove the point that, right from the beginning, a great deal of how children act is inherited.

Knowing that your teen came into this world with good family characteristics can be satisfying. And if some characteristics are not desirable, it's a relief to know that not all his problems are your fault.

Try as we might to raise each child in a similar way, we often say, "I can't believe these two were born of the same parents and raised in the same family! Are we just lucky or unlucky in the combination of genes that came together?"

The closer you look at child-rearing studies, the more you realize the nature-nurture question does not have a simple answer. One study shows that infants abandoned by their disadvantaged parents and adopted by upper-middle-class parents averaged 14 IQ points higher than their siblings who were left behind with their original parents. Yet the siblings left behind were also four times more likely to experience failures in school.

Adoption provided a bonus for these kids, but in the Colorado Adoption Project language abilities of adopted children were correlated with the intelligence of the biological mother even though they had not seen each other since birth. But how much the new mother imitated and responded to infant vocalizations also predicted language development in these same children. Genetic effects are strong but can be modified by motherly (and fatherly) attention.

Every child arrives with a genetic code, but family circumstances will make fundamental changes right from the start. A first-born child is likely to respond to the clear field with an assertive and take control attitude.

The second child finds the field already occupied by the first child and, like the genetic influence, his situation seems to be a given. Reacting to the competition, a second child is likely be the very opposite of the first: shy, laid back, and more interested in a small social circle instead of the social whirlwind created by the first child. If a third child comes along, the field changes for the second, and attention turns to the baby of the family. Number two, now relegated to "middle child," is often a bit of a rebel.

So what does all of this mean for parents dealing with kids at tomorrow's breakfast? Birth order and genetic factors are useful tools, but a parent's opportunities for change are in setting the limits, carrying out consistent consequences, and providing encouragements—right now. Because the tools give parents better insight into their teen's inclinations and his view of the competition, they can be tolerant and look for chances to help strengthen each person's self-respect.

The potential for change is in how the child is welcomed into the world— even for a teenager, it is not too late for changes. The genetic advantages and disadvantages that he brings along, although already determined, can be nurtured by parents who give time, tolerance and tender care during the crucial first years and on through the growing-up years.

4. The most important games have life-long effects

Parents might say the most important game is getting the latest homework done or finishing the chores that have been let go for a week (month?) already.

The eating game might be a parent's next thought. Parents will argue for fruits and vegetables while hoping to limit the fat, salt and sugar. But without the management of exercise, the long-term prospects for good health are dim.

Everyone knows the statistics about sedentary children with too many hours of TV and computer games. And the schools are little help now that many school exercise classes have shrunk to a token 30 minutes a week. But the most shocking statistics show increases in deadly diseases related to laziness started in childhood.

Dr. Ben Hurley, University of Maryland professor of kinesiology, concludes, "The one thing that seems to deteriorate quickest with inactivity is insulin sensitivity." Once insulin sensitivity goes down, diabetes will follow. Type 2

> Type 2 diabetes has reached epidemic proportions in American children, while only 40 years ago, it was a disease of middle age. In the same 40 years, childhood obesity has tripled.

diabetes has reached epidemic proportions in American children, while only 40 years ago, it was a disease of middle age. In the same 40 years, childhood obesity has tripled.

In studies of daily routines of 50,000 adults, every two hours of daily TV-watching was linked to a 14 percent increase in the risk of diabetes. On the other hand, a habit of an hour of brisk exercise each day was linked to a 34 percent decrease in the risk of diabetes.

The *Nutrition Action Newsletter* reviewed the baggage of sedentary habits children bring to their risks in adulthood. Among the 1.2 million Americans who have heart attacks each year, the lack of exercise, learned in childhood, is the main culprit. In a study that tracked 40,000 women for five years, heart attack risk was reduced by half in those who walked briskly for at least an hour a week. The same exercise reduced high blood pressure and stroke risk in 75 percent of the subjects in the five years of the study the newsletter reported.

How can parents help their children live long and healthy lives? The Mayo Clinic's specialist in physical medicine, Dr. Edward Laskowsk, says, "If mom and dad exercise, it's a powerful stimulus for a child to exercise." He suggests parents play physical games—tag, Simon says and dodge ball—regularly with their kids. Run with them. Run like a gorilla, walk like a spider, hop like a bunny. Plan family vacations around activities—hiking, biking, camping instead of visiting a place just to look.

Dr. Laskowski also suggests physical chores. Who can pull the most weeds in five minutes in the garden? Collect the most litter in the neighborhood? Shovel the most snow? "By incorporating physical activity into our children's

> The best predictor of adult activity is the pattern set before they were 15.

lives we set the foundation for a good fitness habit that will have a ripple effect on future generations," says Laskowski.

Teenagers need the workouts, too. The best predictor of adult activity is the pattern set before they were 15. Muscle wasting begins before 40 for women and by 50 for men. Without exercise you lose 6 percent of your muscle mass and 15 percent of muscle strength each decade after that. When should you and the kids start? Now.

5. The game of: "You're responsible for my bad behavior"

Advice columns often print letters from parents describing their offspring's unusual and shocking behavior. Sometimes you have to shake your head in disbelief. Certainly in many cases both child and parents need professional help. But when all the complications that are only briefly told in the newspaper are explored, explanations usually revolve more around parental behavior than the reactions of their children.

> Parents, and sometimes the offspring also, expect too much magic and are impatient or even angry if the prescription includes effort on the part of the people involved.

Why would a child behave in a bizarre way? Answers could include physiological factors, diet or allergies. School adjustment, friends and exercise habits also play a part in the behavior of both healthy and troubled teens and children.

So it's tempting, and often necessary, to cart the teen off to the doctor or psychologist and hope for a magic prescription or surprising insight that will make everything better. The professionals, however, complain that the parents, and sometimes the offspring also, expect too much magic and are impatient or even angry if the prescription includes effort on the part of the people involved.

The "whys" of behavior extend to, and often begin with, "What happens next?" The teen throws a fit, refuses to cooperate, is abusive or demands

> **I was winning, or I was losing, or we were both headed for disaster. The latter turned out to be right.**

undeserved attention and then what happens? Logical consequences or argument? Consistent answers or variable answers and appeasement?

When faced with this question myself, often I can't remember exactly what did happen. My daughter (at age seven) had stopped dead in the toy store in the mall. "I won't go," she said. I said something evasive about getting home. She screamed, "I want it (some toy I can't even remember now) and I won't go until you get it."

"You don't even know what it is," I said, forgetting that my challenge only left the door open for more bad behavior—I hadn't yet said "no," and now she felt encouraged to go full out for victory.

"I do too know what it is."

"OK, what is it?" Of course this didn't resolve anything. I had decided against the purchase, I just hadn't told her.

"It's...the yellow box."

Now she's embarrassed and losing control, but I mistakenly go for the win, "See, you don't know." Now, I was winning, or I was losing, or we were both headed for disaster. The latter turned out to be right. I ended up carrying my kicking and screaming daughter out of the mall, with many scowls and accusing looks following me.

Kids read signals closely, and if they don't hear a clear answer, "No," that has a reputation of being the last word, they assume they can succeed if only they can say the right thing.

The next time, and there were plenty of next times, I was challenged with weird behavior, I tried to remember that my very next reaction is crucial. If the audio says no but the video seems blank, a child or teenager can be encouraged just as much as if both audio and video were indecisive.

CHAPTER 7

Feeding snacks to the tiger

Once you are immersed in teen-rearing, it's easy to forget your own rights. Much of the common disrespect for parents that's shown in fits, tantrums and bad language comes from kids abusing their power and parents forgetting theirs.

1. "Do what I say, or I'll have a fit!"

Tantrums seem to come more often during the holidays. Parents with young preteens usually suspect that changes in sleeping or meal schedules as well as crowds of company are the culprits that set the stage for trouble.

But as the kids grow up, we become more suspicious that they use tantrums as a means to an end, and we are afraid we may be teaching them the value of tantrums.

Parents who avoid copying their offspring's volume and emotion in these moments of confrontation provide a better model and have the best chance of resolving rather than escalating the problem.

If you know your teen is "itching for an argument," then supplying one only enrolls you as a future target. Explanations of refused demands should be short and age-appropriate. Repeating to a three-year-old more than once that Mommy will be home when her class is over, is only feeding snacks to the tiger.

> **B**ut as the kids grow up, we become more suspicious that they use tantrums as a means to an end.

If repeating seems necessary, keep the words and tone of voice exactly the same. No use adding to the entertainment with a variety of conversation.

As every parent knows, the decision to deny the request should not be altered by a tantrum, but often a request from an explosive teenager may tempt Mom or Dad to put off a confrontation with, "I'll think about it," or "We'll have to wait until your mother (or father) comes home."

It's not in a teen's nature to put aside one line of activity and take up another while waiting for an answer to come down from the parental powers. Instead of switching to a new activity, the childish (teenish?) thing to do is cling to the present direction and push for an answer. Nagging is followed by complaining, then frustration and attack, and then the whole tantrum.

A parent's defense is usually to talk, cajole, plead and threaten—providing additional bad behavior to be imitated. As the delay continues, the behavior of both parent and child gets worse.

Parents are often surprised by tantrums just when they think the kids should be most satisfied and happy. But the disruption of routine can be a trigger just because it's confusing or because regular sleep and meal schedules are changed. Also, childish expectations are often unrealistic and disappointment is inevitable. Keeping these reasons in mind can help a parent to be patient when tantrums occur at odd times.

While holidays and company can cause the tantrums, during the off-holiday weeks, some teens get cranky when competition from a sibling is the focus. Others may have a metabolism that turns them into grouches just before supper. An early serving of the veggies or salad, holiday or not, may make a difference.

Here's a good place to keep family notes for a week or two. You may find that food shopping with your teenager right before dinner is always trouble. Or that homework arguments late in the evening produce the most problems.

The best solutions will come with avoiding known situations that trigger tantrums and setting a good example for teens not yet mature enough to handle disruptions that come with holiday schedules.

Another argument for prompt decisions is that they allow less time for a tantrum to develop and for parents to give in. With delayed decisions, parents are tempted to hold out until bad behavior gets worse. Giving in then is certainly a move in the wrong direction. Delays in decisions and giving in to expanding tantrums develop the childish willingness to try to manipulate others by making them miserable.

Many parents I know have used the "all stop" method with success. The term comes from the Navy when the ship's captain commands, "All stop!" and all engines, whether in reverse, slow, or full speed, are shut down and the ship is dead in the water. For tantrums it means no progress is possible until the tantrum stops—no discussion, no alternatives, no argument. Mom merely says, "We're in 'all stop' until you stop this tantrum."

> It's not in a child's or teen's nature to put aside one line of activity and take up another while waiting for an answer to come down from the parental powers.

The pitfall to this approach is that most of us will not completely stop. We are tempted to continue to talk, cajole, plead and threaten—especially if the tantrum gets longer and louder. If this attention is part of your teenager's reason for tantruming in the first place, then we're going in the wrong direction again by providing attention only for escalation.

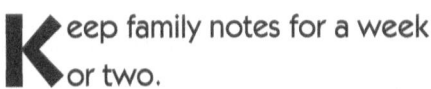

And speaking of escalation, parents need to guard against escalating their own volume and anger, thus providing additional bad behavior to be imitated.

2. Why is he so stubborn?

Parents looking for a little cooperation or a simple apology for a mistake often hit the stone wall of stubbornness. "It's amazing he would rather give up TV and be sent to his room than say he's sorry!"

At a time when confrontation and volume are likely to escalate, a slower pace and lower voice will make the situation easier—not always successful, but easier. Here are three of the most common situations that start the upward spiral of misunderstanding between parent and teen.

1. The Misunderstood Defense. Most confrontations begin with a childish mistake. You would think a teenager would own up to the mistake, fix it or say he's sorry and that would be the end of it. But young blunderers have big egos and are thinking first of all, "What are you saying about ME?"

Teenagers are not very good at expressing exactly what they mean, so confusion reigns. What they intended as a defense may look like offense to their parents:

"Now you spilled your drink. Pay attention to what you are doing."

"I was paying attention, chill out."

"Chill out? Now you apologize or go to your room!"

The teenager who meant to defend himself but did it in an offensive way is now tempted to dig in and resist. Parents are tempted to do the same.

A better strategy would be to help with the defense instead of demanding, "Say you're sorry!" Mom might say, "What bad luck. Too bad the glass was so full. You'd better get a towel for that spill."

Better to teach him to clean up his own mistakes than merely have him learn to chant, "OK, I'm sorry."

2. The Power Struggle Mode. "I don't have to do what you say!"

"You had better do what I say or you'll get the consequences!"

"You can't make me!" ... and on it goes.

Instead of arguing about who's got the upper hand, Dad might explain how to compromise on power. "If you want me to give you a ride to school and to soccer practice when you need it, you have to help me sometimes. You need to come halfway."

This is not the end of the argument, of course, but at least we have points to negotiate instead of just a struggle of wills. In the power struggle and the negotiations, don't forget the powers you have.

3. The Trap of Falling to Their Level. "I can't believe he's got me arguing about the color of his toothbrush!" At this point it's time to deliberately hesitate. Sometimes a noncommittal nod or grunt is all the subject deserves.

"Mom, are you going to get me the Powerman computer game or not?"

Mom: (acting a little distracted) "What? Oh, no, it's too much money and too violent." The main ingredient in each of the negotiations about Powermans and toothbrushes should be the parent's slow, reasonable pace. Keep in mind that a teen's arguments and defenses often sound like attack. And, to a teen, a parent's corrections often sound like personal criticisms.

3. Parents can be enablers feeding the tiger

My neighbor complained that her 15-year-old, Karah, procrastinated getting ready for school. I could hear the yelling when I went out for my paper on Monday. On Tuesday when I went out, the school bus had gone, and Mom was in her car waiting to deliver Miss I'll-be-there-in-a-minute to school. She had even turned the car around for a quick getaway.

> Keep in mind that a teen's arguments and defenses often sound like attack. And, to a teen, a parent's corrections often sound like personal criticisms.

"She needs to learn to get herself ready on time," she told me later. She had been up for hours; Karah had been up for 15 minutes. Mom was ready and in the car; Karah was not. When she came out, she was angry at Mom because she couldn't find her soccer shoes. I heard her say, "Can we go? I'm late!"

As I watched them leave, I wondered how Karah would learn to "get ready on time." It isn't important to her now because she has a back-up chauffer. She can even abuse Mom about the soccer shoes on their way to school.

I wanted to call after them, "Who is seeing that our disgruntled teenager's life works?" Is Mom encouraging the procrastination and abuse?

Use your power. Too much service given unconditionally is not a good thing. Of course we parents want to provide our kids with soccer shoes, clothes, food, and rides. But we don't have to be first in the car and turn it around to make up for the time wasted by our primping procrastinator. We don't have to do her laundry, dry it, take it upstairs, put it away and then step on the gas when she says, "I'm late."

Should Mom get Karah's favorite cereal at the food store? Make dinner without any help? Take the soccer shoes Karah forgot to her afternoon practice?

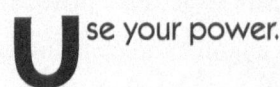

These details go with friendship and respect. They can be left out when the parent abuse card is played. Don't be shy with your kids. If she says, "Thanks for the ride," say, "You're welcome. You help me out now and then, too." Let her know where cooperation comes from.

Karah's mom should speak up about her abuse also, "Karah, if you are late again, you'll have to face the consequences. I'm not driving you, and I'm not writing an excuse." Parents can feel enslaved when the work is too one-sided and the kids expect too many privileges.

Parents can accidentally be the enabler of big mistakes also. One Mom wrote, "Megan (name changed to protect the not-so-innocent), my 16-year-old, and I had a row when I picked her up, and I could tell she had been drinking at her friend's house. She said she knew what she was doing, but I didn't say anything. What can I do? I want her to like me."

Making life easier for a budding alcoholic won't help. The first hint of drinking is not a time for worrying about being liked. It's a time for a tighter leash and a tighter pocketbook—no hanging out unsupervised, no extra bucks for trouble. Where does Megan-know-it-all get money for drinks? She could get it from her friends but that wears thin fast. I guess we know where she gets her transportation, her living expenses, her cell phone and her spending money.

It's time to cut back on the generous services and insist on more accountability from both Karah and Megan.

4. The moody teenager

Cody, age 13, may be in a dark and angry mood on a gray morning, then show a miraculous change after lunch when a friend comes over.

The change is usually temporary and he's soon back to uncooperative and cynical. His mood changes are hard to understand and often a surprise. Since he is a teenager, you'd say he has fits of depression; if he were younger we would call him moody.

Whether moodiness or depression, the problem is usually at its worst when he claims he has nothing to do.

The TV tells teens that most people are doing exciting and usually fun things. The exaggeration provides a depressing contrast to your teen's average day. In the media story, the excitement is produced by an unexpected event which promises adventure. So a teen may have the mistaken impression that relief from boredom will come, not by effort but by fortune. While waiting around for fate to smile, he may get depressed.

Most of us have leftover moments from childhood when we believed a certain thing or person would make us happy. Children are sure that if only they had that certain plastic toy, life would be complete. Later, teenagers are often misled by the media to believe that modeling a certain person, or having a certain companion would do it without any further effort on their part. It takes a lot of adult experience to realize that happiness is a do-it-yourself job.

So the kids will often play a game with us:
Mopey Teenager: "I'm bored."
Mom: "Why don't you go outside?"
M.T.: "It's too cold."
Mom: "You could read your book."

> So a teen may have the mistaken impression that relief from boredom will come, not by effort but by fortune. While waiting around for fate to smile, he may get depressed.

M.T.: "BORinggg."

Mom: "Well, why don't you…"

Mom is usually suspicious that we are in a game of **"I'll bet you can't make me happy,"** but it takes time to finally say, "Well, I guess you'll have to find something to do yourself."

When your teenager gets depressed, avoid the temptation to argue him out of his depression. The argument provides attention for complaining and an opportunity to continue the relatively easy behavior of talking about being depressed as a kind of lazy entertainment. You're also at a disadvantage in the argument because you're talking with the only person who has direct information on how HE feels!

If the TV has implied that other people have a better life, the most productive answer will probably be his own effort to change his activity. A teenager's discouragement may be a reaction to a recent mistake—forgotten homework, poor test score, misuse of work time. In any case, the best help from Mom or Dad will come from sympathetic listening and their teenager's own activity—preferably in an area of success.

> The argument provides attention for complaining and an opportunity to continue the relatively easy behavior of talking about being depressed as a kind of lazy entertainment.

While trying to help your kids with their low moods, remember that long-continuing depression should be taken seriously. Avoid sending the message that if only he would "snap out of it and do something" everything would be better. Belittling your teenager's feelings is frustrating to her and has the danger of overlooking a serious problem that might be lurking below the surface. **When depression continues in spite of extra activities and some parental listening time to explore the problem, it may be time for outside help.**

5. Early bites of parent abuse

Child abuse often starts with a history of expecting too much from a child.

Parent abuse usually begins when parents expect <u>too little</u> from a teenager. Some parents are committed to doing anything to help their teen and will bear any burden. But overindulging is not loving; it just teaches parent abuse.

Babies start out with no idea about consideration for others. "No matter that it's four in the morning, I'm hungry, so I scream to be fed. And don't bother me with the fact that Mom will have to get up and warm it, I want it now!"

Learning how to get attention starts early, but you can't negotiate with a baby, so good parents just try to satisfy them as best they can. Consequently, consideration for others is a new idea to a growing child or even a teenager. When parents become suspicious that their teens are unreasonable, they need to begin helping their teen-terror learn to take care of himself and to be more thoughtful of others.

How do you know when not to give in and instead expect a little consideration and effort from your budding teenager? Start early with lots of talking. Even when you think they are not old enough to understand, language experience and practice is always good.

Even early chores have a social side. Toddlers learning to put their socks on must understand that practice is not a punishment by an obstinate mother. She needs to explain, probably many times, that Mom has other family jobs and his efficiency at this task will be even better than hers. Most of these self-care chores will require a step-by-step approach leaving part of the job (pulling up the socks, for example) for her toddler to do.

One mother stopped to talk to a friend as our PTA meeting ended. I watched as her impatient 15-year-old daughter repeatedly bumped her mother in the back pushing her away and out the door. Mom would not tolerate anyone else doing that. How can the abuse be right for her teenage daughter?

Other behaviors also deserve a reaction. At a Thanksgiving gathering, one mother complained that her ten-year-old son bit her when she didn't provide immediate attention to his requests. "When he bites, what can you do?" another mother asked. "I tried giving him a good talking to, but I made more progress by abruptly leaving him and going to another room without comment."

Mom would not tolerate abuse from anyone else. How can it be right for her teenage daughter?

Mom can't ignore her adolescent snapper when his teeth are planted in her arm, but her friend said when her son started to bite she also left him by himself with no comment. But after that she added an explanation about how she felt and questions about what he could have done about his situation other than biting.

These parent-teen confrontations are not fun, but they are essential if a budding abuser is to learn to be a better person.

CHAPTER 8

Problems with family dynamics

1. Stay-at-home, now or later?

All parents struggle with the nagging balance between staying home with the kids and pursuing a career and life of their own.

New parents feel the greatest pressure to stay at home, and there's no doubt that the kids need you in the early ages. They need care and they need family security.

Kids also need your companionship to balance the thoughtlessness and jibes of friends their own age. Their young friends are inexperienced and have the minimal social skills of the under-10 set. As your children become teenagers, they will be less vulnerable and more prepared to care for themselves.

But even if your teenagers are more handy at taking care of themselves, a case can be made for a responsible adult at home in the pre-teen and teenage years.

Federal labor statistics report that eight out of 10 adolescents have two working parents. The other two out of 10 have the advantage of a parent at home who may be supervising homework as well as their free time. Over 10 million are being raised by single parents, and of these, less than 200,000 are being raised by single-parent fathers.One mother said her son was horrified about the change when she decided to stay home. "What? You're going to be home? You're going to make me do my homework?"

"Yet he was happy to learn I would be here next year when he wants to visit and check out colleges," she said.

But her son added, "It's a real shocker, when someone who's really demanding tells you she's going to be around all the time."

Statistics report that teenage crime peaks just after 3 p.m. The time teens spend on their own before parents come home averages 25 hours each week. A review is in order when this amount of free time is unsupervised.

A mother interviewed in the Washington Post said, "If you're going to do this (stay at home), do it before he stops talking to you."

A second mother added, "Some have the notion that once your child hits five or six, they're cooked. You kind of kid yourself that they're independent individuals without the need for a lot of parental support. It gets harder to see when they need you. Until, that is, things start to blow up." And a stay-at-home father added, "The catch is, you have to be there when they're ready and willing to talk."

> As one father told me, "The fact is I don't want my 10 year-old's 18th birthday sneaking up on me."

Many stay-at-home parents are also work-at-home parents. Often these arrangements are for one or two days a week, giving a parent the best of both choices. The Internet has made this possibility more available for many parents who feel the pressure to be there when their teens need them.

Whatever decision you make about the daily family schedule, give a priority to easy talking time with the kids. As one father told me, "The fact is I don't want my 10-year-old's 18th birthday sneaking up on me."

2. Preventing Mom abuse

"Hey, don't talk to your mother like that!" can be a high moment in a family day. It's not a happy moment, but the parent on the firing line needs the message that her teenager's divide and conquer strategy won't work. Parent abuse will not be tolerated.

Kevin:"I'm going to watch TV now."

Mom: "How about your homework?"

Kevin: "Later, I've got plenty of time."

Mom: "Didn't you say your history paper was due tomorrow?"

Kevin: "Mom, you don't know anything about how long the paper will take."

Aunt Eileen: "Be careful how you talk to your mother. She's had years of experience at school; I think she knows."

Kevin: "I'll do it when I'm ready."

Aunt Eileen: "Well, I can't ride you over to your soccer practice until your mother says you're ready."

Kevin: "You didn't even know about the history paper until Mom brought it up; what do you have to do with it, anyway?"

Mom: "Don't talk to your Aunt Eileen that way; she's concerned about you, too. Now get to that paper so you can make your soccer practice."

Your best protectors are your own relatives, spouse and friends who come to your aid when parent abuse is likely. They should provide parent protection when their best friend is being mistreated, even by a teenager.

Mia: "Mom, is my laundry done?"

Mom: "Just a minute. I'm talking."

Mia: "I need it now!"

Eric: (Mom's close friend) "Take it easy, Mia, let your Mom finish."

Two adults can be stronger than one, and they can provide a model about how the members of the family should treat each other. Eric wouldn't let a stranger barge in and make demands of his friend at a restaurant, and he's not going to sit by when her teenager does it at home either.

How does the parent abuse habit get started? Of course a teen's attitude comes from many sources, but again the relatives, friends, spouse and extended family play a role from the beginning. They can make the effort to help like Eric and Aunt Eileen, or, if they don't, they can be part of the problem.

Eric: "You can't find your keys? I don't believe it!"

Tasha: "Just a minute, here they are."

Eric: "I swear, you would lose your head if you didn't have a neck."

An adult game of **"I-can't-believe-you're-such-a-klutz!"** can be easily absorbed by the kids. Adult friends or relatives who show the kids-teenagers how to abuse their parents are not helping.

Eric: "The car needs some work."

Tasha: "Why don't you take it in Monday."

Eric: "Me? You're the one who drives it most!"

Tasha: "I have to get to work early. You just lounge around until eight anyway."

Eric: "Hey, that cushy job of yours..."

Tasha: "Wait, wait, let's get the car fixed, OK?"

You may think this argument is about car repairs and who should see that it gets done. But a teenager listening on the sideline doesn't understand—doesn't care to understand—the details of dropping a car off for repairs. As with his own conversations, he has his "antennae out," and is more interested in what the conversation says about how the people feel about each other—not the content of the conversation. He often gets it wrong.

So after a simple disagreement on the car, Eric may be surprised to hear Allen say: "You don't like Mom, do you?"

"What! Of course I do, whatever gave you that idea?"

The misunderstanding can be corrected, but the temptation to imitate the attitude Allen heard will linger on. The impression will only be corrected by future examples from you—and from the Erics and Aunt Eileens in your teenager's world.

3. Learning about your parents

Thinking back on our own childhood experiences, most of us are amazed at how little we understood about our parents' struggles. The problems they faced and the adjustments they had to make were not often talked about and their complaints were not passed along to us kids.

In earlier generations the majority of businesses were small businesses and farms, and kids often had a closer view of their parent's work. The education they received included the experience of helping in the family activities that often spread to the business activities.

But in present generations, the "children of the mall" haven't had the same opportunities to see their parents at work. Somehow parents get along with their world of work while the kids focus on friends and school. The connection between school and career success isn't clear and anyway, in TV adventures and sit-coms, success seems to come more from luck than from schooling and hard work.

Without good information, a sympathetic and understanding relationship between parent and teen is not likely. And a teenager's view of jobs and responsibilities is likely to remain childish.

With this weakness in Mom's and Dad's daily model, a teen can develop an unrealistic view of work, money, and career. "They just don't understand the value of money," parents often complain. One step toward a better understanding is to reduce the ignorance gap.

As with his own conversations, he has his "antennae out," and is more interested in what the conversation says about how the people feel about each other – not the content of the conversation. He often gets it wrong.

Taking your teenager to work with you several days next summer is a short-term commitment in time with long-term dividends. Take advantage of the day to point out the skills your job requires. Introduce your teen to other workers and describe what they do. Talk about how you got your job, what you like about it and why you chose it. What other choices did you have?

Teacher: "Duncan, what do you plan to write about in your essay about your summer?

Duncan: "I went to work with my Mom. I met all the people there."

Teacher: "What does your Mom do?"

Duncan: "She works in a clothing store. She says to keep your job, first of all, you have to get along with people. It's hard when customers aren't satisfied or the other workers don't come in."

Teacher: "What did you do there?"

Duncan: "Well, I brought stuff out from the back."

Duncan may not see his visits to Mom's store as highlights of his summer. But the learning about how the workaday world operates will help his school motivation. Although there was no spectacular event, he remembers nearly all the details. Mom probably didn't intend to teach Duncan specific values, but in the time she gave she was a model about getting along with people and working hard—two of the many values Duncan will need to learn.

Mom will also have a greater influence on Duncan at home when he has a more complete view of his mother's abilities. The collection of values Duncan encounters will dominate his attitude as he grows up.

Also, a short trip to reality will widen his experience and point out the practical value of school. He will have more respect for Mom from his visits to Mom's work and a longer and clearer view of what he is preparing for.

4. Aunts and uncles chiming in

With everyone busier than ever, working, commuting, and running errands can crowd out family obligations—especially obligations to teenagers in the larger family.

> She was a model about getting along with people and working hard – two of the many values Duncan will need to learn.

Yet these obligations become all the more important as families spread apart and time becomes scarce. Moms and Dads are not the only adults raising children. Aunts, uncles, and friends of the family also have an effect on the kids.

The part you play in the extended families of others is important. Often remarks from extended family have greater weight because they are less frequent and may seem more credible because they represent the world outside the child's family. Also, another point of view may be welcome without the usual judgment of everyday parenting.

What's your agenda when talking to a niece or nephew? Are you the let-me-tell-you type? Profound remarks that suddenly "get through to" a teenager are seldom accomplished. A slower pace with lots of listening is better.

> Some questions close the conversation because, to a child, there is an obvious easy answer that lets them off the conversational hot seat.

Or is, "How's school?" your predictable question? And then once their comment reminds you of your own childhood, are you off on your own story-telling without giving any more attention to what the teen wanted to say? This may be easy to do because kids are less skilled at this banter and need a slower pace to allow them to get their thoughts together so they can tell you about their experience or feelings.

Questions come in different styles. Some questions close the conversation because, to a child, there is an obvious easy answer that lets them off the conversational hot seat. "How's school?" or "How's soccer?" is easy to cut short with, "OK" or "Good."

Other questions open the conversation because they give the budding teenager a familiar topic that is comfortable. "I guess you're still practicing your music, what part do you like to do best?" This question has a better chance of opening up the conversation without putting your niece under pressure to say the right thing. The topic is familiar and she can have an opinion without the risk of being wrong.

Questions from relatives can also direct the values developing in a young person's mind. If Uncle Ted only asks about sports, then his nephew will tend to put that first, at least in talking to his uncle, and math and science further down the list. And if Auntie Em only asks her niece about boyfriends you can see where that keeps the focus.

Men, more often than women, can accidentally advocate violence or prejudice. Casual remarks we don't really mean can be taken literally by a younger mind, "I could have belted him for that," or "People like that always lie."

Moms and dads in their role as parents should let the relatives in on any strategy that might come up: "We're trying to be sure Larry and Marcie have time at the table to talk." Or, "Ask Larry about his piano practice if you get a chance. He's very interested and getting very good."

So on your next visit with the family, in addition to recognizing the next birthday, donate extra time for talking—ask good questions, take time to listen, and set a good example.

CHAPTER 9

Punishment: before 2 it's abuse; after 18 it's hopeless

1. Should you "get tough?"

Parents using the "get tough" approach to childrearing often cite the severe policies of Japanese schools where corporal punishment is justified by the teacher's "educational motives" and the switch is ever ready on the wall.

If "get tough" means making the hard decisions and sticking to them, I'm all for that. If it means explaining why the enforcement of hard rules and limitations are really in the best interest of your teen, I'm sure we're all for that. But often in the real family situations, getting tough turns out to mean more severe punishments for mistakes.

It is hard to be consistent with this level of punishment. We put in the inconsistencies of warnings and threats and although these add the human element of giving kids a fair chance, the "verbal decorations" also challenge kids to start maneuvering.

> Long-term success with spanking, slapping or using the switch is hard to prove, and both parents and teachers have to look forward to changing the policy as a child-teen becomes too big to hit.

> "Who will win?" becomes much more important than, "What is this about?"

Warnings, threats, and negotiations become part of the game. Have we had it "up to here" yet? Teenagers in the game struggle to stay just short of the blowup but sometimes misjudge the threshold. "Who will win?" becomes much more important than, "What is this about?"

As every parent knows, the next problem with physical punishment is that the kids will imitate. From school violence in pre-teens to road rage in teenagers and spousal abuse by adults, the violence can come from an imitation of parents as much as the media. Mom and Dad are sending the message that punishment is a good (used by Mom and Dad) way to deal with people.

Punishment will tempt a teen to react with silence, deceit, or attempts to win the game. Parents can force their offspring to lose, but along with becoming a loser a teen may also show his frustration by throwing a tantrum, hair-twirling or withdrawing to the private safety of computer games or TV. These stubborn habits are maintained by their usefulness for avoiding contact with the person doing the punishing.

Parents will be left with all the side effects of the insulting, belittling embarrassment that lowers a value of their son or daughter. That's why adults are so insulted if you try punishment on them. With adults we realize the punishment strategy will be resented, and we have to use other ways to motivate good behavior and get cooperation.

Furthermore, long-term success with spanking, slapping or using the switch is hard to prove, and both parents and teachers have to look forward to changing the policy as their teenager becomes too big to hit. Even "educational motives" would not justify hitting a person of 16 or 25.

2. Punishment alternatives

What kind of punishment is effective and useful? One mom told me she had a problem with her son getting into trouble everyday on the school bus. Threatened with "bus suspension," she told her son how much trouble that would cause. She said that if he couldn't ride the bus, she would have to drive him, but she would have to take his little sister along, "And we're not going to drop you off; we'll walk you to your locker with your sister still in her little jammies, and kiss you goodbye." He never had bus trouble again—no extra punishment needed.

One shots. Using such a logical consequence is a good approach, but it can lead to trouble if the threatened consequence is too big: "If you don't stop using that language, we won't sign you up for soccer this year!" Unlike the daily ride to school, soccer sign-up happens only once a season and when such "one shots" are used as a threat, we parents are tempted to repeat the threat in order to milk all the influence we can from the upcoming event.

> Mom and Dad are sending the message that punishment is a good (used by Mom and Dad) way to deal with people.

The threats and reminders become part of a bluff-and-huff game. Once you carry through and disallow soccer or go ahead with the sign-up anyway, you need a new threat to keep control.

Better to allow yourself and your family the enjoyment of single events such as soccer sign-ups and birthday parties without trying to use them to limit bad behavior or produce good. For rules, use a smaller, more repeatable event. For example, instead of threatening to throw out all the clothes you have to pick up (so extreme you feel you have to talk a lot), you could designate a laundry basket where scattered clothes go when Mom or Dad have to pick them up. Once our messy teenager is ready to do laundry, the clothes basket is made available. Any clothes parents have to pick up later are not available until the next basket opening.

Making amends. Most adults get a chance to make amends when a mistake is made—cleaning up the spill or apologizing for the blunder. Lesser mistakes get ignored altogether in the adult world. These are good strategies for kids, too.

> Using such a logical consequence is a good approach, but it can lead to trouble if the threatened consequence is too big.

When all else fails, is physical punishment ever a good idea? A week's grounding sometimes satisfies a parent's frustration, and Mom or Dad may feel that justice has been served, but have we made any headway with the victim?

Of course we are not talking about adults. With adults we try to steer them, advise them, or expect them to fix their own mistakes. The hard line adult punishment approach such as firing an employee, for example, is a last resort strategy, and physical punishment is not a choice at all. It would be outrageous, even illegal, with adults.

Ignoring. Ignoring has to be used carefully because bad behavior has been part of a habit to get entertainment or attention from Mom and Dad. The plan can backfire when inconsistencies creep in. If the usual amount of acting up will no longer get a reaction, the teenager may escalate the volume. Parents may give up ignoring and revert to punishment for this higher level and then return to the ignoring rule only to go back to punishment when the volume again reaches pain threshold. What will the kids learn from that routine?

To make the ignoring plan work, you need to emphasize the positive things the teen does to get legitimate attention.

When bad behavior can't be ignored and opportunities for encouragement are not enough, time out is a good alternative. For children, a little cooling off on a chair or in his/her room as a kind of punishment can work well if the threats and arguments are kept to a minimum. For teenagers, grounding is a kind of time-out.

The trick here is to keep the time-out short. A dramatic long house restriction will require too many threats and arguments. But short groundings are more likely to encourage parents to be quick and consistent.

Many parents have found the act of starting the time-out, putting their teenager on restriction, is the effective part. One minute was enough for older pre-schoolers and an extra grounding day at home is enough for a teenager. The message is sent when the prompt decision is made.

Some parents won't like these alternatives because they will not produce instant change, but then punishment won't produce magic either.

The best parental strategy will include praising the good, ignoring the

tolerable, and reacting with logical, mild, and repeatable consequences to the intolerable. This plan will give teenagers a good model to follow as well as a way to learn, and they will still feel safe risking the creativity we all want our kids to show.

3. Parent power and its limitations

Teen-children believe in magic—either the "Harry Potter" kind or the "Mommy will fix it" kind. Parents have their own brand of magic that says if they keep doing the same thing their teens will change for the better—a version of "The kids will fix it on their own."

My best letter of the year describes the problem well: "Our 15-year-old thinks our car is her personal bus service. She says, 'Drive me' and we do it, but she's not grateful. In fact, she is usually abusive in the car with bad language and a bad attitude. What can I do?"

> **The best parental strategy will include praising the good, ignoring the tolerable, and reacting with logical, mild, and repeatable consequences to the intolerable.**

Parents don't often retaliate when the kids are abusive because we don't want to seem mean or act like a kid ourselves, but yet we feel we have to object. We wouldn't carpool with a grump for long and the same should apply when Grump says, "Drive me."

We agreed on a new strategy. When the next "drive me" demand came up, Mom said, "OK, but I don't like riding around arguing with you, so it will take me a while to work up to it." Sometimes a little honest feedback about not wanting to ride around with grumps is effective—even if you still provide the ride. Also, service was delayed 30 minutes. Maybe little-miss-bad-attitude will learn from that.

When they were finally in the car, grumpy 15-year-old said, "So what do you want to talk about?"

Mom said, "Oh, well, what did you think of that movie last night?" A tolerable conversation began. To keep it that way, Mom needs to compliment

We wouldn't carpool with a grump for very long and the same should apply to kids. her daughter's good disposition when appropriate and be ready to pull back the services when necessary.

Imitation is a big part of disposition in kids. If an example is not set before them, how are they to know what to do or how to do it? Mom has to describe the behavior she doesn't like, and then she needs to set a good example. Mom has to be careful not to play a circular game of "kid is grumpy, Mom gets grumpy, kid copies more grumpiness."

Another parent wrote that his son was depressed and said, "He mopes around here, won't do anything, and won't be talked out of it. We've tried cheering him up and we've tried asking what's wrong, but his reasons are always different—school, bad friends, bored, or nothing to do. His attitude makes me feel the same way."

Again, Dad's example is more likely to have an influence than his argument. Don't worry so much that the kids won't listen—worry that they are always watching.

Yet, prolonged depression should be taken seriously. Few of us spend enough time talking with our children, but if talking about depression seems to be taken as a kind of sick entertainment, it may be time for someone else to do the talking—a counselor.

Diet and sleep habits play a large part in next-day depression. The National Sleep Foundation suggests teens and young adults should drink no caffeine, especially late in day. They also suggest less food and fluids before bedtime, no late heavy meals, and no nicotine. A good example and a reasonable routine can make a big difference.

Whether you have a grumpy teenage passenger in your car or a depressed one on the floor in front of the TV, these solutions are not easy to follow every day. The epilogue of this book (page 313) suggests starting a regular parent group where problems and possible solutions can be aired. We all need help and perspective from other parents.

There are no training requirements for raising children. With our driver's license and our other professional certificates in our pockets, we often oppose any childrearing license except marriage. Many believe in a free right to have children without any requirements from our community—even school. Maybe we're afraid of government interference.

One in 30 children in our neighborhoods is abused and neglected, But most of us are unsure where to draw the line on interfering. What would be your thoughts on the following case? A mother and daughter enter a supermarket. An accident occurs when the daughter pulls the wrong orange from the pile and 37 oranges gain their freedom. The mother grabs the daughter, shakes her vigorously, and then slaps her.

What is your reaction? Do you ignore the incident? After all, it's a family squabble and none of your business. Or do you go over and advise the mother not to hit her child. How is she likely to respond? If she rejects your advice, do you insist? Call the police?

Now suppose the girl was not that mother's daughter. Would you act differently? Suppose the daughter was 16 and yelled for help when her mother slapped her. Calling the police sounded extreme before. What if she was almost 21? Must she wait for her birthday to qualify as a victim deserving protection?

Whose rights should be considered first, the mother's rights to mother as she sees fit or the child's right to be protected from violence and abuse?

4. Mind your model of safety

You may not always notice how teenagers imitate the adults around them because they imitate the style more often than exact actions. Attitudes toward others, conversational style and temperament are the durable characteristics of teachers and parents that are copied. The family atmosphere develops from these regular reactions and imitated attitudes.

Parental reactions, critical and angry or fair and loving, are copied by the kids in

> Don't worry so much that the kids won't listen – worry that they are always watching.

their responses back to the parents and on to others. The routine habits recycle through the family, and everyone reaps a little of what they sow. Loving, pleasant, uncritical reactions give everyone a better day.

We have all seen parents who continually ride their children: "Blow your nose." "Tuck in your shirt." "Don't touch." On the other hand, we have all seen parents who never react and let their teenagers go their own way, ignoring responsibilities at home and school and showing no consideration for anyone else.

Parents who show consideration and admiration for their children usually have a positive and less frantic family situation. A mother who balances criticism with encouragements and frequent compliments is more influential and, by imitation, her kids help provide a better family atmosphere

Imitation is not always recognized for the powerful influence it is. Parents may spend much of their time watching and cautioning their teens. "Don't touch that. Stay away from that. Be careful." When it comes to child safety, parents, possibly for their own peace of mind, overestimate their own success. Peter Ehrlich, a pediatric surgeon at Children's Hospital in Morgantown, WV, summed up his research saying, "Unfortunately, just because a child has a bicycle helmet does not mean he will use it."

> The routine habits recycle through the family, and everyone reaps a little of what they sow. Loving, pleasant, uncritical reactions give everyone a better day.

Ehrlich found that while 70 percent of parents said their children always wear a helmet when riding their bike, only 51 percent of their kids wore them. Twenty percent of the kids say they never wear a helmet, while only 4 percent of parents said their children never wear one. The determining factor is their parent's example.

Parents want their children to be safe and at times will engage in wishful thinking to feel they are getting better results than they are. For example, Ehrlich also asked about car safety. Parents said their children wore seat belts

92 percent of the time, yet their children reported wearing them only 72 percent of the time. And 82 percent of the parents

> **T**he determining factor is their parents' example.

said their children always sat in the car's back seat, but only 43 percent of their kids said they did.

Of course, reprimanding the kids is easier than setting the right example, but it's the example that is always the most effective in the statistics. From seat belts and helmets to road rage and bullying in school, the parents' lead is the best predictor.

Teenagers also follow their parents' lead with other dangerous behaviors. Teens of alcoholics are three times more likely to become alcoholics. Smoking follows the same trends, the National Survey on Drug Use and Health reports. In our population, 450,000 will die of smoking and 100,000 will die of alcohol abuse—every year. On the average they will die 26 years earlier than their normal life span. In comparison, 6,000 died in the terror of 9/11.

A 32-year-old who was pulled over at night for driving an ATV on a public road while drunk and without lights, was asked why the ATV had no lights. His excuse: "It's my Dad's." He might have used the same excuse for his drinking habit.

Grades in school seem to follow the same trends. Teens of parents who had good grades in school have better grades. And children of parents who attend school conferences also have better grades. Watch what you're doing. The children are.

Most parents feel their childrearing record for last year was less than perfect but they remain the best influence on their kids this year, even if they don't always feel successful. A recent national survey by a nonpartisan research group, Public Agenda, in a poll of 1,600 parents of children 5 to 17, only 40 percent said they were doing better than a "fair job" in the past year.

> **F**rom seat belts and helmets to road rage and bullying in school, the parents' lead is the best predictor.

> **P**ositive influences will have to come from Moms and Dads.

When it came to the reasons for coming up short, parents listed "negative societal influences" first and then worries about too little family time. Cost of living came in third.

Most parents felt they could not count on either the society or the media for positive influences. I guess positive influences will have to come from Moms and Dads.

Parents in the study said even prime time TV was a negative influence on their children, yet most were not willing to do much about it. For example, only 22 percent said they ever "seriously considered" getting rid of the TV and half said their kids had a TV in his or her room (40 percent of 5- to 9-year-olds; 50 percent of kids over 10).

Both parents and teachers know kids have to be encouraged, so when the kids are not watching TV or computer monitors, the adults in their lives usually step in to inspire and encourage them. In our own experience, on the other hand, we parents know that as adults, once we're past the reward of payday, praise, encouragement and other positive reinforcement are hard to find.

Here's a good resolution: Find something to compliment, appreciate, and encourage each day. Tell your teen you noticed when he made a successful effort—cleaned up extra dishes—said something nice to his brother—got ready for school without complaints about clothes and lunches.

This "behavioral smile" is contagious; the kids are likely to copy your effort and the smile style will recycle through the family.

> **P**arents in the study said even prime time TV was a negative influence.

CHAPTER 10

Negotiating

1. When do they become "deserving?"

"Chris has taken to helping in the kitchen! He's twelve and does a good job. He made his own scrambled egg the other morning. I told him how impressed I was, and he made one for me!"

What fun it is to impress your parents! Chris loves to help with cooking, doing a little on his own and having his parents say how great he is.

Since parental approval is such an emotional high point, it is a shame some parents often begrudge their kids "too much" of this kind of reward. Reward and reinforcement are terms that may sound too mechanical because the words imply a contrived influence on behavior. But the most frequent reward your offspring will receive is your admiration and appreciation. Parents who are generous with these "rewards" are the most effective.

Yet many are still uncomfortable with the notion that selfish benefit is required to get children, or anybody else, to do the right thing. "They should do it because it's right, shouldn't they? They know it's good for them! They had better be glad they have a good home and a chance to learn and get ahead!"

Isn't this the way we all feel sometimes? We can't believe that kids would pass up an opportunity for personal growth or a chance to contribute just because there is no payoff.

It's children and teenagers we're talking about, of course. Employees who are asked to work a little longer or teachers asked to carry a larger load deserve rewards for their extra work. And our boss who expects a little overtime for nothing just doesn't understand our personal financial situation!

As a matter of fact, the higher you go, the more reward is expected for any effort. Managers and school principals don't feel respected unless they make more money. Corporate officers and members of Congress worry that lower salaries for them would bring in people less competent than themselves; and CEOs demand golden parachutes of stock options for the "proper incentive" to do a good job up there on top. So the higher ups commonly get more money and appreciation, while both money and appreciation become scarce for the "less deserving" and, of course, the kids.

Some parents object to the idea of rewarding teens because it might spoil them. But remember a spoiled teenager did not get that way because too much was provided. Many teens in families with small incomes are spoiled, and many teens with the benefits of wealthy families are not spoiled. A parent's routine reactions to their teenager's behavior determine the habits. Parents who pay attention to the highlights of what their teenagers do, will find plenty of opportunity to provide a deserved compliment. But if obnoxious behavior is "required" to get attention, then obnoxious behavior will be the rule.

> The higher ups commonly get more money and appreciation while both money and appreciation become scarce for the "less deserving" and, of course, the kids.

2. Rewards, punishments and threats

We all know what bad behavior is, but it's harder to pin down our expectations of good behavior. Bad language, for example, is much easier to spot in a family moment than a good attitude expressed toward a brother.

So we may encourage good behavior now and then, "Get that homework done and we'll have popcorn with TV after supper!" But bad behavior usually gets most of the attention, "If you're going to talk like that, turn off that TV and you can just forget about dessert."

We all understand the popcorn reward as positive reinforcement, and the no-dessert routine is a punishment strategy. But the most common strategy—the negative reinforcement strategy—is to use a mild threat, not just to intimidate bad behavior but also to motivate good behavior: "Clean up those dishes or there will be no TV tonight!" Now Mom's son may get busy on the dishes to avoid losing TV time, or he may hope to avoid the dishes and the threat because he thinks Mom is bluffing or she will forget.

This starts a destructive, competitive game: if he does the dishes, Mom wins. If he procrastinates and she's bluffing, he wins. If he procrastinates and Mom carries through with her threat, everybody loses. This example of negative reinforcement uses Mom's negative threats to motivate (reinforce) her teenager to do what she thinks he should. Since most of us are not very good at coming up with new threats or carrying through on the old ones, the situation seems to call for a lot of talking, nagging, and threats.

A teenager can use negative reinforcement, too. Parental requests are often met with a lot of flack or even threats. If the resistance succeeds, the daughter avoids the request and Mom or Dad avoids more obnoxious behavior by making fewer requests. Not a satisfactory outcome but one that is likely to be repeated, if it works.

A son's threats and lack of compliance make up his version of "flack" and some parents would rather give in (make the bed or take out the trash themselves) than "take all that flack." There's no payoff for Mom, just the avoidance of more resistance and flack.

A game of flack can go on a long time because it attracts attention and it's a little entertaining. Now if it also works in getting out of requests now and then, we are well on the way to building ourselves a real problem.

If your own life is surrounded by such negatives, you would probably explain most of what you do by saying, "Well if I didn't make his lunch (drive him to school, wake him up three times in the morning), there would be a price to pay." People who feel they are always avoiding a "price to pay" tend to remain in an unhappy rut.

If there is a mild form of terrorism this is probably it. Victims of negative reinforcement may never change because they have learned to take no risks. If you have this kind of situation in your family or marriage, it's time to talk about a change. Otherwise victims in the game are likely to think of leaving as soon as they can.

"If I don't do what he wants, would he really throw a fit as he sometimes has? Or is that time past?" Could I just tell my husband, "I really don't want to go shopping again this weekend" and get away with it? Would my wife really blow up if I said, "Let's just take in a movie instead of going over to the Smith's?" Or is it just a row I have remembered too long?

> Negative reinforcement is a mild form of terrorism.

Negative reinforcement looks for mistakes where "getting mad" or other threats can be carried out. To change this strategy, a parent or spouse needs to balance it with specific compliments and appreciation. Highlighting the good and the successes has a more durable effect and presents a better model to be imitated than a habit of posturing and bullying. In the long run, it makes for a happier family atmosphere.

Incentives or bribes? Some parents would tell you that rewarding children for good behavior is not good because it reduces their natural motivation and makes them into little counters of nickels, dimes, and M&Ms. If this were true in the adult world with its salaries, bonuses, overtime, and awards, our country would be in more trouble than it is and almost completely out of true dedication to a job well done.

How can it be that praise and support for a job well done is good for employees but bad for kids? Of course it is not bad; rewards, especially social ones such as compliments and appreciation, used carefully and generously, are essential to a person's development and to a good parent-teen relationship. There's more than a little prejudice against children in the spank-'em-don't-pay-'em attitude.

You might say much of life runs on the fear of mild punishments for coming up short. But punishment is intended to reduce behavior, not motivate action. Once the threat of punishment is withdrawn, as when a punitive teacher leaves the room, any power the threat of punishment had evaporates quickly.

Also a whack now and then is certainly a lot easier than looking for moments to praise and reward. But soon he will be too big to whack, and he will confine his efforts to whatever produces the benefits, the satisfaction or the pay.

The confusion over both rewards and punishments is in choosing an appropriate reaction for the nature of the behavior at hand. If a teenager is already interested in the task, such as a wanna-be rock star's interest in practicing her guitar, then offering money for practice time is obviously out of place. It ignores the musician's dedication to her craft, and if her natural interest is distracted to some payoff, then interest may very well go down hill. The satisfaction needs to come from improved performance and appreciation by those who hear it—including parents.

> There's more than a little prejudice against children in the spank-'em-don't-pay-'em attitude.

Teachers have learned the value of staying alert for successes and keeping the threats to only the necessary. Let's look at an example with a younger child, I think you'll see some similarities to your teenager:

Teacher: "When I do the multiplication cards with Gavin today, instead of threats I'll ignore all his foolishness and concentrate on his success."

(Later) "OK, Gavin, let's try those multiplication tables."

Gavin: "Oh no! Not again!"

Teacher: (Ignores Gavin's remark, gets out the cards.) "How about this one?"

Gavin: (Looks at "4 X 10") "Just add a zero! Just add a zero," he sings loud enough to get a laugh from others in the room.

Teacher: "That's right, but not so loud." (Oops, that slipped out. Gavin smiles a devilish smile.)

Gavin: (Beginning his most frequent behavior, foot swinging.) says "Forty." (Springing his favorite trap of good and bad behavior mixed together.)

Teacher: "Good." (With as little enthusiasm as possible.) "How about this one?"

Gavin: (Swings hard enough to kick the desk and stares in an exaggerated way at "9 X 9") "Could be eighty-one."

Teacher: "Yes, but don't…" Teacher realizes the imminent error of attention for kicking and falls silent. Gavin kicks the desk again but gets no reaction.

Gavin: "It is eighty-one."

Teacher: "Right you are and that's a hard one, too!"

Careful work and selective attention to Gavin's reactions during these sessions can be a true test of patience for a teacher or parent. Leg-swinging is likely to escalate to kicking before Gavin gives up, and he may return to it now and then when boredom sets in. The teacher, withholding attention for bad behavior, watches for the sign of boredom and terminates the session when it seems there will be no more opportunity for positive reinforcement.

It is difficult to be consistent and frequent with praise and admiration. As one mother said of her drummer son, "I already told him last week that I liked some of his music. What else can I say?" Mom needs to come up with more ways of saying it. "Your teacher says you're doing great! How can you do those complicated beats, they're terrific."

> The teacher, withholding attention for bad behavior, watches for the sign of boredom and terminates the session when it seems there will be no more opportunity for positive reinforcement.

Punishment for poor performance is not often subjected to the same analysis as reward. Possibly this is because we already know that punishment is not likely to have a positive effect on motivation, and certainly won't soothe the fear and loathing a teenager will have for learning situations that threaten punishment.

When I came home from high school in the afternoon, I developed the habit of cooking some part of the family supper before my mother came home. I never got a single nickel for doing it. I did have the appreciation of my Mom's and Dad's comments at dinner. I still do a lot of cooking. If Mom had reduced the praise and offered, instead, a dollar for every dish I prepared for supper, I might have lost my motivation as soon as I had enough dollars for the moment.

In the long run children grow up and become too big to punish but also too practical to waste time on unrewarded efforts. Mom and Dad's most powerful influence will always be their thoughtful reaction to the next effort of their children.

> Certain foods turn out to be the culprits more often than others.

3. Magic, diet and strange behavior

We would all like a magical answer to bad behavior and sometimes there is one. But often we are not willing to stay the course with a new approach because the effect is not immediate. For example, take the connection between bad diet and bad behavior.

"Dajon, my 15-year-old, often turns into a complete grump," his mother told me. "At other times he gets so hyperactive we think only medication would help. But four weeks on his new diet, and he settled down. He's still a little hyper, but a lot calmer."

Dajon was taken off all drinks with caffeine or added sugar. His diet and his disposition were carefully recorded everyday with special notes on fats, salt and sugar. He was found to be agitated by sugar and caffeine and aggravated to the point of tantrums by eggs, of all things. Certain foods turn out to be the culprits more often than others. Eggs, along with oranges, chocolate, wheat, tomatoes and milk are near the top of the list.

The Institute of Child Health found that of 78 hyperactive children like Dajon, 70 percent reacted to food additives, 64 percent showed adverse reactions to chocolate and milk, 57 percent to oranges, and 45 percent to wheat products.

In another study, Patrick Holford, a nutrition expert, found that nearly 90 percent of hyperactive children showed improved behavior when unnecessary additives were eliminated from their diets and essential vitamins, vegetables and fruits were added. Holford also explained that some chemical additives are "anti-nutrients;" that is, they actually rob children and teenagers of important minerals such as magnesium and zinc. Holford also cautions parents to be wary of "juice drinks" that are not 100 percent fruit juice. These products usually contain sugar or other sweeteners—most often Aspartame.

Thirty years ago Dr. Benjamin Feingold first proposed that artificial flavors, colors and preservatives could cause hyperactivity. Lately, some circumstantial evidence supports this connection. For example, in Europe fewer than 20 food additives are approved for use and only one child in 2,000 is diagnosed hyperactive. Compare this with the United States where more than 4,000 food additives are in use and one child in every four is diagnosed hyperactive. The majority of scientific studies have linked hyperactivity to these food additives. Some studies have not found any effect, but hyperactivity is not easy to define and measure.

Nevertheless, 70,000 new compounds have been invented and distributed into our food, air, and water since 1950. Only a few have been tested for their effect on human behavior. Our children and the rest of us are part of one massive uncontrolled clinical experiment dedicated to not finding any problems.

The Center for Science in the Public Interest reviewed 24 scientific studies and concluded that food dyes and certain other foods adversely affect children's behavior. Dr. Marvin Boris, one of the authors, says, "It makes a lot more sense to try improving a child's diet before treating him or her with a [suppressing medication]." He urged the Department of Health and Human Services to encourage parents and professionals to improve children's diets rather than depend on drug treatments.

4. Our expectations of boys and girls

Subtle messages can steer children toward their strengths or away from their opportunities. These messages about our expectations of sons and daughters creep in and imply who they are supposed to be.

Sending the right messages is part of a parent's job, but some unintentional messages can be misdirected. Girls often hear: "Are you happy?" Boys are more likely to hear: "Did you win?"

Girls hear, "Is your hair attractive?" and boys hear: "Is your hair combed?" Girls: "Don't eat too much." Boys: "Don't eat too little." Girls: "Exercise to look better." Boys: "Exercise to be stronger." Girls: "Be friendly and pleasant." Boys: "Be competent and capable."

In spite of recent changes in attitudes about equality, our expectations of boys and girls differ. And the world has different expectations of them. What we emphasize to boys as they grow differs from what we emphasize to girls. This is partly out of consideration for them and partly out of our desire to prepare them for a world we know still has sexist expectations.

One family told me of a conversation with their teens when the kids were picked up from school. It went something like this:

First Teenager: "I got my math papers back today, and I got more right answers than anyone!"

Parent: "Wow, that's great. I hope you'll have time this weekend to study more so you can stay out in front."

"Oh, I can keep up with them easy." (Is this a boy or a girl?)

"Well, to stay at the top, you have to keep at it." (Is this Mom or Dad?)

Second Teenager: "Mrs. Brown said we have to choose a final project for science class, either one of our chemistry experiments or a physics demonstration."

Parent: "Physics can be fun." (Mom or Dad?)

"My friend Jennie is doing a chemistry project."

"Wouldn't you like to be with Jennie?" (Mom or Dad?)

"I guess you're right."

What we emphasize to boys as they grow differs from what we emphasize to girls.

From the attitudes expressed, you might guess that the person in the math class is a boy, and Teacher Brown's student is a girl with a mom focused on social aspects of the class. From the outside, it's easy to tell one teen is encouraged to be concerned with success, while the other is encouraged to be comfortable. Hopefully, Mom and Dad are making their presumptions based on experience, not gender.

Parents should try to show a positive attitude toward the activities that fit the individual. Then they can encourage each teen to develop his/her very best, without too much concern for fitting common expectations. Without some care, it's easy to steer a teen toward only certain interests and hold him or her back from others.

As the attitudes of teenagers develop, their expectations of the opposite sex also take form. Without corrections from Mom and Dad, rowdy sons can learn abusive attitudes toward women, for example. Or a daughter can become cynical about her career prospects and settle for a marital situation with less opportunity than she deserves.

The sources of sex differences are found in both the environment and our heredity. Of course, there are real differences. Each child has a unique profile of potential talents and abilities. The parents' role is to encourage the discovered highlights and inclinations of each child while carefully avoiding the stereotypes and prejudice that only reduce the courage to face new challenges.

One letter from a concerned father asks, "Is it okay/normal/good for my 13-year-old son to be interacting so much with girls?" He said his son, I'll call him Erik, had many boy friends but, "At school lunch, eight or ten boys will be sitting at one table, but there's my son at a table with six or seven girls. Is there a way to guide him to spend his time with boys? When I was his age, I shunned girls and thought 'boys rule.' Is he just better adjusted than me?"

Erik is adjusting well, but he needs his dad's help in getting along with girls—not discouragement. If radio host Don Imus had more of Erik's experience in his boyhood he might have saved himself great embarrassment when he insulted young women basketball players. Such negative attitudes are dangerous baggage as Imus found out.

The youngest generation in the workforce was born after 1990. They have no experience with the exclusions of women as combat soldiers, as CEOs, or as presidential candidates.

Since the majority of students in medical school, law schools, and graduate schools are women, you need to learn to get along with all the people, not just the male half. Erik's dad can help by setting a careful example and avoiding thoughtless "Don Imus remarks" that imply that some group is unworthy or lacking potential.

Review your messages to your teens, both girls and boys. Comments that say women should watch their figure but men can have another beer are unhealthy for the boys and promote a value system for girls that is too shallow.

5. The gender gap

From toddlers to teens, boys are different. They are five times more likely to have accidents with bikes, sticks and baseball bats and are also five times more likely to get into trouble at school. Later on, they are four times more likely to have trouble with the law. They cause more teen-driving accidents and get most of the traffic tickets. They also have lower grades in school and are more likely to drop out.

There are exceptions, but generally girls develop social skills more rapidly, learn to please adults, teachers and parents, and surge ahead in school grades.

Men and boys need good role models before them in school, also, to keep them looking ahead and not giving up in the high school years. Without a college education the divorce rate is 50 percent; with college it is 25 percent. Crime rates among those who have not gone to college are five times higher than among college graduates, according to the Bureau of Justice Statistics.

A boy's inclination to give personal interests and entertainment top priority, while giving school responsibilities and social obligations short shrift, will cause problems in his school years and in his marriage later on. He needs encouragement to tackle the hard tasks in school and, when school is out, to keep his social priorities.

We need to sell both genders on the valuable applications of lessons taught in school. If no obvious connection between what is going on at school and what is important at home exists, we have a tough sell and the chances of a boy, or girl, sticking with it through college are diminished.

How about putting their history studies to use in planning the next vacation? What towns along the way have interesting history to offer? What science could your kids apply at home to repair jobs, to the garden or to the next computer technology Mom is thinking about buying?

The gender gap in college applications is greatest among minorities and lower incomes—just where you would expect the application of schoolwork at home to be least. The kids can't run only on the fumes in the tank that say, "Some day, you'll need this to get a job." They can get a job without all that education, but can they get a life?

> They can get a job without all that education, but can they get a life?

I recently attended a Bar Mitzvah ceremony for a friend's son. In this ritual, when a boy reaches 13 and has completed a prescribed series of studies, he is accepted as a man with his father in the synagogue. What a wonderful rite of passage! Too many boys in our community never receive such an endorsement and long for that recognition and respect.

Most parents, teachers, and counselors believe boys are slower in developing social skills and therefore may attract less support, acceptance, and admiration than their sisters. Some believe boys don't want the gushier praise; they only want to be recognized for the competence they have.

The support doesn't need to be a big fanfare. For most teens it can even be a little understated. The message doesn't need to be highlighted, just consistent. But if most opportunities are missed, a teenager's effort can quickly drop off.

A strange effect of sexism in our culture is that girls often show better adjustment in childhood than boys partly because girls make an earlier contribution to the family, particularly in the domestic chores. They enjoy early appreciation and are encouraged to do even more.

A son, in contrast, may feel ignored and search for some way to prove his worth, a way to show off. What will he find? If Mom and Dad don't help, temptations may come from a teen's friends who encourage risky behavior and have mischief on their minds.

Positive support is the major advantage parents have in competing against the peer influence of a teenager's friends who encourage and criticize without much thought.

> If Mom and Dad don't help, temptations may come from a teen's friends who encourage risky behavior and have mischief on their minds.

Gripe as both sons and daughters may about chore assignments, schoolwork, and learning social skills, our recognition of their successful forward steps will help maintain their satisfaction with themselves and will insulate them from risky behaviors that peers may encourage later on.

6. What is your discipline style?

Good and bad parenting styles are common topics among parents. When a story comes up one will say, "That's not how I would handle it" or, "I would want to be sure he got the message that (his behavior was not acceptable) (I set the limits) (he is still loved)."

It's hard to put a parenting philosophy into words and even harder to change it. For example there's the "I-set-the-limits" style that keeps the focus on guarding against excessive rowdiness, rule infringements, etc. This style can lead to a parent who feels like a policeman watching for mistakes.

Then there's the "Isn't-he-lovable" style where the parent thinks her teen can do no wrong or if he is wrong, he's too cute to reprimand. The "Oh-what's-the-use" style is the same but without the "cute" compliment.

The "I-just-want-to-get-through-the-day" approach is popular with harried parents who try to ignore most problems and use moment-to-moment negotiations for the rest.

I favor the balanced style that says, "Highlight the good points, it shows you like them, but be firm and consistent during the bad moments, it gives them security."

One father told me: "I've always felt I just didn't know where to start with Carlos. He always did so many things wrong!"

"So what did you work on first?" I asked.

"Everything, I guess—all his mistakes. Whenever I had the chance I went after something. But later, when the "shotgun" approach didn't work, I sharpened my focus and lowered my expectations. I tried to catch him being good, doing right on some little things. When I got realistic about what Carlos might do right, he improved and we got along better, too!"

Carlos' father switched from "why-aren't-you-perfect?" to "you-do-some-things-really-well." It requires more tolerance and patience, but the relationship between father and son is much improved. He'll not LEARN if he doesn't DO. And he won't DO if every attempt is criticized.

When to let your child take over some responsibilities is the hardest part of a parenting philosophy. It's tempting to hold on to control as long as you can. But it's dangerous to suddenly switch to "you're grown up now; it's your responsibility" when your teenager graduates from high school.

Better to start early. List the responsibilities your teen can do now: make her bed, lunch, and phone calls; clean her room; buy homework supplies; arrange rides to school and activities; make dental appointments; keep a bank account; choose a summer camp.

Psychologists worry about our modern society forcing adult concerns on children too early. We should not be tempted to force financial, social, or career concerns on young teens as a means of "growing them up." But gradually giving over responsibilities that they are ready to master will increase their abilities and their self-respect.

> He'll not LEARN if he doesn't DO. And he won't DO if every attempt is criticized.

Since most errors occur when a person tries a new task, parents may procrastinate when they should risk giving over new responsibilities. Mistakes are a part of learning. Give your teenager responsibility now, gradually, not abruptly on the steps of a college dormitory, or in the back of a church just before a ceremony. And with each new responsibility, keep the praise and incentives handy.

Most of the parents who write me describe day-to-day discipline problems with the 3- to 16-age group. Parents complain about frequent tantrums and a lack of cooperation. They feel they have lost control of their kids.

Since kids live for parental approval and attention, how is it that so much control is lost? Six parenting principles can help improve these daily family interactions.

Principle 1: Acknowledge specific good behaviors. Most parents can easily list the bad behaviors they find objectionable but have only a vague idea of good behaviors they hope for. So "hitting his sister" may be high on the bad behaviors list. Concrete incidents of such mistakes come up often along with "screaming loud enough to stampede cattle," "dragging the dog by his tail," and the list goes on.

Good behaviors such as saying something nice to your sister, talking in a normal tone, or petting the dog are often not specified at all so if they occur, they are not likely to be detected or attract much attention. If you have nothing good to look for, you probably won't find it. So create a good list, at least in your mind, and pay attention to it.

Principle 2: Limit your reactions to fits, snits and tantrums. Your reprimands may not have the negative effect you intend. There's always a challenging, maybe even entertaining, side if parents try to be too creative in their reactions. All parents suspect confrontations are, in part, entertainment. Keep your reprimands plain vanilla.

Principle 3: Avoid punishment. Punishment doesn't teach much and it's likely to be imitated. Then everyone's attitude gets worse.

Principle 4: Like your children. Of course we all love our children, but do you like them? Do they know it when you do? To be "cool," kids may ignore your compliments, but the long-term effect will still make a difference. It's easy to criticize but the result may be a teen who says, "She just doesn't think I'm good enough." As with good listening habits, liking habits are part of the overall parental attitude a teenager will take to heart.

Principle 5: Watch your conversational habits. It's not easy to turn off the TV or interrupt your work when you hear, "Can we talk?" but your full attention is important. Face up to your conversational partner, not "in their face" but looking at them and showing that you are paying attention.

Principle 6: Make sure the boys have the right encouragement. Insist on both boys and girls doing their chores. Chores and homework of all kinds develop their skills and their enthusiasm for work done successfully.

7. When parents disagree

How to raise the kids is a common source of marital conflict. It comes right after the most frequent disagreements and arguments about money.

Parenthood is learned on the job with an added dose of our own childhood experiences. So Mom and Dad are likely to have different standards and thresholds for patience and tolerance. Keeping the complaints list short and specific can help.

José is 12 and his parents have different approaches to parenting. In general Mom's rules for Jose are more liberal than those applied to his sister, Bella, who is 15. But Dad seems less tolerant of José's mistakes than Bella's.

Mom says her husband is very strict. He criticizes their teenagers' posture, eating habits, and conversation. He comments on their selection of friends, when he thinks they are wrong, and where they should go and not go. He imposes strict curfews—often the biggest problem.

Their differences are most troubling when it's time for discipline—which usually means punishment:

José: "Grounded for a whole week?"

Dad: "That's right. I told you to be in by 9:30."

José: "That's not fair."

Mom: "He was only ten minutes late, maybe a whole week is too much."

Dad: "Don't interfere in this, he has to learn." (José stomps out.)

Mom and Dad's disagreement can tempt José to argue and look for loopholes. He may even try to recruit Mom to his side causing even more problems. Dad's discipline strategy doesn't seem to have a positive side.

When parents get a chance to talk over their strategies, it's tempting to skip the topic for the sake of being pleasant. Progress can come from the following ground rules.

1. Make a very short list of only the top two or three problems worthy of parental effort. Decide on a consistent reaction to these problems and agree to ignore the less important ones for now. Often parental disagreement is exaggerated by a long list of complaints.

2. Keep the list specific. Don't list attitudes or general characteristics, but only actual behaviors such as, "He comes in late," not, "He is irresponsible." It's hard to pin down general attitudes or characteristics because they don't happen at a particular time. As a result, parental reactions occur at irregular times when one parent has "had it up to here" and the other has not.

3. Avoid blaming each other for the mistakes of your child. It won't help and the kids will pick up the idea that others can be blamed for their mistakes.

4. Be specific about the good behaviors you expect. If you know exactly what is bad but only have a vague notion of what is good, which are you likely to find? We've all had a boss with this problem.

So while creating a short complaint list you can agree on, highlight some likeable habits to look for as well. When one couple added that part to the list, their son said to me, "I knew they loved me; I didn't know they actually liked me!"

There will be arguments still, but the family atmosphere can be improved if parents limit the complaints list to the priorities and remain on the lookout for success as well as mistakes.

SKILL 3

Steering Through the Minefield of Bad Habits

Mom is barely home with the new baby when confusion about the basic three—eating, sleeping, and, a little later, toilet training—begins. All of these are such natural and necessary behaviors you would think they would be the easiest tasks for parents to teach and children to learn. So you would suppose teenagers would be through with all of this. Instead, all three are troublesome territory right through the teenage years. This is because parents have limited control and limited information about their children's real moment-to-moment needs of the basics. Yet they still have a strong desire for everything to go just right for the sake of their offspring's health and hygiene.

CHAPTER 11

The Early Basics

1. Why are the basics so much trouble?

Since almost all adults end up learning the basic three, we know the job is eventually accomplished. Why is it, then, that the basic three, particularly the eating and sleeping part, are often trouble until the kids are 20 or 30? As all experienced parents know, emotions get in the way when it comes to perfecting the basics.

Eating, sleeping, and elimination have special characteristics beyond just the essentials for health. Keep in mind these five aspects of the basic three.

1. The basic three are somewhat out of the control of parents. You can't force someone to eat, sleep, or use the bathroom.

2. The only direct information about the moment-to-moment need for food, sleep, or elimination comes from the not-very-reliable son or daughter and is not directly knowable by parents.

3. The behaviors are somewhat out of the control of the child-teen as well. Other conditions, deprivations, and feelings enter in. Neither children nor teenagers can feel hungry or sleepy any time their parents think they should.

4. The basic three are partly driven by even more obscure conditions and experiences that may seem irrelevant. Even with us adults, our eating, sleeping, and bathroom activities are related, in a way not completely understood, to coffee, tea, excitement, boredom, depression, worries and distractions, too little or too much exercise or the need to escape an unpleasant situation—just to name a few.

5. Being private activities, the basic three also comprise the last bastion of self-control and privacy of one's own life. They are the last places any of us, child, teenager or adult, will tolerate interference.

2. Basic number 1: What, when and how to eat

Eating occurs naturally for the first year until it dawns on our newest offspring that there's power in the control over when and what to eat. The resistance starts even before a child can sit up when he blathers a drool down his front just for fun.

The cuteness wears thin when a few months later he starts throwing unwanted food at the cat and you say, "No, no, eat that. It's good for you." The first skirmish of a 20-year diet battle has begun.

Often parents worry the children don't eat enough. To urge them to eat more, parents may turn to threats: "Eat the rest of your beans or there will be no dessert." Or they may appeal to love: "Eat it for Mommy." One client-adolescent of mine had a 200-pound problem from trying to please. He said to me, "The more I eat, the more Mom and Dad are satisfied."

While parents may urge their children to eat more, they are not likely to urge them to eat less. But the risk of an American child-teen endangering his health by eating too much is actually the greater long-term risk. Eventually, we all have to learn to listen to our bodies, not our Mommies.

Too many young people are obsessed with weight loss and appearance. One Canadian study of 11-year-old girls found that 44 percent were on a diet to lose weight and a study from Exeter University found that of 37,000 girls between

12 and 15 years old, 57 percent listed appearance as the biggest concern in their lives.

Childhood obesity (that is, 20 percent above normal, healthy weight)

> **By the time our children are adults, half will be overweight and one-third will be obese.**

has risen from less than 10 percent of children 8 to 18 in the 1980s, to more than 15 percent in 2000. By the time our children are adults, half will be overweight and one-third will be obese. Anorexia (refusal to eat) and bulimia (purging after eating) is also a growing problem in many families.

Sometimes we worry they eat too little. The Center for Health Statistics estimates that about 9,000 children are treated for bulimia (purging) each year and about 8,000 for anorexia (dangerous refusal to eat). In the first year of college the percentage of bulimics can rise to 18 percent of women (4 percent of men). Even at the earlier ages of 12 to 18 over one percent may be anorexic. Onset can be as early as 10 (Jane Fonda revealed that her secret bulimic habits began at 12, sometimes bingeing and purging 20 times in one day).

My grandmother and my mother constantly worried about the eating habits of us kids, but they gave no thought at all to their own example—Grandma didn't even set a place for herself when she served large family dinners. "I'll be fine, just eat," she said.

Control is often at the center of the battleground over eating habits. Both parent and teenager may struggle for power and try to keep control of who eats what and how much.

No one is likely to tolerate interference with his eating habits. So troublesome food rules at the dinner table can easily become mere power struggles to see if Mom and Dad can really win. The price of admission to the clean plate club may be too high for the family to pay.

The eating disorders of teens and adults usually have some roots in this issue of control. One daughter told me, "They (parents, teachers, relatives, and nearly everyone else) tell me what to wear, when to wear it, when to study and when to go to school. But they can't make me eat and they can't make me not eat. And I'll prove it. I'll eat all I want or I won't eat anything at all!"

When parents insist on too much control, a teenager may rebel and may ignore his or her own body signals about when to eat and how much.

Left on their own, all family members will make diet mistakes. Outside of the home, food temptations will be bungled, but the overall diet will not be determined by an occasional slip-up at the convenience store or fast food restaurant.

Take control where you have it—at the food store. Shopping for food is usually a parent's job. This is where Mom and Dad have the most control and influence over the family diet, not in table arguments. The choices of pints instead of gallons of ice cream, peas instead of peanuts, and fruit instead of candy, can make up a better diet going home. Better to make good choices at the market (low fat, salt, and sugar) and leave the family mealtime conversation for other topics. If it's not in the house, they can't eat it. If you provide healthy snacks in front of the TV, they will (still) come.

Left with the selection you provide, most kids will hold to a reasonable diet with a few mistakes, just like adults. Focusing too much on eating is treading on dangerous ground. You also give up a mealtime the whole family could enjoy.

One Mom said, "My children just want ice cream and snacks—nothing that's any good for them. I buy fruit and vegetables but usually end up throwing half of it away."

She said her four kids eat a half-gallon of ice cream and a package of 12 snacks every week. "That's 26 gallons of ice cream and about 600 snacks a year," I said.

Mom said, "Well, it sounds like a lot, but what can I do?"

If Mom didn't buy unhealthy food, the kids would still fuss, but they would have to eat their fat, salt and sugar elsewhere and settle for fruit juice pops instead of ice cream at home; water in the fridge for drinks; baby carrots and celery for snacks.

Other food-serving strategies. When cutting back seems to be in order, sometimes buffet style serving at home is best. Everyone gets what they want on their plate, but the extra food is not in front of them on the table. Even if some family members return for a refill, the amount of food they take is likely to go down when compared with how much they would take with all those serving bowls at arm's reach.

Another good strategy is to serve one course at a time—salad with nothing else yet on the table, then another course. The advantage of this routine is that food has more time to get to the body sensors that signal fullness. Fast eating usually means over-eating and bad choices.

One mother told me that her son's routine choices improved when she gave him part of the cooking chores. Once he began cutting up salad additions and boiling the vegetables, his choices at meals were gradually wider and more reasonable.

Table manners are best taught by infrequent corrections and by example. You wouldn't tell a dinner guest to, "Be sure to eat all your asparagus and don't use your knife to eat mashed potatoes." Table nagging the kids can easily become the primary dinner confrontation. Teenagers in this game will learn to use food to resist Mom and Dad's control or they may eat to please them. Neither outcome is healthy preparation for a lifetime of eating.

If your teenager is healthy and in the normal weight range, you can encourage happier mealtimes and de-emphasize a teen's preoccupation with appearance by keeping argument and urging about food at the minimum.

Some children with problems related to eating too little and many have the problem of eating too much. Eating too much of the wrong foods has become epidemic in America, and the statisticians tell us that 2004 was the year obesity took over as the No. 1 cause of early death in the United States.

> Teenagers in this game will learn how to use food to resist Mom and Dad's control or they may eat to please them. Neither outcome is healthy preparation for a lifetime of eating.

3. Meal time should be family time

In a study of 5,000 teenagers, Dr. Maria Eisenberg of the University of Minnesota Medical School found that family meals together make healthier kids and healthier families—even in families that don't have great relationships.

"Just the eating together part is related to healthy outcomes," said Dr. Eisenberg in her report in the Archives of Pediatrics and Adolescent Medicine.

Staff in the study asked teenagers how often they had eaten with their families in the previous week. In another part of the interview, they asked whether the teenagers thought their parents loved them and whether they could talk to their mother or father about problems.

The researchers also asked about grade-point averages and other behaviors—did the teenagers drink, smoke, or ever think about suicide?

For years experts have known that strong families often dine together and strong families make strong kids. Not just bones and bodies but stronger character as well.

"Each additional meal together per week has some benefit to the kids," Eisenberg said. So if supper has to be delayed until a late family member is home, it's worth it.

Mealtime is a good opportunity for parental listening. Save your complaints about your adolescent's behavior for other times when siblings won't be there to chime in, confuse the message, and place the blame.

The effect was strongest for girls. For example, half of the girls who hadn't eaten with their families in the previous week said they smoked cigarettes, compared with only 17 percent of girls who had eaten with their families every day. For boys, the rates were 36 and 22 percent. Alcohol use and suicidal thoughts showed the same trends in both boys and girls.

Even after factoring out the questions about strong family connections, the kids who had regular family meals still fared better than those who never ate with their families. In short, these meals make an independent contribution to kids' health and happiness beyond strengthening the family connection.

Of course, teens will select poor diets when left on their own. Any parent could have told us that. Eating together gives some control of diet back to parents.

Keep the family meal in your family routine. And keep the routine clear of other activities. TV during dinner doesn't promote good conversation.

4. Even teenagers don't know what's good for them

Animals seem to have an instinct for what to eat and how much. Youngsters seem to have lost that instinct, if they ever had it. But animals have the advantage of only a few choices whereas American children and their parents are bombarded with choices everyday by the media.

On the whole, young American Moms watch the diet of their babies carefully. But once the children have a say, the diet deteriorates because there are many conspiracies to lure the kids away from the right food choices. Supermarket displays in the checkout lines, TV, movies and food courts in the mall all do battle with what Mom and Dad want their kids to eat.

The U.S. Department of Agriculture's Center for Nutrition Policy and Promotion measures the degree to which a person's diet includes daily servings of the five major food groups: grains, vegetables, fruits, milk products, and meats. Proper limits on cholesterol and salt and fat consumption are also taken into account. By age 15, the average score in the fruit category, for example, is only 50 percent of its healthy level in infancy. Also by age 15, only 12 percent of the girls meet the dietary recommendations for milk servings.

> Giving in to the "He knows waht he needs" parental approach leads to the worst habits. The kids don't know.

Giving in to the "He knows what he needs" parental approach leads to the worst habits. The kids don't know. Across all categories of the Healthy Eating Index, less than 30 percent of children over five years old maintain a good diet.

We all know teenagers are shortsighted, but parents are often shortsighted too. Of course health habits influence the sick days from school, but childhood habits also influence their life expectancy in later years. Before the teenage years are over, a child's longevity may be determined by habits that have already done harm.

Early body weight and eating habits influence the longevity number. For every pound overweight your child is as a young teenager, his prospects for longevity are reduced a little.

Neither teenagers nor children make good advisors when shopping for food. Food shopping is where Mom or Dad have the most control and influence over the family diet. They shouldn't give it up.

Give the kids a chance for a long life. You might think that once the kids grow beyond your protection it's up to them to take care of themselves. But how long they live as adults has a lot to do with how they live, and eat, right now.

Even short-term changes make a difference in health. At the American Heart Association annual meeting, Dr. James Barnard reported that teenagers on a 13-day low-fat, high-fiber diet, with exercise, lowered their cholesterol 25 percent and blood fat triglycerides 41 percent.

Everything we do is balanced against the effort and inconvenience to do it. All behaviors, even getting out the donuts or hot snacks, have an inconvenience. You have to get a plate, find a fork, warm the food up, and get a drink to go with it. The notion is called "response cost."

So keep the healthy food handy and ready—fruit on the table, ice water instead of soft drinks in the fridge. Let the fat, salt and sugar be the ones that are least likely to be bought at the supermarket and the most troublesome to get out at home. The kids will buy other snacks, but at least at home your diet and theirs' will be better.

> You have to get a plate, find a fork, warm the food up, and get a drink to go with it. This notion is called "response cost."

5. Basics 2 and 3: Bedtime and toilet training problems still hanging on

Parents treasure those free moments when the kids are in bed, and no demand, sibling fight or childhood disaster needs attention. But naps evaporate from the daily routine by the age of five or so and bedtime gets later. Bedtime, and then getting up the next morning, often become the most dreaded arguments of the day.

Struggles over bedtime seem inevitable because parents know the long-term consequences that can include grumpy kids the next day, and nearly unconscious teens as well as children stumbling about getting ready for school in the morning. The kids are always focused on the here and now and don't care about tomorrow morning's consequences.

Of the basic three, eating, sleeping and toilet training, sleeping can produce the most confrontation because so many factors can change the needs of a child-teenager and the demands of parents.

Arguments at bedtime usually have their cause in the day already done. TV and computer game hours may have replaced outdoor activities. Yet if vigorous exercise comes too close to bedtime it may create insomnia instead of making sleep more welcome. When these bedtime problems arise, keep a daily record for a week or two in order to recognize eating, exercise, and TV habits that can interfere with sleep.

Eating too close to bedtime can also interfere with sleep, and as adults know from experience, particular foods can disrupt sleep. Caffeine, sugar or even too much plain water in the evening can keep a person up.

To smooth future bedtimes, parents may need to design a new strategy. Your best hope is in determining which activities play a role in your teen's sleep pattern. Look first at diet and exercise routines. Snacks with caffeine such as a glass of soda or a piece of chocolate should not be part of the diet of a teen with sleep problems.

A daily chart that records both the activities that might be related to sleep (exercise, diet, exciting or frightening TV) and a note on how the bedtime routine went on that day can provide a better understanding. Also record what your teenager drinks, particularly those drinks with sugar or, please forbid it, caffeine.

For 30 percent of kids who have sleeping difficulties the problem is intensified by bad diet and disrupted routines. Each night, we all go through different stages of light and heavy sleeping. There are moments when we are awake, episodes so brief we don't remember them. Has your teenager come to expect conversation or computer entertainment if he or she wakes up, or stays up, at night?

Many counselors provide the following tips for both children and adults:

1. **To keep your body's routine**, try to go to bed at about the same time each night and get up at the same time each morning including weekends.

2. **Avoid heavy meals, caffeine, chocolate, and exercise before bed.**

> One embarrassing experience can worry a teenager for years about where is the next handy bathroom.

3. **For children, a relaxing routine before bed is important,** such as a warm bath and a reading session. Avoid exciting or upsetting TV in the evening.

Depression, hyperactivity and other adjustment disorders in teens are also often caused by disrupted routines and bad habits connected with dieting, exercising and sleeping.

Bad dreams, digestion troubles, and breathing disorders such as apnea account for some problems, but the majority can be helped by adjustments in family habits.

Toilet training and bedwetting. Psychologists back to Freud have considered toilet training a crucial childhood experience. For most of us, toilet training acquired some of its importance from the natural reaction of parents to the disgusting and embarrassing outcomes of mistakes. So the emotions arise first in the mind of the parent and only later in the mind of the child-teen.

When to use the toilet is the last place an older child is likely to tolerate any interference. Yet even young adults can make a distracted miscalculation. One embarrassing experience can worry a teenager for years about where is the next handy bathroom.

For older kids, you may need to remind them about what causes problems. Too many juices or soft drinks after supper can set up bed-wetting problems. If a child insists on water at bedtime, put only the amount you want him to drink in the glass. He may not have the long-term sense to stop halfway down the glass.

Late-evening snacks can add up to bad nights even for adults, but teens, still on short-term satisfaction, may not see, or want to see, the connection. Stomach cramps, sleeplessness, and even general restlessness can be caused by the extra ice cream, popcorn or just extra helpings at supper.

6. Other basics they need to know

Should you get serious about chores? The most dangerous thing on earth is a human being with nothing to do. A teenager may not cause as much havoc as an adult, but a teen delayed from moving on to new challenges has a surprising ability to find trouble. So as soon as it is reasonable, encourage and reward your kids for making their bed, cooking a meal, washing the car, and looking after a younger sibling. Start early to build their self-respect and their pride in capabilities as soon as it's reasonable.

When is reasonable? Earlier than many would think. It's not when a teenager can finally do a perfect job. Of course a youngster will make mistakes and some dinners will be a disappointment, as will room cleaning and grass mowing, but that only means someone is benefiting from practice.

Negotiating chores is not a family highlight, but doing them will give your teen pride in his abilities and reasons for caution when a friend suggests a dangerous habit. The family routine is essential to a teen's insulation from bad habits. If your daughters and sons think they are worthwhile and capable, they will feel they are contributing, then they are more likely to take care of themselves and shun self-damaging habits.

Parents are often hesitant in handing over the daily chores of life because they can do these chores better themselves. They may also feel guilty if they insist that their child/teen take part. Other parents are often inclined to protect their teens and children from chores as if the chores were an evil to be concealed as long as possible.

Completing the drudgeries of life is, in fact, one source of satisfaction that wards off depression. With kids,

> **The most dangerous thing in the world is a human being with nothing to do.**

this benefit is often missed because the verbiage that goes with chores is usually negative. Both parents and teens talk of "chores" as burdens to be carried. That's true, but the benefit to psychological health should not be forgotten by a parent facing resistance from a growing-up teenager prone to being grumpy.

Boys, in particular, are often overprotected from chores and suffer feelings of exasperation at having nothing "really worthwhile" to do. Remember, most teenagers believe the only "really worthwhile" things are on computers and cell phones.

Parents can teach the value of chores like all others, by example, and by seeing to it that their daughter or son gets opportunity and encouragement for his or her domestic efforts. For a boy, there may be unrecognized sexism in denying him training for everyday chores. He may not know he is being shortchanged. He may complain all the way through making his bed, but the effect on his self-respect and his value of himself will improve with every competence he acquires.

> Completing the drudgeries of life is, in fact, one source of satisfaction that wards of depression.

When an adult refuses, let's say, a drink at lunch, what is the most common excuse? "Sorry, I can't, I've got a lot of work this afternoon, I have things to do." The implied self-evaluation is: "I have important things to accomplish (skills to use). I am too valuable!" Where will a boy or girl learn that?

I met one of my 13-year-old friends in the mall the other day, but he couldn't stop to talk. "I told my friends I can't hang out at the mall today. I make dinner on Tuesdays, and Mom and I already bought the stuff!"

And when he is tempted to try some self-degrading or self-damaging drug he will be a little more likely to value himself and believe he has too much to lose.

7. Allowing practice

The essential ingredient to child-rearing is a parent allowing practice. Practice in turn, makes success possible. And from success you can learn a new satisfaction and respect for yourself.

"Corinne, could you set the table for supper?"

"Mom, I don't know where all that stuff is."

"Start with the silverware."

(Corinne puts out the silverware.) "Why do I have to do everything?"

"Now the plates."

"OK, can I go?"

"Now these glasses and serving spoons and you're done!"

Later, Corinne's brother says, "That was good."

Mom: "Thanks, Corinne helped."

Corinne : "I set the whole table!"

In spite of the flack at the beginning, Corinne has added a practice session and another small ability to her growing up. She has another reason to feel valuable, another reason to think carefully when the dangerous temptations come along.

Keeping a daily record of your teen's behaviors is a frequent subject of this book. None of us welcomes the inconvenience of doing this no matter how worthwhile, but it keeps the arguing to a minimum and, if the chart includes chores the kids already do, the incentive is there from the beginning.

A software product called "Easy Child" makes the recordkeeping easier. "This week's points equal next week's privileges," is the slogan of the people selling "Easy Child" on the internet. The software includes charts for parents to track agreed-on tasks while a privilege chart lists the earned points and their value.

The producers of the Easy Child materials also subtract points for negative behaviors such as arguing and fighting, but I think subtracting from the total produces increased arguing and weakens the value of the points just as the weakening dollar can ruin our economy. If points can evaporate, they can also lose value. Better to keep the point system and the punishments separate.

Don't reject the reward idea as "bribery." We all have lots of reasons for going to work this week and one of them is

Withholding pay from some devalued age group, race or gender has always been a bad, unproductive policy.

the pay. Withholding pay from some devalued age group, race or gender has always been a bad, unproductive policy.

8. Emergency basics

The basics of everyday living also have their dangers even at the older ages. Parents should have training and information about emergency situations.

My youngest daughter, in her 30s and sitting in an outdoor restaurant, was stung by a bee. Within one minute she had red areas on her skin. In two minutes she called me on her cell phone and asked if she should "do something."

In five minutes she had trouble breathing and her dinner companions made a crucial early decision to step over the privacy issue. They insisted on taking her to a nearby hospital. One person called ahead and two others started moving her to their car. In another five minutes they were at the hospital but she was unconscious and not breathing! With a shot and other treatment she was recovering only 20 minutes after the sting.

Most of us would have waited too long. I would probably have denied the possibility of a true emergency and hoped the problem would clear up. I would not know what to do and she probably would have died.

Many children and adults have these life-threatening allergic reactions to bee stings or foods. When the reaction begins, cells of the immune system release massive amounts of chemicals—particularly histamine. As with my daughter, the skin frequently shows symptoms first—hives, itching, swelling and redness. Blood pressure drops and the individual may faint. His or her nose, mouth and throat may become obstructed by swelling. Bee stings, peanuts, other nuts, milk, eggs, soybeans and fish products are the main offenders, says the University of Michigan Health System website.

> In another five minutes they were at the hospital but she was unconscious and not breathing!

Marc S. McMorris, M.D. and director of Michigan's system, recommends that people with potentially life-threatening allergies be evaluated by their primary care doctors, and subsequently referred to an allergist, to determine if they need to carry an aggressive therapy such as an epinephrine auto-injector.

> Jeffrey's eyes started tearing, but he said nothing.

Choking is a similar and more common childhood emergency. Five-year-old Jeffrey watched his brother being silly at dinner making bubble noises in his milk. Jeffrey laughed and at the same time took a bite of meat, the most common culprit. He stopped talking, put his hands to his throat and tried to stand up.

Mom demanded, "Jeffrey, what's the matter?" Jeffrey eyes started tearing, but he said nothing. He was choking and could not speak or breathe.

In 2001, the Office of Communication estimated that over 17,000 children under 15 were treated for emergencies related to choking on toys and food. More than one in every 100 died.

Nearly 80 percent of the children who die each year from airway obstructions are under five years old. Jeffrey was in danger of dying from the most common cause of all accidental deaths among young children—choking on food.

> Choking is a common childhood emergency.

Would you know what to do for Jeffrey? If you called 911, how soon would help arrive? What could you do to save Jeffrey while you wait for the paramedics?

Should you tip his head back or forward? Should he lie down? Should you give mouth-to-mouth resuscitation or should you try the Heimlich maneuver? Exactly how do you do these procedures? If Jeffrey can talk a little, should you still slap him on the back or would that only risk more choking?

If you know the answers to these questions and you are practiced in these skills you are among the very few. There's no time to learn during an emergency. Less than 5 percent of parents will ever take the time to learn the emergency procedures for heart and breathing difficulties. But for those who do, they could raise the survival rate of the victims by as much as 40 percent when, for example, CPR (Cardio-Pulmonary Resuscitation) is applied correctly.

The American Heart Association's course, CPR for Family and Friends, is offered at most local hospitals and explains treatments for both choking and health-related problems. The three-hour course explains what to do and gives you practice in doing it.

We all have to do our best to prevent these problems. If an emergency comes, be informed and ready to help.

CHAPTER 12

Their privacy, your responsibility

"Jasmine, put that video game down and get to your homework."
"Just a minute, I almost have the bonus points."
"If I have to come in there…"
"Can't you just leave me alone?"

Replace video game with TV, CD-player, video iPod, eating junk food or just plain fidgeting, and you have the collection of arguments that fill many parenting hours. Children and teens do not have complete privacy because their view of what is safe, appropriate, productive or useful has not yet surfaced above what is fun.

1. "I know what's good for me, just leave me alone"

A teen may give up piano lessons when the first few lessons produce no laudable success, but then he or she may lock onto the immediate feedback of video games that have no useful result at all. Why can't they see the difference in long-term benefits between developing musical talent and a computer obsession?

That may be the most perplexing question for parents in this generation. Piano practice is work. It is only appreciated much later. Video games are fun right now, but too private for anyone to ever care. So the kids choose video games for the immediate entertainment and get depressed later. Can't they see that? No. Their short-term view doesn't reach that far ahead.

So how can you steer your teenager away from wasteful habits and toward more productive activities when the advantages have not yet appeared on his or her short-range radar screen?

You can't just leave a boy or girl alone because they don't know what's good for them. They're not likely to follow your advice either, unless they are motivated to do it, and kids are not easy to motivate. They often shrug off parental praise and admiration because they don't want to appear weak or in need of "outside" support. But left to their own perception of what is good for them, piano practice is likely to be replaced by video games and homework may be replaced by TV. A teen's motivation to follow better directions will have to come from immediate success with useful activities. How can a parent's reaction help?

The answer is in the response to, "What happens next?" In the video game, the points immediately build up or the Klingons are killed off. In the beginning of piano practice a teen learns only the scales and an unfamiliar song—Mom says it's wonderful but that's parental praise, and they know why she's saying that. For most kids, piano lessons require a creative teacher who assigns up-to-date attractive songs in a surmountable format early on. It's the early success that will keep the practice going.

Chores require the same attention to what happens next. If Farrah makes her bed or Alana takes out the trash, the help should be recognized. For teens, this means a little more than just, "Thanks."

Dylan: "I'm hungry. When's supper?"

Mom: "Not right away, I have lots to do. Want to help?"

Dylan: "I'll just wait."

Mom: "Have one of those crackers. How about rinsing the asparagus and getting it started?"

Dylan: "It's not my thing."

Mom: "Not mine either, but give me some help."

Dylan: (grudgingly) "OK."

Mom's weak request, "Want to help?" doesn't produce any assistance. But later when she requests directly, "…give me some help," she gets a little cooperation. This is a small step. It will not assure his adjustment in college. It may not even result in remembering that asparagus needs to be steamed. However, it may bring Dylan a little closer to family responsibility and some conversation with Mom. If he burns the asparagus, so be it.

> The answer is in what happens next.

2. Computer companions, game addiction: "Why do you spoil my fun?"

Technology gives us conveniences and more time free of drudgery, but it also creates addictions that eat away our time. Computer companions can fill too much of a teenager's day.

I asked my grandson, "How many times have you played World of Warcraft today?"

Without missing a button or looking up he said, "I don't know."

"Did you win the fourth game before this one?"

"What?" His eyes are still glued to the little screen.

"I was wondering if there is any trace of memory about previous games in your mind." (It's tough when your Grandpa is a psychologist.)

"Grandpa, I have to focus on this to win, OK?"

He was right. He needed to focus to win. But the focus on the mindless repetition of a computer program will not give him self-confidence or make him happy. In fact, you have probably noticed that after such a session, your adolescent's mood is usually worse, not better.

The newest games may be more addictive, but even our grandparents were concerned about the effect of the media on their children, whether it was the radio or the movies. Violence, shallow values, simplistic answers to life's questions, and relationships too sexual and too oriented to looks and popularity, were prevalent way back then too. By the 1950s, TV was beginning to squander hours of every childhood day, and the concerns were intensified.

Even when family time gets its turn, it can seem tame after hours of exciting computer games and TV programs with problems solved every 27 minutes.

Now the kids have computers and iPods for companions, and the struggle with the media has escalated. Media can take a lot of time away from the family. Even when family time gets its turn, it can seem tame after hours of exciting computer games and TV programs with problems solved every 27 minutes.

Like the TV challenge to parental influence, computer companions subtract from exercise and real experience with social skills, friends, and life's stresses. As a source of information, the computer companion can become more credible than parents or teachers. And the computer companion of teenagers can slip in a lot of information unobserved by their parents because computers are usually more isolated from family traffic than TVs and therefore less supervised.

Here's another place where parents need to set limits on how much and what kind of programs (TV or computer) their teens watch and use. Put violence off limits and make it a habit to look over your son's or daughter's shoulder frequently. "What are you watching?" is still a legitimate parental question even if the screen is a monitor and not a TV.

Parents may be tempted to use VCRs, TVs, and computer companions to keep the preteens and teenagers busy. While TV and computers are not necessarily bad time fillers, their best role is as a basis for family discussions to be sure boys and girls come away with a realistic view of the programs.

Kids are often disappointed when the real world doesn't measure up to the excitement of TV and computer games. Parents, on the other hand, are often disappointed that TV and computer games don't measure up to the real world where success requires work, relationships require respect, and risky behaviors produce logical consequences. So the subjects can provide a lot of opportunity for discussion of character-building values. Since the media programs also provide a potential for disagreement, parents need to keep the discussion pleasant and avoid turning the conversation into personal criticism.

Projects and crafts that have concrete results are good competition for the computer companion and are much more likely to attract attention and admiration from others as well as strengthen a teenager's value of her own usefulness. Her value of herself gained from her own successes and discussions with you will protect her when she is tempted by those dangerous teenage behaviors.

3. Bad movies: "All the other kids are going, why can't I?"

Often when a parent hears "But Mom, all the kids are going," the subject is a movie of questionable quality. Many films aimed at kids put parents in the position of judging movies they have not seen and don't want to see.

You can't rely on the ratings because they often avoid any responsibility with "parental discretion advised." Dedicated parents, the industry evidently feels, should set aside a few hours a week to make judgments that TV and Hollywood producers find too financially risky to offer.

A well-turned shoulder and a sigh in bed can bring complaints from parents worrying about what is going on in the minds of their teenagers when they view a love scene. Yet a bullet in the bad guy's head gets only a shrug because parents presume their kids know the bad guy is getting his comeuppance. After all, he is the bad guy, isn't he?

But the violence is also inflicted on insignificant guards, lowly gang members or other pawns in the movie plot. The message is, "If they're bad or if they're not important, violence is OK." It's becoming clear where teenagers learn their lessons in violence.

The film industry leaders spend millions to lure the kids to the latest vicious gore. Yet they take no real responsibility and leave it to the parents and the community to suffer the consequences.

> **K**ids are often disappointed when the real world doesn't measure up to the excitement of TV and computer games. Parents, on the other hand, are often disappointed that TV and computer don't measure up to the real world.

The struggle between parent and teenager over "media control" often starts with those PG-13 and R-rated movies. Many parents tell me they avoid most (not all) of the arguments by saying, "PG-13 movies are allowed only after I have learned about the movie; no R-rated movies allowed."

For older kids you could drop the restriction on the PG-13 movies, but if you spend all week telling your son or daughter how to act toward others, it's not productive to then permit a weekend PG-13 movie that sends the opposite messages: that parents and other adults are dolts, problems can be solved if you have the right weapon, and, for happiness, follow the money.

Some PG-13 stories can show growth and good sense, but the usual plot revolves around a smart young man and a more level-headed girl who are out on an adventure. The parent, teacher, or police chief is a little on the stupid side and can be easily duped. Mix in a preposterous car chase where no one (of any consequence) gets hurt. Add a great explosion (all are fine in the next scene), helicopters and bad language (always grabbers), a little romance and/or sex (this is where the "PG-13" comes in), and you have the recipe for a summer blockbuster.

> **D**edicated parents, the industry evidently feels, should set aside a few hours a week to make judgments that TV and Hollywood producers find too financially risky to offer.

In the end, some villain gets what he or she deserves and the parent figures realize just how smart this girl and street-wise rascal really are. Girl and Rascal are heroes and probably never have to go to school again.

R (Rarely acceptable for children) movies can be good learning experiences and entertainment for teens who are ready to understand them. Kids under 15 are not ready for R movies and will only remember that sex was glorified, violence was intensified, and the language was terrible.

Many movies provide a chance for productive conversations on sensitive topics that are otherwise too personal. Keep these conversations on the movie and resist the temptation to focus on your teenager and her opinions. If good parental listening habits become routine, even a discussion of a bad movie can be a time when information flows to you and provides a better understanding of your kids as well as providing your teen with a clearer view of the issues in the film.

Kids under 15 are not ready for R movies and will only remember that sex was glorified, violence was intensified, and the language was terrible.

The many sources of entertainment accessible to kids are difficult to evaluate. You need help from your fellow parents to sort out the good from the bad and the ugly in films you haven't time to see.

Here's another place where a Parent Support Group (see page 313) can be a pool of information exchange and discussion. Not only can a group discussion help with movies, it can be a source of comfort and satisfaction to know that others have problems similar to yours.

4. The video obsession

The Kaiser Family Foundation conducts ongoing surveys of the activities of children and teens and also asks hundreds of children to keep seven-day diaries of their media use.

Since 1999, time on computers and video games has doubled while TV has increased only a little—probably because the maximum is already near. Sixty percent of those between 8 and 18 have the TV on during meals, and 51 percent of families have the tube on all the time whether anyone is watching or not.

Teenagers often have TVs in their bedrooms (68 percent) and usually have a VCR, DVD or video game player as well (50 percent). Also, 20 percent have premium TV channels and 20 percent have internet access in their rooms.

What can parents do? They should know what their children are watching and set down some rules. The rules should put limits on the violent and sexual content. Only 20 percent of seventh to twelfth graders report that their parents enforce TV rules. They must be right because only 6 percent of parents use V-chip screening to restrict TV content and only 10 percent check parental advisories on music or video game ratings.

Nearly half of the under-18 set have gone to an R-rated movie without parent permission. And 65 percent have played Grand Theft Auto—that controversial game of crime and violence (beating up prostitutes and killing police officers).

The American Academy of Pediatrics recommends no TV for children under 2—not even "Barney" or "Sesame Street"! This academy of 55,000 doctors also recommends that even older children should not be allowed to have a TV or a computer isolated in their room.

They said direct interaction with parents and other adults is necessary for healthy brain growth in teens as well as babies and toddlers. This interaction is also essential to development of social skills and intelligence even in teenagers.

The effects of TV on physical health have led many doctors to take a "media history" along with the usual medical history questions—time spent on movies, computers, and TV shows.

Over 1,000 studies show that exposure to media violence increases the aggressive behavior in both children and adolescents, the academy said.

The average American child watches 21 hours of TV each week while increasing body fat. Maybe our TV tubbies could start learning how to do the chores they will need to do all their lives—the laundry, the dishes, the lawn, even some of the shopping.

Parents are tempted to avoid the flack, turn on the TV, and do the chores themselves. The contradiction is that while adolescents may whine and moan at the prospect of doing chores, their feelings of self-worth and accomplishment continue to sink with each passing TV hour.

Self-esteem is based on competence. Competence comes from practice. Kids have to learn from their own experience that they can make the family meal, do their laundry, and handle a little money in shopping.

Did I say make the family meal? What a mess that would be! Yes, but mistakes are evidence that someone is trying to learn. The family is the best place for practice with help from Mom and Dad for mistakes and the clean up. Both parents and kids will feel much better after even a below-par supper made by a son or daughter than they will after another hour of TV while waiting for Mom to produce the meal.

Teens are not good managers of their conflicts between being lazy and being useful, and parents can easily play into the wrong side of the equation for the sake of convenience. Instead, begin steering your teens toward usefulness, self-sufficiency and self-respect now. If the kids can't make the family dinner, at least they could set the table, get everyone's drink, or prepare one of the servings.

One college freshman told me he was quitting college because, "I can't take care of my own laundry; all those settings confuse me, and then all my underwear keeps coming out pink!" When I joked that he could throw away the old underwear and just buy new, he took me seriously and blurted out, "I don't know my size!" The little number on his elastic had followed him around for 18 years, but he took no notice of it because Mom handled all of that.

So tomorrow start on the laundry, the shopping, the lawn, and the meals. The TV can wait.

TV can also wait because, despite clear and unshakable evidence that violence on TV results in violence in real life, the media moguls continue to insist that their shows have no effect on children.

Then they point with pride to increased sales of cars, medications and fast food because of the commercials aired with the shows. They justify advertising prices up to a million dollars a minute on Super Bowl Sunday. We are to believe that the commercials influence both children and adults, but the violence in the show itself has no effect.

To maintain that TV violence has no effect is nonsense, of course. Both girls and boys who watch the most TV violence are also most likely to become violent adults, says Rowell Huesmann of the University of Michigan. Huesmann studied 329 elementary school-age children in 1977 when "Starsky and Hutch," "Six Million Dollar Man," and "Roadrunner" cartoons were as bad as it got.

> When I joked that he could throw away the old underwear and just buy new, he took me seriously and blurted out, "I don't know my size!"

Heavy watching of violent TV during childhood leads to more violent adults.

Huesmann tracked the amount of time these kids watched violent TV shows and with the 1977 results in hand, he tracked his subjects again, 16 years later.

Even with controls for other factors such as social class and intelligence, the heavy watchers of violent TV during childhood were more likely, as adults, to throw something at their spouse, or push and grab their spouse. They were also more likely to have shoved, punched or choked another person during the previous year.

Unlike earlier studies, statistics for the girls matched those of the boys—probably because of the violent women role models in TV after the 60's, says Huesmann.

The amount of violence on television is staggering. The most frequent violence is on premium cable shows (85 percent of shows) and on basic cable, 59 percent. Independent networks come in at 44 percent, while PBS is at 18 percent of their shows.

Limiting TV time, even with all the grumbling and complaining that will follow, is well worth the effort. Also, encourage specific activities to fill the void. Hobbies, crafts, and sports all give a teenager a chance to learn new skills and develop pride in his abilities instead of envying the bad habits of TV characters. Invest in good age-appropriate reading materials and, of course, insist on school work before entertainment.

When TV is on the agenda, investigate the programming yourself to determine what programs your teens plan to watch. V-ratings do not flag most violence. Studies by the Kaiser Family Foundation found 80 percent of shows with violence are not rated at all. Yet 55 percent of parents surveyed believe the V-content rating is applied to all shows.

It's worth the effort because these shows send a message that encourages bad character. In violent TV scenes, 84 percent do not depict any long-term consequences; perpetrators go unpunished 73 percent of the time; 47 percent show no resulting harm to the victims and 58 percent depict no pain. Even 37 percent of the children said that "bad shows" are "too violent and gory," says Mediascope's National Television Violence Study.

CHAPTER 13

Setting limits

1. Couch potato tubby: "I'm tired, can't I just watch my show?"

Obesity is an unpleasant word reserved for body fat that's out of control. If your teenager is a couch potato tubby headed in this direction, how can you help?

For children and preteens, obesity is reached when total body weight is more than 20 percent fat for boys, 32 percent for girls. Normally, two out of 10 children are in this category, but the number can reach eight out of 10 if both parents are obese.

In 1970 we fed ourselves on 3,300 calories each day. That was the production consumed from farms and food companies in the United States in those days. Now we are up to 3,800 calories a day with buster burgers, super-fries and the large gulp.

The extra 500 daily calories (equivalent to an extra banana split every day) has added 10 pounds to the average weight of a teenager compared with just 10 years ago, says the Pediatricians Research Group of Woodlands, TX. It's not surprising when you consider we tempt ourselves with over 10,000 new food products each year—mostly candies, snacks, soft drinks, baked goods, and ice creams.

No doubt the food pushers both at home and in the food business deserve some of the blame for the obesity problem. TV with too many commercials about food and computer sessions with too much junk food next to the keyboard should also share the blame. These habits keep the little butterballs inside, inactive and close to the snacks.

Of course exercise enters in. Teenagers who report more than five hours of TV per day are five times more likely to be overweight from lack of exercise than kids watching less than two hours each day. Snacks during TV, say, a small bag of potato chips each day, will add a half pound each week. Not much, until you think that it totals up to a 26-pound weight gain each year. Ten years equals 260 pounds.

> The best single predictor of adult obesity is the average number of daily fat-storing hours of TV during the teenage years.

Parents need to encourage and model good exercise routines. The best single predictor of adult obesity is the average number of daily fat-storing hours of TV during the teenage years. Since this problem has been growing for 40 or 50 years, we now have a generation of parents who have grown up in the super-consumption society and they set a poor example. So parents are part of the problem, but they can also be part of the solution.

"Rebecca, turn off that computer game and go outside and get some exercise."

"It's too cold and anyway I'm right in the middle of this."

"Get your coat and gloves and shovel some of that walk before your father comes home."

"You don't go out there, why should I?"

"OK, I'm getting my coat too. We'll do it together."

A parent pitching in with her daughter gets double bang for the effort.

Family mealtime should also be more than calling the kids for a feeding. Turn the TV off and put away the video game. Take extra time for meal conversation so you can catch up on their news. It also gives food time to signal, "enough."

2. Weight gain causes other early problems

Our poor eating habits are pushing other disease statistics. Diabetes, characterized by high blood sugar levels from defects in insulin production, afflicted 6 percent of the population in only four states in 1990. By 1995, nine more states were added to the list, and by 2000 only seven states could boast that less than 6 percent of their populations were diabetic.

The Center for Disease Control calls obesity and diabetes the "Twin Epidemics." Diabetics have twice the death rate of non-diabetics, twice the heart disease and stroke rates, and 12 to 24 thousand amputations, incidents of kidney disease, and blindness each year.

Diabetes used to be considered an adult disease of body weight too high, but now one in four children shows early signs of Type II diabetes and 60 percent show at least one risk factor of heart disease. Childhood obesity also accounts for 50 percent of the new cases of sleep apnea and asthma, the Surgeon General reports.

> In 1982, only four percent of children were overweight and childhood depression was rare.

3. Thumb and finger exercise is not enough

Childhood depressions, teenage suicides, and overweight problems have all tripled in the last three decades, and they are all statistically related to lack of exercise.

In 1982, only four percent of children were overweight and childhood depression was rare. By 1994 16 percent were overweight and five percent were being treated for depression. In 2001, 25 percent were overweight and 10 percent were depressed. By the way, 25 percent is exactly the same proportion of surveyed children who report they don't participate in any vigorous activity at all.

Schools have cut back on their help with this problem. The National Institute of Child Health and Development reports the average third grader has only 25 minutes of exercise each week while the institute recommends 30 to 60 minutes each day. Only one-third of public schools now have physical education classes more than once a week.

The inclination to hang out in front of the TV, computer, or Gameboy has put our kids at risk. The Mayo Clinic's Children's Health Center says that TV-watching, now up to 25 hours per week on average, is the biggest culprit in exercise-related health problems of teenagers as well as children. Middle class children average more than 30 hours per week. Video games and computers are the next biggest culprits. The clinic's doctors estimate that 60 percent of the childhood obesity cases they see are directly related to too much television and computer junk. They make the following recommendations.

1. Limit TV and other "high-tech" entertainments to make sure outdoor time and action get their share of each child-teen's daily schedule.

2. Keep up your own exercise habits as a model for the kids.

3. Promote physical education in your schools.

Many school psychologists and counselors would add these other suggestions:

4. When birthdays and holidays come around, give gifts that encourage exercise. A gift of another video, CD or violent game for the button-pusher set is not in the best interest of your child, niece, nephew, or grandchild.

5. Encourage casual and informal sports at home as well as the ones offered in the time-limited school schedule.

6. Encourage trips that produce exercise—hiking, swimming, and setting up camp.

Do it not only to control weight and as a hedge against depression but also to build muscles, increase flexibility, and to just feel good.

Jerry Seinfeld once said his most prized possession was his replica of his first bicycle—a vintage Schwin that he felt was his ticket to freedom on the streets of his New York neighborhood. How many children today would value their bike that much?

4. Rhythmic habits: Quit bugging me, I can't help it

Although rhythmic habits are sometimes symptoms of severe childhood disorders, normal children and adults have rhythmic habits, too. Occasionally tapping a pencil, swinging a foot, or rocking to music may annoy parents but it's too trivial to merit any attention.

When a habit grows and becomes troublesome, most parents can remember its beginning as a less frequent event. This can be a case of parents trying to fix a non-problem and now they have a problem!

A behavior that started as just fidgeting became a gimmick for attention and then a way to express exasperation at the parents. "Getting through to" the parents now produces a reprimand, a kind of negative attention supporting bad behavior in a situation where positive attention seems unlikely—at least to a child-teenager.

> Occasionally tapping a pencil, swinging a foot, or rocking to music may annoy parents but it is too trivial to merit any attention.

An occasional correction or request to stop an annoying habit is not likely to do much harm if the parent's emotional reaction can be kept in check.

Todd has been banging his foot on the chair leg at dinner for three minutes.

Mom: "Todd, stop kicking the chair—it's a bother when we're eating."

Todd: "I can't help it."

Mom: (Still in a very quiet tone) "Well, if you can't help it, you'll have to eat in the small chair with your feet on the floor. Did you finish your picture before dinner?"

Todd: (Still kicking the chair) "Yeah, it's a boat."

Mom: "A boat. I'd like to see it after we're finished. Please don't kick."

Todd: "I told you I can't help it."

Mom: (Still very calmly) "If you continue, you'll have to be in the little chair. That's one." (The count-out begins.)

Todd may have to go to three and then to the little chair this first time. Later, if his kicking as a ploy to get Mom going doesn't work, he'll stop or at least keep his excess energy habits at a tolerable level.

> If Mom only comes up with these interests when Todd acts up, you can see where that will lead.

Mom is right to provide another direction for Todd's focus by asking him about his picture. These other topics will have to become a regular part of Mom's habits before the chair kicking or another reason for kicking is likely to start. If Mom only comes up with these interests when Todd acts up, you can see where that will lead.

A teenager's nail-biting, hair-twirling, face-rubbing, and lip-biting can produce a running battle with a parent, "Stop that. You'll just make a sore."

Her offspring stops momentarily and says, "No I won't. Leave me alone."

Then he or she resumes and Mom resumes, "I said stop it." Teenager then hesitates long enough for Mom to be distracted and then begins again.

Where does such useless behavior come from? At first it can be just the random squirming and wiggling of an adolescent that produces the reaction, "Stop that fidgeting!" Later on, when he/she has learned how to get a reaction, the fidgeting develops specifics: hair-twirling, scratching, or ballpoint pen-clicking (for the older ones).

Another side to fidgeting has been shown in several psychology experiments repeated many times with both people and animals. In one example, a laboratory white rat is trained to press a lever for food. He soon learns that the food is only given for lever presses after long intervals of about two minutes. In the meantime there is little to do but wait. What to do, what to do? A water bottle is available, but he is not thirsty. But, faced with nothing to do, he drinks (remind you of anyone you know?).

But he does not just sip. He may drink up to two times his body weight while waiting for the "food intervals" to pass. You can see that this experiment requires regular wipe-ups.

All that was needed to stop the extra drinking was to shorten the waiting time—down from 2 minutes to 30 seconds and the excess water-drinking was gone. Pay-offs came more often, there was work to be done, and our rat had no time for fooling around.

So fidgeting has two possible explanations. One, it could be used to pass the time as our furry waterholic does or, two, it could gain attention as a child might use chair-kicking to attract attention.

Paying attention to other, more desirable behaviors will be a good strategy in either case. "Jumping on" fidgeting behavior will always be a dangerous habit for parents because bad behavior thrives on attention. If the fidgeting is not important, let's not make it so.

Another solution for fidget habits is to reward the lack of fidgeting. For example, one mother told me she promised her son two dollars if he could refrain from nail-biting long enough so that his nails would need clipping. Because this demand seemed a bit too large for a first step, she also promised 20 cents for each individual fingernail that needed trimming because it had been allowed to grow.

Such a direct motivator must be used carefully.

> **Bad behavior thrives on attention.**

There is always a tendency to add reminders with a little nagging in addition to just applying the rule. In the child's view, he needs more attention, and also in his view, any kind of attention will do—even nagging from Mom or Dad with reminders about payoffs.

If we now come along with a new strategy to ignore fidgeting so that the child-teen's usual attention-getting solution will no longer work, then we need to make an extra effort to find acceptable behavior that will deserve attention.

5. Is a Linus-comforter an obsession even if he's a teenager?

Kids have favorite things. We don't mind. A blanket, an old Pooh Bear or even a rusty toy can serve as a security post in the swirling waters of life.

Thumb-sucking sometimes goes with the blanket fetish, but as the months and even years go by we parents can get sick of our teenager's increasingly ragged scrap. Then we'll try anything. Should we throw the darn thing in the dumpster? Take it away and allow it only at bedtime? Or should we just lock it up?

Should we throw the security blanket in the dumpster?

Even in the Peanuts comic strip, Lucy says to Linus, "If only you knew how nauseated I get every time I see you holding that stupid blanket!"

Adults have favorites, too. I know a man who takes his home pillow on business trips. Another who keeps a blank check in his wallet, won't mow the lawn without his wallet in his hip pocket and also wears only one kind of underwear.

I know a woman who keeps an unopened bottle of 100 Tums in her car and adds another—not when the first one is empty, but when it is opened.

Should we lock up the pillow, blank checks, wallet and Tums bottle? Of course not, these folks are adults and have a right to do as they please.

When should you cross over and start interfering? How far do you want to go in meddling with your teenager's habits? When is it a problem? And is it your problem or your teen's?

The world presents a lot of stress and our kids don't understand much of it. They need their routines to manage the turmoil.

Parents have judgment calls to make about these mild compulsions and need to do occasional soul-searching to discover if the problem is only in the mind of the beholder. If Lucy bites her fingernails but not excessively, maybe Mom should tolerate it. But if Linus insists on taking his blanket to school, it could be a problem for him and his parents.

Talking, nagging and threatening about such comforters may become rewarding entertainment for a teenager—even while he is arguing and objecting to the corrections themselves. A conscious choice can clean up the family airways. Threats, not carried out, only increase the stress: "I'm going to throw that blanket in the trash!"

Instead of relying on threats, it's better to use smaller consequences that are so mild you can use them repeatedly without hesitating or feeling you are too harsh.

A creeping deadline is sometimes good: "After lunch, your Pooh Bear is off limits until 2 o'clock." For week two announce a new time limit, 2:15; then 3:00,

4:00, 5:00, and until after supper. Bringing in a reward is often a good encouragement: "When the time is over, we'll

Talking, nagging and threatening can become rewarding entertainment for a teenager.

have your afternoon treat (before giving Pooh Bear back)." Fading is also often a good strategy. "All knuckle-cracking has to be done upstairs" (later, only in his room, then only at his desk)—no limit on the frequency this time, just a limit on where.

Both the creeping-time and shrinking-place fading strategies have also been used successfully with adult smoking habits. If all of this seems like too much for your teenager's problem, it may be time to stop the nagging as well.

6. Sports fanatics: "Coach says I have to go; will you drive me?"

How can parents defend against a sports fanatic who believes his favorite activity should be required of all persons on the planet? And the kids, to show the proper spirit, should be enthusiastic at practice and hyper-manic at any meet, match, game, or tournament.

Our family game was soccer, but I think the lessons I learned will apply to whatever your sport is. My wife, three children, and I all played on different teams. But when I started coaching, I began to notice problems.

I saw myself as a reasonable coach, but I had to change my habits to calm down and see the big picture. I tried to avoid outbursts that made me similar to those other coaches going crazy when one of their players committed a health-threatening foul in complete innocence.

These other coaches—not me, of course—could be fanatics. Three practices a week, one game, and sometimes more on the weekend. Often a road trip was also involved. If I suggested my kids might miss a practice or game for a family event, you would think I had said something disloyal about our country!

The first fatherhood lesson I learned from all of this was: "Beware of the fanatics." With the bribe of a team shirt, a coach can take your daughter or son away from you. Any extra scrap of time left over for family will have to go to

> If you call number 14 for pushing and add, "Be careful, Mark, that's dangerous," Mark is personally embarrassed, surprised you know his name and has the nagging fear you're going to tell his mommy!

homework, which is constantly in danger of coming up short. Family time for dinner? What are you, un-American?

So consider limiting the formal, outside of school, activities to one fanatic. That way your family will have at least two nights a week free of exhaustion and available for family activities.

Lesson number 2 came when I started refereeing. With pre-adolescent players ranging from the size of a small chicken to a pro-football lineman, you would think that controlling the players on the field would be the major challenge to health and safety, but that is not the biggest referee problem.

The wild, screaming, would-be-player-parents create the most trouble. Since a foul could go for or against their perfect and innocent child, parents are sure the referees are wrong 50 percent of the time. And although most parents have never played the game, they are quite sure that as soon as they find time to read the rule book, they will prove that their little darling would never "foul" one of those other little ruffians.

As ref, one trick to controlling the players is to learn names. If you call number 14 for pushing, he is likely to be innocent, incredulous, and grumpy. If you call number 14 for pushing and add, "Be careful, Mark, that's dangerous," Mark is personally embarrassed, surprised you know his name, and has the nagging fear you're going to tell his mommy!

The prospect of controlling parents, on the other hand, is dim. You can award free kicks, penalty yards, or free throws for infractions by players in various sports, but for parents, you will need to ask them to volunteer to referee. I have seen a dozen parents vanish in an open field when the word "volunteer" comes up.

The last rule I learned from soccer is to remember why the game is being played in the first place. Once parents take their child's success as a personal confirmation of their own success, all maturity is lost in the screaming. Many of my players were so embarrassed by their parents' behavior, they asked to be taken out and substituted as soon as their parent arrived to watch.

So enjoy the game, not just for the success of your own offspring and not just for the score, but for the whole game. Help your child keep the game in perspective by your example. After all, it is just a game, isn't it?

CHAPTER 14

Meds, drugs and diets

1. Medications: "I didn't get my pill today, can I help it?"

What's the answer to those annoying outbursts from the kids—the crying fits and the hyperactivity?

Even when medications are part of the solution, parents and physicians still worry about side and long-term effects and hope to add natural long-term remedies that will provide a more fundamental adjustment.

Parents may view the problem as a product of unfortunate circumstances. For example, a parent will say, "He has a hard time behaving because he was upset when his father and I divorced." Or, "He was upset when I remarried." Other parents suspect that bipolar symptoms exist on one or both sides of the family tree. Others complain their child-teen rejects discipline because his or her father won't cooperate with his mother or both parents agree with his teacher who said, "He might be ADHD (attention deficit and hyperactivity disorder)."

Of course any of these speculations could be true, or partly true, but regardless of underlying causes, changing a child-teen's behavior using careful parental reactions may hold the only hope for long-term improvement.

Studies by the U.S. Department of Agriculture show children and teens guzzle 64 gallons of soft drinks a year with an average of 38 milligrams of

> **P**arents may view the problem as a product of unfortunate circumstances.

caffeine in every ounce. For adults, it's coffee and, if it's fancy coffee, the caffeine may be as high as 200 milligrams per cup.

After the temporary boost in energy, there's the inevitable drop in energy and disposition that follows. A re-supply of caffeine will produce another burst of energy, but an addiction is beginning to form just to avoid the down-turn-aftereffect. Addiction is fundamentally a negative reinforcement effect.

Hofstra University professor, Jennifer Schare studied 400 preschoolers for a year and found that the heavy users of caffeine had more "uncontrollable energy," which could be diagnosed as ADHD. If caffeine is occasional, provided at school but not at home, for example, a "bipolar disorder" might be suspected. At school he is wired and always in trouble, but at home he calms down, but is grumpy. Caffeine effects, and the additional sleep disturbance that comes with them, provide pharmaceutical companies with a host of prescriptions for "disturbed" children.

Physicians often recommend less than 100 milligrams of caffeine—about two ounces of most colas—for the whole day. Why they recommend any at all is hard to understand.

In addition to a diet that contains caffeine and sugar in large quantities, food allergies can add to the problem. In the United States, all that extra food has about 7,000 new additives which have been approved, and most were not heard of a century ago. By contrast, Northern Europeans are now two inches taller than Americans without the fat that we've put on and only about 70 of our 7,000 food additives are legal over there. That may explain some of our expanding allergies.

The National Institutes of Health reports that 50 million Americans suffer from allergic diseases and 54 percent test positive for one or more allergens. The most common disruptive culprits in children's diet besides caffeine and sugar are sugar-laden junk foods, milk products, citrus fruits, tomatoes, bananas and certain food additives.

Food intolerances occur when the digestive process rejects a certain kind of food. Other problems are food allergies where certain (usually stomach) tissues are irritated by the food. In either case, keeping careful records of what your teenager eats and when he acts up can identify foods that produce behavioral side effects.

A teenager who is sensitive to particular foods is likely to be more frequently irritated by parents, teachers and siblings. He or she is not likely to understand that disrupted sleep and the resulting unhappiness may be an additional allergy symptom along with his/her runny nose, stuffiness, wheezing, stomach ache, itchy eyes or muscle ache. Even his or her parents may not recognize the connection.

Parents should be cautious in focusing on one solution for a troublesome child. Here's one true example.

When Jeff was 6, he was a model child. He was easy-going and seldom any trouble at school, but when he started second grade, he became agitated and impatient and fought with other students. Tantrums became a daily burden at home and school. At home the tantrums usually built up around bedtime or later at night when he woke up restless and irritated.

Had he been assigned to a bad teacher? Did something happen at home?

I knew Jeff's mother well. She was a steady, dedicated and loving mom. Because of the surprising change in Jeff's character, I asked her to keep a record of everything Jeff ate and when disruptions happened. Although Jeff was already on some medication for his disruptive behavior, Mom took it as a challenge to note every scrap and snack that he had. In six weeks her records showed a peculiar but common event: every time Jeff had pizza, his behavior got worse.

So we started the pizza experiment. No pizza for two weeks and the frequency of his tantrums went down a little, but his troubles at school and home continued.

The most common disruptive culprits in children's diet besides caffeine and sugar are sugar-laden junk foods, milk products, citrus fruits, tomatoes, bananas and certain food additives.

Our expanding diet in the U.S. certainly helps us to find allergies.

There was no dramatic result until Jeff's mom (remember, she's the dedicated type) declared all tomato products off limits. That's not an easy task when you think about all the sources – ketchup, salads, pizzas, spaghetti, casseroles and the list goes on. But it turned out Jeff had an allergy.

Without tomatoes, Jeff's old self started coming back, but every time he slipped up (one time we discovered tomato in the salad dressing), the irritations returned. To protect Jeff (and everyone else), the whole family went off tomatoes.

Where do such allergies come from? It's a mystery how we get these sensitivities, but our expanding diet in the U.S. certainly helps us find them. Oranges from Florida are not just a holiday treat any more, and milk no longer comes from a farm in your county. You can't even be sure your food comes from this hemisphere. The more food sources you sample, the more likely you are to take in something that disagrees with you.

Jeff, by the way, grew up to be an emergency room physician. He is still his easy-going self, and he's still off tomatoes.

Certainly diet, allergies and parental habits play a role in these problems. Even if medications are already a part of the answer, a record of bad behavior as well as allergic reactions, variations in parental habits, diet and possible sources of the allergies may show other parts of the problem.

Nevertheless 350 million doses of Ritalin, Adderall, and Dexedrine will be given this year in the United States to control bad behavior in children—triple the doses given in all other countries on this planet put together. In many cases these medications are helpful, but allergy testing and careful recording of everything a child-teen eats and the time he eats it can show aggravating sensitivities that can be avoided.

Even a teenager diagnosed with Autism or ADHD is not merely afflicted with one wrong process. Diet and what happens next still influence bad habits. The thoughtful use of reactions and consequences, watching for good behaviors to highlight, and encouraging self-esteem through useful tasks, all remain a part of the answer to bad social habits.

Seasonal Affective Syndrome (SAD) turned out to be eight-year-old Kaylee's problem discovered when her Mom kept records over the weeks of a fall semester. As the days grew shorter, Kaylee's temper grew shorter, also. When a set of bright fluorescent lights were added to her dark morning hours, Kaylee's behavior improved.

Kaylee also had problems with psychoactive substances—sugar and caffeine. Along with Mom's reactions, these sources are nearly always a part of the answer.

Prescriptions can be a convenient answer to common rowdiness, sleeplessness and school problems, but medications can cover up other causes.

Start with a record of the most likely culprits: caffeine, sugar, chocolate, eggs, and milk products. Draw up a chart with the days marked down the side and hours across the top. Tape it on the refrigerator.

You need to record the time and date of every little bit of these foods that your adolescent eats. Very small amounts can trigger reactions. Many adults complain of sleep problems or headaches after one cup of tea even in the early morning while others have problems only if they drink tea or coffee before bed.

Also, record any other factors that might be relevant. The kids will not see these connections in themselves. One teen who had violent tantrums over the slightest problem turned out to be allergic to chocolate. Even a small brownie after school extracted a price in the family evening. The source wasn't discovered until Mom brought in three weeks of recordings of his snacks, meals and tantrums.

Another Mom complained that after her always-pleasant son turned four, "he became mean and angry and yelled a lot." She agreed to record her rating of his behavior every hour they were together – 1 for very nice, 2 for just a slight problem, 5 for getting mad about something trivial, 10 for a full, losing-it tantrum—usually more than one a day. She also recorded everything he ate at all snacks and meals. Eggs turned out to be a big part of the problem. No hives, no itchy eyes or stomach aches, just irritation and prickliness.

Since behaviors are partly controlled by what happens before and after, I also ask parents to include a column on the record for the events just before and after the problem behavior surfaces. Two hours of TV right before the melt-down or an entertaining argument with Mom every time our not-so-little terror delays his homework can indicate an answer that would help as much as any pill.

The solution will also have to include what is good about our problem-teenager's behavior. What do we want to encourage and how can we encourage it? If he does his homework, then what happens? Do we look it over and admire the work or go on to getting dinner ready because, for the moment, the problem is solved?

Medications can be life savers for parents suffering with a severely disturbed child. Drug companies have a right to be proud of the help they provide. But it is not right to belittle environmental effects just because medications can reduce the symptoms.

> The source wasn't discovered until Mom brought in three weeks of recordings of his snacks, meals and tantrums.

Every parent has been amazed by a healthy teen finding 200 ways to sit on a chair, 10 ways to lose his hat, and 30 ways to tangle shoelaces. Activity, even hyperactivity, seems to be just part of growing up.

But one child in ten suffers from behavioral disorders such as attention deficit/hyperactivity disorder (ADHD), separation anxiety, or social phobia. And about 3.4 million U.S. children under 18 are said to be seriously depressed. Ritalin and similar medications are life-savers and family-savers for those situations in which a child or teenager is extremely agitated for long periods every day.

2. Drugs and other troubles after school

The prime time for juvenile crime is from 2 to 6 p.m. You might think it would be at night, but for this young age group, a survey found violent juvenile crime peaked between 3 and 4 p.m. "Fight Crime: Invest in Kids of California," a nonprofit organization, conducted the survey of their state's law enforcement agencies in 1999.

Even in the rest of the nation, after-school hours are the most dangerous for serious car accidents involving teenagers as well as juvenile crime. Vandalism, theft and violent crimes are reduced when kids attend after-school programs. Without continued support from parents and school for a variety of after-school programs, the troubles multiply.

Some parent groups (see page 313) meet regularly to talk over their teens' situation at school and plan a sharing of after-school supervision. Parent groups can have healthy effects and relieve the loneliness a parent can feel if things start to go wrong. Parents also gain strength from these talks and from agreements to enforce standards for TV and computer time and other activities.

After-school programs are not the whole answer to the drug problem, but an understanding of the many circumstances that sometimes influence drug taking can help.

We were all shocked in the 60's and 70's to find drugs becoming common in affluent schools. We should have known that these would be the most obvious targets. Addicts need money, lots of money, and they hope to get it from your kids. A pusher isn't interested in a kid who doesn't have much money. Your teen should not carry any more money than necessary to school or on afternoon outings.

Parents should also stay informed about the money their teens have. How much does she make from her job? Where does her money go? Better spent on clothes and fun than available for trouble. Just some conversations about weekly activities ought to keep parents up to date without prying. If things don't add up, both parents and counselors should get nosy. Changes in your teen's appetite, hours of sleep, and symptoms that seem like an allergy or cold but linger too long, should be explored.

Some parents want to show their children that Mom and Dad are "cool" about drugs. Parents who approve of their own drug use or misuse of medications and alcohol encourage an irresponsible attitude in their kids and set the stage for trouble.

Remember that talk about drugs and other adventurous and dangerous activities is a favorite topic for all healthy teenagers. They need this free conversation as a way of exploring these topics easily. Parents and other adults around the teen should not react too impulsively to just talk and save dramatic reactions for a time when the concrete evidence of drug or alcohol use is in.

Volunteering for after-school programs is helpful and allows parents another opportunity to learn what's going on with their children. Contact your school about its programs. Even an afternoon each week can be a worthwhile contribution.

3. ADHD, Ritalin and diet

As a treatment for Attention Deficit Hyperactivity Disorder (ADHD), Ritalin increases nervous system alertness and thereby increases focus and ability to concentrate. Millions of prescriptions for Ritalin are written each year to treat ADHD. The use of Adderall and Dexedrine is not far behind Ritalin in the totals for ADHD treatment, up 2,000 percent in the last nine years.

Yet a study by Drs. Adrian Angold and Jane Costello found that the majority of children and adolescents who receive these medications do not fully meet the criteria for ADHD—even with the expanded criteria for ADHD approved in 1994 by the American Psychiatric Association.

Many parents have made medications their first solution to behavior problems. Dr. Lawrence H. Diller, pediatrician and author of *Running on Ritalin: A Physician Reflects on Children, Society and Performance in a Pill*, concludes: "How we deal with our kids' problems reflects our thinking and a much larger problem in our culture." An editorial in the *Journal of the American Medical Association* reported that drugs have tripled for children under five, increased 170 percent for five- to 14-year-olds and 300 percent for the 15- to 19-year-olds.

Many parents want a solution that requires no more work and attention than making sure the troublesome youngster gets his medication. Physicians also hope prescriptions will do the job. Conversely, the business world hopes to sell caffeine, sugar and additives, regardless of the behavioral effects. Limiting these in your teen's diet may be more effective than medications with no proven track record with young persons. For ADHD children who are temporarily so hot-wired they can not be reached and cannot be taught, Ritalin can be a godsend. And a day in school can go much better for a child who would otherwise wreck every project and every lesson for the other students.

When the absolutely necessary parental time is added, a teenager in need of medication can develop and adjust to life and soon leave the medications behind. With teenagers, you will have to defend a distinction between "drugs" and medication.

Parents need to keep a close eye on the possible sources of problems to be sure medications continue only when, and only as long as, needed.

4. Birth circumstances and health

In a study of childhood aggression, Richard Tremblay of the University of Montreal followed 572 families with 5-month-old babies until the children were over 42 months old. He reported that children tended to be more aggressive if the mother gave birth at age 20 or younger or if she was a runaway, involved with police as a teenager, smoked during pregnancy, or came from a low-income household.

Mothers were concerned that their slip-ups or circumstances during pregnancy were being blamed for their child's aggression. But studies that find a relationship between a characteristic of Mom and later behavior of her child may not mean Mom causes the problem or the success. For example, we know mothers shouldn't drink any alcohol during pregnancy, but even fathers who drink alcohol during their wives' pregnancies are also more likely to have

> Studies that find a relationship between a characteristic of Mom and later behavior of her child may not mean Mom causes the problem or the success.

problem children. Of course, the statistic is not the result of a physiological factor directly inflicted on the child by Dad's drinking, but it is likely the result of fathers who continue to act out aggression and set bad examples.

Babies of teenage mothers and infants who have low birth weights show a higher risk of suicide later in life, Swedish scientists reported in 2008. Studying more than 700,000 young adults, researchers at Karolinska Institute in Stockholm found that infants born to young mothers and those who weighed 4.4 pounds or less at birth were twice as likely to try to kill themselves. Birth weight doesn't directly cause suicide attempts, of course, Dr. Danuta Wasserman of the institute said, "The results show we need to monitor and support young mothers during pregnancy and later to help them with the emotional and practical support they need [raising their children]."

The children of the study were born between 1973 and 1980 and were followed until 1999. Of the 600,000 studied, about one percent, 2,000 men and more than 4,700 women, attempted suicide and 400 men and 166 women succeeded.

The influence of other factors such as large families and low levels of education, suggest that the influence of family circumstances and parenting time and style are the fundamental basis for the statistical relation between birth circumstances and the health and happiness of the children.

Financial support of programs to help young mothers is an investment that will reduce the necessity of future welfare support from the community.

5. Depression in teenagers

The behavior disorder of clinical depression occurs in 4 percent of preschoolers and in about 20 percent of teenagers. The numbers for teens are probably higher than 20 percent because we often brush off their complaints saying they "always talk like that."

The statistics vary partly because the definition of depression varies. Preschoolers don't know the word and, with teenagers, the perception of the word depends on when you talk to them and what they say.

Yet 19 million people complain of depression enough to make it into the clinical medical records. In 2005, 118 million prescriptions for antidepressants were written, twice as many as in 1995, says the Center for Disease Control.

Preschoolers are the fastest growing market for antidepressants. Yet the British Journal of Medicine reported no scientific evidence that antidepressants work for children. For children under 18, Britain has banned all but Prozac which is used for complicated emotional problems.

Of course we all get the "blues" and "feel down in the dumps" from time to time. The solution is usually an increase in physical activity—sports or exercise class—or just a change of scene.

For many of us, and especially for teenagers, diet can be a part of the problem. A 12-year-old boy half the weight of his Dad, can get far too much sugar from a candy bar or an overdose of fat or caffeine from a portion that would have no effect on his father.

Mental habits can also influence clinical depression. While adults can take encouragement from looking ahead to summer activities or vacations, teenagers are shortsighted. If homework is due tomorrow morning, depression can develop because the prospect of friends coming over tomorrow afternoon is too far in the future as is any upcoming weekend fun.

A teenager's active imagination concerning the magical powers of Harry Potter or the dreams of becoming a soccer star serve an important anti-depressant purpose for a person who has not yet developed the necessary foresight to form realistic goals beyond next week.

In cases where dreams of future success are not enough to pull a grumpy teenager out of depression, a review of activities, diet and mental habits may help parents understand the cause of their teen's depression. Jennifer Conner, psychologist with the Oregon Counseling Organization, lists symptoms of depression such as fatigue and lack of energy

> A 12-year-old boy half the weight of his Dad, can get far too much sugar from a candy bar or an overdose of fat or caffeine from a portion that would have no effect on his father.

nearly every day; bad temper, irritability; fear, tension and anxiety; drop in school performance; repeated physical complaints without medical cause (headaches, stomach aches, aching arm or legs) and changes in appetite or sleeping habits.

Of course all of these behaviors occur in all children, but excessive and continuing amounts of bad habits deserve attention.

Conner suggests seeking immediate professional advice for serious symptoms, but most depression is usually temporary. Allow your teen space and time. Keep caffeine at absolute zero. Alcohol use by children is never appropriate. Learn more about any medications your teenager is taking. Discourage meal skipping. Regular meals are a crucial part of your teen's ability to cope. Maintain regular sleep for the same reason.

Take time to be a part of your adolescent's physical activity. It will help you as well as them, and it will be an opportunity to listen and understand.

Every parent needs to save time for giving attention, communication, and companionship. Consistent supportive attention for a teenager having a low day can make the difference between a habit of depression and a habit of bouncing back.

Communication can be just what the doctor (should have) ordered when a teen needs to tell someone how scary the world sometimes seems. And companionship helps in moments when TV heroes and stars are unattainable and a teenager needs a friend.

The best thing to spend on your kids is time.

CHAPTER 15

Sad, bad habits

1. The SAD behaviors: sex, alcohol and drugs

The more concerned your teenagers become about their privacy the more your suspicion might grow. Learning the signs of trouble and helping your offspring avoid bad directions is the number one challenge in the teen years and even the pre-teen years. Steering someone who is almost out of your control is a hard assignment for parents. To prepare for those risky years, parents need to know the danger signs, and they need to know themselves.

When it comes to those dangerous behaviors, drugs often produce the most tragic stories, but when counting statistics about abusers, alcohol wins. Alcohol abusers are defined as persons whose drinking habits produce poor work, excessive absenteeism from work or school, and complaints from friends and family. One quarter of our teens become alcohol abusers by the time they reach college age. And alcohol-related accidents remain the biggest killer of our pre-teens and teens until they pass college age.

What's a parent to do? You can't protect your kids from every temptation, but you can make sure the right messages are sent:

1. Don't send the message that alcohol is a problem solver: "I've had a tough day, I need a drink."

2. Don't send the message that alcohol is necessary for social situations. Using alcohol for its relaxing effect only postpones learning better social skills.

3. Don't send the message that behavior under the influence is somehow more genuine, natural, or free because it's more emotional and less thoughtful. Just because behavior is less filtered doesn't make it better. Inhibitions have been learned from experience, and thoughtfulness is a valuable human quality. When teens depend on alcohol to break down social inhibitions, the breakdown of sexual inhibitions is the next bad habit. In surveys of teenagers, intoxication is the most common explanation given for unsafe sex.

Now, about those drugs: Watch the money. The drug business is about money. Where can an unemployed addict get $75 a day to support his or her habit? Recruiting a new user—your teen—is one of the best sources of money. Pay attention to the amount of money your teenager has. Drug pushers look for buyers with extra money, so your teen should carry only the needed amount to school or stores.

Watch your model. Your kids are always imitating you. Set an example for your sons and daughters to follow in the use of tobacco, alcohol, and drugs—including medications. Teens imitate the most. Review your habits for the sake of your kids.

Watch your teen's habits. Paying attention can keep you up to date on any temptations. In addition to the money situation, changes in sleeping and eating habits, friends or secretiveness about friends can also be a sign of trouble.

One dad recently told me he made a point of regularly calling the parents of his son's friends. As a single parent he liked to compare his experiences with what others were going through.

As much as you think your children will never abuse alcohol or take drugs, you need to know the signs. Unfortunately all kids show some of these signs from time to time, and it doesn't indicate drug or alcohol abuse. The difference that deserves attention is a cluster of abrupt changes in these signs:

1. Unusual, unexplained need for money, or money missing from the house.

2. Changes in friends, eating habits or sleeping that don't make sense.

3. Lack of concentration, extreme agitation.

4. "Cold symptoms" that just don't go away—red eyes, runny nose, increased infections.

5. Changes in appetite, cravings.

6. Changes in fatigue, hyperactivity, appearance, becoming sloppy.

7. Unusual clumsiness, shortness of breath, coughing, peculiar odor to breath or clothes.

One mother's story began: "John started going with those older kids last summer and suddenly he didn't care how he looked; he was sloppy, always sniffing, getting up later every day, and he lost interest in everything—even soccer!"

This mother found drug paraphernalia in her son's room the first time she looked! The cluster of changes in social habits, attitude, and self-care were enough for her to investigate.

> The difference that deserves attention is a cluster of abrupt changes in these signs.

2. Ten to 20-year-olds back on the bottle

Often a parent first discovers a teenage drinking problem on the morning after:

"Boy, do I feel terrible this morning!"

"Are you sick? What did you have when you were out last night?"

"Ah, just the regular stuff."

"Quin, you must have had something different from the same old stuff." It will probably turn out that Quin was tempted by a few beers for short-term fun and now he has the day-after long-term misery.

Looking beyond the short- to the long-term consequences is one measure of growing up. Even parents can have trouble looking ahead to drinking problems:

"Let him have a little beer, what harm can it do?"

> **S**tay informed on every occasion, about how your son or daughter is going to get home from a party or other activity.

"As long as it's in the house and nobody is going to drive, I guess it's OK."

Drinking habits often produce strange excuses: "I couldn't help it, I was drunk" is a common teenage misunderstanding of responsibility.

Traffic laws don't excuse the drunken driver of responsibility and often teens don't seem to understand that drunkenness is not an excuse for stupidity. Nevertheless the most common excuse a teenage girl gives for getting pregnant remains, "I was drunk."

But drinking and driving continues to be the most dangerous fall-out from the drinking habit. All parents dread that terrible phone call in the middle of the night: "This is Officer Jones of the State Police, your son has been..."

What can parents do about the alcohol menace?

First, stay informed, on every occasion, about how your son or daughter is going to get home from a party or other activity.

Second, disallow all social events with alcohol.

Third, support and respect the laws concerning drinking and driving and the officers who enforce them—the next car they stop, just in time, may have one of yours inside.

Strict laws do work as I found out during a celebration with my wife's large family in Norway. Her cousin accidentally picked up her husband's wine glass by mistake and touched it to her lips. Her face showed near terror as she realized what she had almost done! She was the designated driver for her part of the family that evening and, in Norway, the road blocks and breath tests for any alcohol consumption are inescapable.

In the Norwegian courts, any evidence of alcohol and the automatic fine is two months salary! That can't be brushed off even by the wealthy. Results of behavioral tests and blood levels determine the jail sentence (up to one year) to be added to the fine. The law is strict and drinking and driving is rare in Norway compared to the United States.

Our legislators have a responsibility to provide an effective law beyond unenforceable suspensions and trivial fines manipulated by DUI lawyers.

Some will say their freedom to judge their own drinking and driving is more important than a few deaths, but they are wrong and we should say so.

It only shows a prejudice against the young to crow about getting tough with teens because of their 14 percent of the drunk-driving fatalities and then wring our hands and coddle the adults responsible for the other 86 percent.

It's not enough to complain about alcoholism and drug addiction and then demand prescription programs for anti-depressants and hyperactivity drugs for the kids. How many excuses for overuse of medication can you give your teen and still maintain an anti-drug argument?

Parents may see a clear distinction between medications and illegal drugs but a teen may not. The distinction becomes even less visible if medications are abused at home.

Despite their eagerness to help, drug company advertising often tempts parents to try risky medications. The pharmaceutical companies are in the business of developing and selling drugs. So it's in their best interest to sell antidepressants for the glum, tranquilizers for the overactive, and diet pills to anyone who will take them.

Their point of view may not be in the best interest of our kids because often these over-prescribed drugs are sold to a wide range of people over a long period. On the other hand, antibiotics and other specific medications are sold for temporary problems. When faced with the choice of researching and advertising medications for temporary problems or medications for a lifetime, drug companies will go where the money is.

Even prescription drugs can be abused in spite of your doctor's refill limitations and dosages. The implied acceptability of such missteps creates a dangerous precedent for a son's or daughter's future excesses.

Teenagers naturally lean toward short-term

> How many excuses for overuse of medication can you give your teen and still maintain an anti-drug argument?

benefits. Parents have the job of teaching their kids to see the long-term consequences.

One mother objected to her doctor's refusal to continue prescribing tranquilizing medication for her son. She said it helped him stay on task, even if he was far beyond the trauma of the car accident that had started the medication. She didn't buy the arguments that her son might become dependent, or he might find the distinction between his medicine and street drugs arbitrary.

Of course even child-management medications are necessary in some cases. But be careful with the message that goes along with these remedies. "I can see you're upset, you need your pill," sets a precedent that may be hard to break. Better to keep the comments and the dosages as low as possible.

3. When should your teen start smoking?

We all know smoking shortens life expectancy on average by about a half-day for every day a person smokes. Of course, every smoker thinks he is an exception. My uncle surprised us all by living to be 80 and died with his pack of cigarettes on his night stand, but he lived a miserable coughing life of emphysema.

Recently my doctor asked me when I had stopped smoking. I said I knew the exact day—Thanksgiving, November 22, 1962. He said, "Oh good, you know the date. It gives me a chance to use my tables to show how long you are likely to live."

"One day makes a difference?" I asked.

"Not much, but every day of non-smoking after quitting makes a little difference—even after 45 years." Suddenly I wished I had quit earlier.

The human mind in action is a wonderful thing to watch. One Mom told me, "I never smoke around the kids, it's bad for them."

She is right, secondhand smoke is bad for kids but so is first-hand smoke and so is her example. She can't smell it on herself, and it's nice she has reduced the smell of her kid's clothes, and if there's any left over, the kids will probably air out before school lunch.

But the example has been set, and I'm sure the kids got the message. Of the 3,000 kids who start smoking each day, about two-thirds have parents who smoke. "It's up to them, isn't it?" one smoking father said. Not exactly. In the United States, 24 percent of adults who are smoking parents have over 60 percent of the kids who start smoking.

> Of the 3,000 kids who start smoking each day, about two-thirds have parents who smoke.

The number of daily first-time smokers hasn't changed much over the years, but now most begin quitting in their twenties. So every day only 900 start a lifetime of smoking—600 are offspring of smokers.

I haven't seen any plans for tobacco companies to go out of business, so I guess they are counting on somebody's children to fill in for smokers who die off. If your teen delays joining the ranks, there are good consequences.

For example, two teeth. Yes, smokers lose, on the average, two more teeth per decade than nonsmokers. So just delaying smoking from eight until 18 should save two teeth! Of course another 12 teeth are goners in the decades between 18 and 78.

If your children delay smoking until 20, then, in addition to saving two teeth, they are likely to delay turning prematurely gray as well, since smokers are four times more likely to turn gray prematurely. Also delaying smoking will put off balding since men who smoke are twice as likely to be bald or balding as non-smoking men.

In the long term, smokers have thinner, less elastic skin which means more wrinkles than nonsmokers. So children who wait until 25 to start smoking should look ten years younger at age 50 than reunion classmates who started smoking at 15. I guess that's an advantage.

But starting young has other consequences. For example, young smokers have twice the likelihood of colds, flu, and respiratory disorders each year. Young smokers are also much more likely to try marijuana, and teens who have tried marijuana are twice as likely to try other drugs.

If your teenager delays smoking until 30, other statistics kick in. First, he or she is likely to forget to start smoking at all (more than 80 percent of starters begin in high school, 90 percent before 21).

So when should your child start smoking? The later the better, but never is better than later.

The increasing number of quitters has decreased the American adult smokers from almost 80 percent in 1948 to 44 percent in 1964, to 29 percent in 1987, and about 24 percent today.

For all those ex-smokers, the health and longevity benefits start coming right away.

After 20 minutes without smoking, blood pressure decreases, pulse rate drops, body temperature of hands and feet increases to normal.

Eight hours after quitting, carbon monoxide levels in the blood drop to normal and oxygen level increases to normal. After 24 hours the chance of heart attack decreases. After two weeks, circulation improves and walking is easier.

At one year, the excess risk of heart disease is decreased to half of someone still smoking—not good but better. Five years and stroke risk is back to that of a non-smoker. Ten years and lung cancer risk is down by half. Fifteen years and risk of heart disease is reduced to that of non-smokers and so is death rate.

So what is the best thing a smoking parent can do to steer the kids in the right direction?

Quit.

When it comes to bad habits the most effective help you can give your teen is to set a good example. Give your teen a chance for an active life as well as a long one. Set the right example. Insist on no smoking, reasonable eating, no alcohol and regular exercise in the growing years.

4. When can you relax and count on his common sense?

You would think if you could just get the kids safely through childhood, the chances of a terrible accident would go down as their common sense kicks in.

The truth of the matter is that the older your teenager gets the more likely he or she is to be injured.

A recent study by Ezekiel Emanuel and David Wendler from the National Institutes of Health shows that daily hospitalizations, emergency room visits, and even deaths per million increase very slowly through childhood and pre-adolescence.

Among American teenagers, football injuries top the list at 3800 injuries per million occasions of participation. Soccer is next at 2400; then basketball at 1900; cheerleading 1700; baseball, 1400; and skateboarding, 800. All of these injuries become more frequent as the kids go through the teen years.

Before they reach the 15- to 19-age group, the daily death rate among children is about one per million per day. In the late teens it skyrockets to 10 per million per day. Why is that? Because of cars, of course. Hospitalizations jump from two per million per day to six. Even emergency room visits—a good measure of childhood accidents—jumps from 30 to 60 per million per day from the early teens to the late teens.

All that we do to protect our children by using car seats, then seat belts, then looking both ways crossing the street and being careful with scissors, all of this, is overwhelmed and swept aside by the risks of driving and riding with reckless friends.

May through August is the most dangerous time. We would expect that this one-third of the year would produce one-third of the accidents or winter weather would take more than its share, but 42 percent of accidents occur during the summer. The National Safe Kids Campaign's study of data from 1991 to 1996 concludes that summer is more dangerous because "kids are not sitting at their desks in school in a protected environment, the days are much longer and the exposure (to risk) is more."

The kids of driving age are by far the most dangerous group. The girls are now incurring

> At one year, the excess risk of heart disease is decreased to half of someone still smoking – not good but better.

All of this, is overwhelmed and swept aside by the risks of driving and riding with reckless friends. almost as much risk as the boys. In 1990, 160 of every 1000 girls wrecked their cars and by 2000 the number was 175 per 1000 per year. The boys are steady at 210 per 1000 drivers per year.

The National Center on Addiction and Substance Abuse reports that the girls drive more and drink just as much—48 percent of girls drink; 52 percent of boys. For the first time, high school freshmen girls nudged out the boys for first place in reports of regular drinking in 2000—41 percent of girls and 40 percent of boys.

What are your plans for your teenagers and how are they being supervised this summer when they go for a ride? Nothing else you have done to protect them during all their growing-up years counts as much as your answer to this question.

5. Bad language habits: "Oh, come on, Mom, "screw" is just a word"

How can you stop that terrible language? As I left the mall one weekend, I heard the lowest gutter language from a group of almost-teenagers.

In a desperate need for identity and to "be somebody," these preteens selected the worst examples from movies and TV that often justify profanity as ordinary and realistic. This from the same movie people who have conferences about how to make punches sound "better" and conjure horrible fights without blood or hospital stays and amazing car chases through traffic and pedestrians with no injuries, tickets, lawsuits, or insurance problems. Profanity is actually rare in public conversation; movies are not realistic.

Outside the media, the purpose of a teenager's copy of bad language is, I guess, to impress the listeners or to emphasize what is important. But heaps of swearing added to whole sentences of "like" and "you know" result in no emphasis at all and an impression of mindless ignorance devoid of adequate vocabulary.

Some teens give the impression that they have lost respect for themselves as well as anyone listening when they bury themselves in a mud of bathroom talk and profanity left over from their recent childhood (interrupted only this morning, I think).

What's a parent to do? Most teens have better manners, but some shouldn't be brought to a mall without a gag and a leash.

How does this habit get started? First, you have to have a group. Teens usually don't have the confidence to engage in this sleazy patter alone and, anyway, most of it is intended to impress their friends. While they may say they don't care about the opinions of others, the whole show is staged to impress others. When on their own, they try a more acceptable strategy to blend in. Of course, they really do care and try desperately for the admiration they long for.

Parents can help solve this confusion by maintaining a good model through the transition years, objecting to the trash language and defending other members of the family when they are abused by it. "Don't talk to your Mother like that!" can be a great family moment even if not a pleasant one.

If profanity is not accepted and no bad model for imitation is handy at home, this embarrassing phase of a teenager's years will pass.

I think most kids expect their parents to keep up the standards while they try out low, or no, standards. As a matter of fact, kids would be embarrassed if their parents imitated the not-yet-grown generation.

One mother I know tried everything to clean up her daughter's language. Nothing seemed to work until her daughter's friend stayed for supper one evening. As the meal started, everyone went into shock when Mom said, "Pass the f***ing potatoes."

Later her daughter said, "Mom! I can't believe what you said in front of Brad! What were you thinking of?"

"Isn't that the way you talk sometimes? I was just trying to fit in."

"No, no, don't try to fit in. Just be Mom, OK?"

It's a satisfying story, but the best strategy I know is to "Just be Mom (Dad)." Hold to your standard and object to language abuse as you would any other abuse. Your example will win out.

When your grown-up sons and daughters say, "I can't believe I said that, I sound just like

> **"Don't talk to your mother like that!" can be a great family moment even if not a pleasant one.**

my Mom (Dad)," you will want them to be thinking of the best of your behavior, not some sleazy profanity.

CHAPTER 16

Other dangerous temptations

1. Are the kids ready to try risky behaviors?

Have your teenagers started leaving home yet? Yes. Even our preschoolers move out of our control a little when they say, "I can do it myself!" And teenagers will struggle with independence, testing the limits and trying out their new skills as they acquire them.

A preschooler who insists on putting on his own shoes even when he can't get it right, will insist on his own choice of cereal tomorrow and his own school clothes in a few years. Later on, as a teenager, his struggle will be about curfews, cars, and then his own apartment and choice of a medical plan.

One thing you can count on in teen-rearing is that the kids will move out eventually, but you can also be sure they will never completely leave. Leaving will still be in progress at 30! Some of us grandpas still have 40-year-olds who call back to go over old topics.

When will they be ready and how painful will it be—for them and for you? It depends on how much they learn from you and how much tolerance you learn from them.

Whatever time it is, it's time to teach your teenagers more about life skills—from getting dinner ready to handling money to getting along with friends, lovers, and bosses. The more they know, the better they will feel.

> **Leaving will still be in progress at 30!**

What did they learn about life's skills today? Your time dedicated to this training counts. A recent study by the National Institute of Child Health and Human Development showed that while quality child care improved language and memory skills, children who spent over 30 hours per week in day care are more demanding of attention, more aggressive, and generally less socially skilled.

Child care is here to stay in this era of single parents and two-income families. The balancing need is for parents to set the right social examples when they are together with their children and teens. And they need to teach the character and moral development that was short-changed in day care years.

Your time and example can counter whatever shortcomings may show up in the teenage years. Put in at least as much time on discussing social situations and daily responsibilities as you do in helping with homework and math already practiced in school.

Happiness and contentment are elusive, and they can be missed if either teen or parent is too afraid to move on to learning new skills. Dr. Spencer Johnson's book, Who Moved My Cheese?, told a simple story of two mice and two friends who look for happiness and fulfillment (the elusive "cheese") in many situations. They find it, lose it, and find it again. The story has many good lessons for children as well as teens about overcoming the fear of changes in life such as, "Smell the cheese often so you know when the cheese is getting old."

Your teenager will always want your companionship, but as it is with adults, the need may be disguised under an assertion for independence and opposition to control. Just because a teen asserts independence at an early age, doesn't mean companionship is unimportant. The struggle in growing up is a confusion of emotions—fear, desire for control, desire for acceptance by others, and anxiety about security and something called happiness.

Be patient as you and your teenager each look for your own kind of "cheese."

2. When should dating start?

Parents of every generation are shocked when the subject of dating first comes up. Some kids will start probing a parent's resistance before they are 12 while others just drift into their own social habits later on in the upper classes of high school.

The trouble comes from the details. Curfews, cars, the activity, and the friends involved. Kids think in terms of black and white, "Will doing this or that be dangerous?" If it's not immediately life threatening, parents should have no objection, right? And if parents suggest that anything could go wrong, the kids say their parents don't trust them.

Parents consider more of the risks and possibilities than their teens. What could happen and what is reasonable at this early age? Once again it's a teenager preoccupied with "Me" taking all restrictions very personally, while his parents are trying to teach him about worldly and long-term risks.

Most teens are not ready to even think about these serious questions. So until they are well into high school, the rules should not change. No outings without trusted older adult transportation. No evenings "hanging out" with no plans and no rules.

Boys Town Press publishes *There are No Simple Rules for Dating My Daughter*, (available at parenting.org or go to Amazon.com), a 200-page practical look at teen issues from unmasking sexual con games to what to wear and where to go. Authors Laura Buddenberg and Kathleen McGee help teens come to some healthy attitudes about good relationships and bad ones. Without the preparation for exploring and knowing your own feelings, dating may be only a fantasy to keep your teen popular with the crowd.

When my oldest daughter, Pam, was 17, I asked her how her date had gone. "Not good. He introduced me as PAT! He hadn't even taken the trouble to get my name straight. He spent the whole evening talking about himself. He never asked a single question about me."

Pam recognized the signs of trouble. And at 17 she knew enough about herself and dating to make good decisions. Teens at younger ages may think that a bad relationship is better than no relationship at all. With this idea in mind, a teen will put up with a lot.

Questions and stories help keep communication flowing.

Dad: "How was the date?"

Joey: "OK, but Jennifer and I just don't get along so well anymore."

Dad: "You're having some rough spots now."

Joey: "Yeah, she likes those horror movies. We always have to do her thing."

Dad: "What did she think of your new shirt?"

Joey: "OK, I guess. She didn't say. Sounds like she doesn't care, doesn't it?"

Dad: "A little." Dad's listening helped and when Joey is ready, he'll find someone who cares more.

Buddenberg's and McGee's book poses good questions for a church or school class. It brings out many danger signs that can help a young person recognize trouble and know themselves well enough to avoid bad situations. Parents can learn how prepared their son or daughter is for the dating scene by discussing the questions raised in *There are No simple Rules for Dating My Daughter*.

3. Pregnancy: What about the father?

May is Teenage Pregnancy Prevention Month. Parents and teachers in the United States should be particularly concerned about the problem. We have the highest annual teen pregnancy rate in the industrialized world—55 of every 1000 girls between 15 and 19 per year—two times higher than Great Britain, eight times higher than France! Half will end in abortion. The other half, after some natural terminations, will cost a lot.

The first cost is the burden on the family, the altered life plans and career plans, the grief, guilt, embarrassment, blame, charges, and demands on the girl, the boy and parents of both families.

Next is the cost to taxpayers. About $37,000 for each teen birth over the lifetime of the mother and child. Sexually transmitted diseases (STDs) cost a huge amount more for diagnosis and treatments.

So your daughter has a 1 in 20 chance of becoming pregnant before she is an adult, and both sons and daughters are at three times that risk for STDs. This is not just a "girl problem."

How should a parent talk to his or her teenager about this? See page 28 for a discussion about those first talks with young teens. Before starting a conversation with your older teen, a little self-inspection is in order. What do you want to say to your teens about their responsibilities in a relationship? What message does your son get in the non-serious moments about his attitude toward women and sex? What do you want to say to your daughter about contraceptives? Abortion? At what age do you want to bring these topics up?

Alcohol is the most common excuse young women give for making the big mistake. What attitudes should a parent model on this subject?

When it's time to get serious, remember all those listening skills. Keep your pace of conversation slow. Reserve your answers and advice until your teen has a chance to express his opinion. Before you give all your guidance, you need to learn what they know, or think they know. Remember that one session on this topic will not be enough, so conclusions with "You should...," "Don't ever...," and "Be careful not to..." don't have to be said in the first conversation.

Take your time on this subject, it may be the most important part of your influence on your teenager's future. If your emotions take over, you may never hear from him or her on this subject again until she (or he) has something to announce to you.

For fathers in unwanted pregnancies, the most common excuse is, "I just didn't think she would get pregnant." But now that the deed is done, who do we expect to be responsible? Usually it's the girl. And all too often the surprised new grandparents will also have to take charge. What about the father?

Pregnancy is not just a "girl problem."

With teens, we are tempted to think of the dad as a rowdy irresponsible youth that we wouldn't want near the baby. But the fact is that in 90 percent of teen pregnancies, the father is over 20. These dads are adults using childish excuses.

If we are going to coerce mothers to have their babies, then the fathers are going to have to help care for them. If Mom is now going to spend her time worrying about food, child care, discipline and all the other concerns of child-rearing, then it's only fair that dad carry half the burden.

"You can't just force a guy to go over and pitch in on child-rearing when he doesn't want to." Oh? Why not? We don't mind forcing the girl to take on the burdens.

> If your emotions take over, you may never hear from your teen on this subject again until she (or he) has something to announce.

The dads get off too light. Child support is only money, and all parents know that money is only a small part of bringing up a baby. Often the father believes he (or his parents) can simply write a check and then they are free to go out for beers.

Child care everyday, diapers, school functions, sports, homework help and being there to provide love, support and the time all children need, these are the realities new Dads need to face up to. It's true that if men could get pregnant, abortion would be viewed more leniently. But if reckless fathers truly believed they will also have to spend days, evenings and weekends caring for their children, then they would be more careful with their temptations.

He's not fit to raise a child? If you were not fit to drive it would be off to traffic school for you. If Dad lacks some parenting skills (he evidently has the first one) he should be off to baby school to learn the rest. Both young Moms and Dads will need guidance and lessons.

Child care training needs to be part of every high school program. Senior high school days ending at noon is madness on several counts. Getting a dose of real life could easily be worked into their school schedule.

I asked one protester of planned parenthood whether he thought fathers should be required to take more of the responsibility. He said, "It's about life, not just awkward child care arrangements." Of course it is about life, but as a male he thinks it's not about his son's life.

The next time a man or boy thinks, "I just don't believe she'll get pregnant," he should know that the consequences could change his life as much as hers.

4. Thinking is not dangerous to your health

A teenager's curiosity and imagination can take his thinking in unusual directions. Sometimes a teen's thoughts may make him or her suspect there is something wrong with his or her "basic personality."

Recently one mother wrote that, "A week ago my 11-year-old son said he might be gay because he wondered how big other boys' penises are. What should I say? He seems very upset about this."

The truth is that sexual curiosity is no different than curiosity about space travel or terrorism. Mom's pre-teen needs to hear that his curiosity about anatomy doesn't mean he will grow up to be gay, straight or otherwise any more than his interest in space travel means he will be an astronaut. He needs to hear it's OK to think—even about unusual things and even without conclusions.

If Mom's routine reaction is critical and she says, "Put that out of your mind," her son could conclude that thinking can be dangerous and he ought to quit it. That will leave him open to many dangerous fanatics that troll the troubled waters of the teen hangouts.

"So Mom, do you think I could be gay?"

"No, it's not likely. Why would you think so?"

"Well, I wonder if boys are all the same, you know, down there."

"That's a long way from being gay. The rest of your body isn't the same as everyone's so I suppose everyone is different. When you're grown, you'll know better how you feel about people, marriage, children and lots more. It's not a simple black and white issue as your friends might think."

Take your time in these conversations. Keep your pace slow and remember that no conclusion needs to be reached today; that's why families last a long time.

Avoid criticisms that are likely to be taken personally and internalized by your teen. "What makes you think that? Why don't you pay more attention to what you're saying? What were you thinking of?" will only discourage easy conversations and encourage more secrecy.

> **Take your time in these conversations. Keep your pace slow and remember that no conclusion needs to be reached today; that's why families last a long time.**

Centering on the personal also leads to the "quick fix" approach, "Why don't you...You should try...Think before you talk..." Such advice and criticism has the potential of closing a conversation before your teenager has a chance to sort out what he has to say. Regardless of their quick snippy comebacks, the kids don't have your vocabulary or your way with words. They need time to discover how they feel and to put it into words.

What attitudes toward women do you want your son to learn? What suspicions of boys would serve your daughter well and what ones lead to trouble?

Set a good example when expressing these opinions and attitudes. Your model will have the most influence, and it will set the stage for their relationships in the years to come.

5. Sex and curiosity

We parents know sex is a big problem among our teenagers, but too many of us hesitate to provide much information. We are afraid of what the kids will do if we tell them too much, but we all suffer the consequences when they know too little.

The percentage of women 15 to 20 who are sexually active is about the same across our country as it is in other countries. About 80 percent of women have sex before 20, 60 percent before 18 and less than 20 percent before 15. The same is true in Canada, Sweden, France and Great Britain, reports the Washington Post.

The national differences come when you look beyond the sexual activity and consider the pregnancies, births and the abortions that are produced. In all of these categories, the United States is at the top of the list. Our birth rate among teenagers has declined steadily from 1991 to 2002, but it is still higher than that of any other developed country. The price is terrible.

About 600,000 unmarried American girls will become pregnant this year. While caring for the baby, only one-third will receive a high school diploma; less than 2 percent will have a college degree by age 30. Later on, their baby boys will be 13 percent more likely to go to prison and their baby girls will be 22 percent more likely to become teen mothers themselves, according to Family First Aid which also offers help for troubled teens at familyfirstaid.org.

Why are we failing so badly? I include all of us in the "we," not just parents of girls, but parents of boys as well. Our brief, sometimes totally absent, sex-ed curriculum ignores too many gaps of ignorance, creates too much unhappiness and too many failures among the child mommies and daddies and the babies they produce. Without any knowledge and without contraception, a sexually active girl has a 90 percent chance of becoming pregnant this year and a sexually active boy, usually not underage by the way, has a 90 percent chance of causing it.

Our silence is to blame. Out of embarrassment or misdirected morality, we support abstinence without getting into details. So we have created generations who are miserably ignorant about sex. Intelligent and "with it" as we think we are, we are embarrassed and intimidated when it comes to sex. "If we don't talk about it, it won't happen" is a label we put on sex, pregnancy, and even sexual diseases.

Like attentive sheep dogs, we hope to keep those in our care in line, frightened and huddled together. The dog has all the responsibility, the sheep have none. They just hope the dog will go away.

The parent-as-sheep-dog comparison breaks down as parents turn their attention to other important matters. The sheep dog never turns his gaze from the flock. Parents don't have this luxury and must teach responsibility to children who eventually go it alone. That's why we must risk the

Intelligent and "with it" as we think we are, we are embarrassed and intimidated when it comes to sex. "If we don't talk about it, it won't happen" is a label we put on sex, pregnancy, and even sexual diseases. embarrassment and teach the details of sex education, the responsibilities and the consequences.

When one trapped and scared teen was told she had herpes, she said to her doctor, "How could this happen? We never actually did it. We just, you know, fooled around and, anyway, I took one of Mom's (birth control) pills."

Loose talk about sex seems to get more outrageous every day. Many parents find it unbelievable.

Fifteen-year-old Brandon: "When are you going to come across for me, Pia?"

Pia: "Leave me alone. And don't talk like that, it's disgusting."

Brandon: "All your friends do it."

Pia: "Oh, I don't think so. And how would you know?"

Many girls face this kind of harassment everyday at school. Boys are not immune to it either as girls get bolder. This part of our culture encourages lots of problems—date rape, for example—and puts pressure on teens who see more and more approval of casual sex in movies and on TV. The pressure is often not friendly. More than half of the girls under 15 who had sex said they were forced into it.

Parents are not always helpful with these problems either. The American Family Research Council surveyed 10,000 families and found that 52 percent of children between 5 and 17 have bedroom TVs and watch more than 7 hours each day on average. In contrast, conversation with parents averages only 38 minutes each day. Who's winning the influence competition here?

What can parents do to help their teens be safe and careful in times when sexually transmitted diseases can be deadly, and pregnancy can change life's direction in a single evening? Should I have said evening? Evidently I shouldn't have since teenage sexual activity, like teenage crime, peaks between 3 and 4 p.m. each day.

A parent can start, first of all, by keeping the high-tech out of the bedroom. TVs and computers should be out where the family can see what programs are being used or watched. Secondly, parents should review arrangements for supervision for after-school activities. And then, they should reserve time everyday for just family talk.

6. Who points the way through the dangerous temptations?

TV and computer game violence and terrible movies set examples we could do without. Peer influence also plays a role, providing second-hand information and a magnified influence over the dangerous impulses of our teenagers.

But after all the influence of media, peers, and newspaper reports of crime and horror are counted, the most important risk factors that show up strongest in the tragic statistics are the example that Mom and Dad set.

Social science research has an inherent problem in connecting a teenager's bad behavior specifically to her parents. Nevertheless, parents are more likely to be singled out for attention by these investigators and more likely to get the blame in the resulting statistics.

But even though American social scientists tend to study what is in vogue or easy to investigate, I suspect that they are right on this one. Parents are the number one influence.

For example, the Child and Family Welfare Association of Australia studied 4,000 families and found that 40 percent of teenagers drank and most did so in the presence of their parents – not secretly without parent permission, as the myth often implies. This continues in spite of our own National Institute of Alcohol Abuse studies that show the three leading causes of death in the 15- to 24- age group are, in order, auto crashes, homicides and suicides. Alcohol is a leading factor in all three. Also the institute

Teenage sexual activity, like teenage crime, peaks between 3 and 4 p.m. each day.

reports, adolescents who begin drinking before 15 are four times more likely to develop alcohol dependency in adult life.

Many parents find it easier to let teachers do the teaching and preachers the preaching. But even these parents will do most of the teaching themselves by their example. They are always on stage; their views, attitudes, and disposition are the ones most likely to be copied – even by the teenager who says he will never be like his parents.

Whatever your views on the rights and legal wherefores concerning posting the Ten Commandments in schools, look for opportunities to talk over the values expressed in the commandments with your son or daughter. As a parent, you have the most influence. By your example, you teach your version of respect for others and the principles of character every day. The TV, movies, and even the posters in school lag far behind parental influence.

> The TV, movies, and even the posters in school lag far behind parental influence.

In order for your teenagers to explore their opinions and form their own view of good character, they need to tinker with many ideas. If every remark is criticized, if every conversation is treated as a game where each remark requires another correction until Mom or Dad wins, teens will avoid the game, say less and think less.

SKILL 4

Teaching School Strategies

"I don't wanna go to school anymore."

"Zack, you have to go to school."

"The kids are mean, I don't like anybody and they don't like me."

Why are some teenagers satisfied with school while others find it so objectionable? Of course there are as many answers as there are teens, but parents can help with the adjustment. In addition to academic skills, the ability to make friends and get along with classmates can be taught. Medications may help explosive kids, but medications can also insulate a person from learning and practicing social skills as well as school subjects. A student may become dependent on the drug and miss his chances to deal with everyday frustrations.

CHAPTER 17

School adjustment and separation shock

Lack of social skills and success in the classroom can isolate a teenager and create a dread of every school day. It takes creativity to resolve these problems. The tips in this chapter can help a parent with a teenager who needs more good days and fewer bad ones.

1. What can you teach your teenager about getting along at school?

At age five, I was shocked when my parents left me at the door to a kindergarten classroom full of other selfish five-year-olds. They were self-centered and not at all like the helpful and serving parents I left behind.

Suddenly all my companions were immature children. They didn't care if I had my juice and cookie. Mom and Dad would care. Unlike Mom and Dad, the other kids didn't drop everything and listen when I yelled (of course, I only made reasonable demands) they just continued doing their own thing! I wasn't the center of attention any more.

All grade school newcomers face these adjustments to being on their own. They develop new ways to fit in, get their measure of attention, and deal with a new school, new friends and other kids who are not so friendly. But many need to be taught the specifics of making friends, cooperating in a class, and working out problems with unfriendly classmates.

It's not easy. How would you like it if all of your friends had the social skills of grade schoolers? They don't, do they? And when high school comes along, what if all your friends had the minds of 14-year-olds and you had only 14 years of experience yourself?

> **Many need to be taught the specifics of making friends, cooperating in a class, and working out problems with unfriendly classmates.**

Most kids adjust by focusing on a few friends and coming to an uneasy truce with the rest. Other kids may have trouble getting on the same wavelength with anybody.

A bad adjustment at school makes for an unhappy childhood and begins a torturous journey through the teenage years. Some teens may learn to dread school and perform poorly. They need to know how to make school life more enjoyable. Here are a few helpful hints to pass along to them.

Hint 1: Develop a compliment habit. Withholding compliments, whether out of inattention, jealousy or a fear of embarrassment, is a mistake—even if the one giving the compliment is only 15. While waiting and hoping to be admired themselves, kids often neglect the other person's yearning for a kind word. Even that nasty kid in the last row hopes for some positive companionship.

Hint 2: Make a "friendship list." To better understand the impression students have on others, school counselors sometimes ask students to write down why they like certain people and not others. If you have a troubled teenager, ask him or her to make such a list of the qualifications for friendship.

While appearance and being cool will be high on their list when thinking of themselves, teens usually list different characteristics when thinking about why they like someone else. The most common reasons teens mention are: someone they admire, someone who likes them, someone who is available and who is a reliable companion.

Hint 3: Learn to listen. Parents coaching their teenager should ask: "Where do you look when talking with a friend? You don't want to stare at them, but if you look away too much, the other person thinks you don't care. Your eyes, reaction, and posture say a lot about how you feel." Everybody needs time, wants to be liked and has a story to tell. Friends need to listen to friends.

> They need to know how to make school life more enjoyable.

Cool, sarcastic, angry, or bitter people make interesting characters in movies and on TV, but teens should realize that in real life Ms. and Mr. Cool are not well liked because they show little concern or interest in others.

The quick comebacks, put downs, and ridicule that make up sitcom jokes don't produce good school friends or a warm family life. Parents need to set a good example. No one feels safe when every comment risks ridicule.

2. Risk-takers have to feel safe

Every new dog owner knows that you have to start out carefully with a new puppy. The little fellow is just bubbling with activity, some of it is cute and most of it is wrong. He won't do anything you tell him, but if you react with too much anger, you may need the carpet cleaned again. Even a loud sneeze can traumatize him.

In the long run, he may get over the trauma, but his willingness during training will be tentative if he develops a fear of reprimands.

When I was training dogs for the army in the 60's, the dogs were screened for natural ability, "willingness," the army called it. The test was simple. Did the dog stay in front of his handler when he heard a loud noise up ahead? Did he show a natural curiosity and attention to whatever his handler did? If the answers to these two questions were yes, he stayed. If not, he was rejected and sent back to his civilian owner.

If he managed to stay in training, the army rule was, "If he's right, praise him; if he's wrong, correct him; but if he's not yet wrong let him continue what he's doing." Correction was usually putting the dog in the place he should be or going back to an easier training step where praise was more likely. Effective trainers were consistent and quiet.

The rules are similar when a teenager is learning something new, but you can't reject a teen and send him back to his previous owner, although the thought may have come to your mind. So for a teen to succeed in learning, especially in creative learning, he has to be a risk-taker. And all risk-takers have to feel safe when they are messing about with homework, computers, or ideas. Too much criticism, too much correction, and creativity begins to take cover.

Many adults secretly feel that their creative talents were hidden away because of early reactions from adults, parents or teachers who were too focused on mistakes, deviations, and errors. For some, the message went through at an early age: "First of all, stay out of trouble." It is hard to rekindle that army-dog "willingness" once the stay-out-of-trouble message has been accepted.

In addition to school subjects, the risk-taking factor also shows up in a teen's willingness to try new activities outside of school. All of us have a family relative who approaches life's problems too timidly and stays in old ruts hoping for a magical change or at least, no trouble.

Creativity requires a lot of confidence. That's why most parents instinctively tolerate "mistakes" when children investigate a new challenge. Scrutiny too close and corrections too freely given are often a teen's reason for deliberately selecting activities out of range or out of the interests of his or her parents.

As a child becomes a teenager, a parent's role changes quickly from authority to provider of consequences and then later, to companion and coach.

An effective coach encourages practice. A coach is also a good observer, listener, enabler, and example.

> Too much criticism, too much correction, and creativity begins to take cover.

Good coaching encourages assertiveness and creativity, a coach sets only necessary limits and motivates his or her players to stretch their abilities and take the risks of new approaches and new ideas. This kind of coaching develops a player's self-respect, and with self-respect comes courage to take risks, create new art, explore new ideas, and add the extra effort to expand the spirit.

How to pay attention. Parents often ask their kids to pay attention and then complain that the kids don't respond. Of course we parents don't really want a response; we want attention with no fiddling and no back-talk. Just sit there and look and listen.

Many kids, especially those with attention deficit and hyperactivity disorder (ADHD) find this vague demand to pay attention and do nothing a confusing, even impossible, request.

Adults also find paying strict attention hard. Adults are too social and have too much to say, as any person leading an adult class or a meeting at work would tell us. We teachers can make ourselves frantic coming up with exercises, projects, and new ways to "get their attention" so we can present the next lesson and yet "keep control" of our audience. Once you try it, you will believe in good pay for teachers.

> Corrections too freely given are often a teen's reason for deliberately selecting activities out of range or out of the interests of his or her parents.

The truth is that paying attention is not a natural habit. We are an active species. We are good at telling and not so good at listening. Better to challenge the kids to give new examples, different arguments or suggest related experiences. After all, learning is in the doing of the thing.

Teachers are fond of saying kids remember 10 percent what they hear, 20 percent of what they see and hear, and 50 percent of what they do, see and hear. The percentages may vary among education professors, but the conclusion is right: just "paying attention" is usually not enough.

When I started graduate school I was scared. I had worked very hard to make the minimum grades to qualify for graduate work. I told my graduate school mentor, Dr. Donald Lewis, on my first day that I wondered if I could make it. He arranged to see me every week and asked me to bring my class and study notes. Then he made an odd request. He asked that all my notes be on index cards. Three reasons for this or that theory, four experiments about this or that principle, etc.

In class, I paid attention because I was writing about what I was hearing and seeing—all the time. I even had complete note cards on the talks given by invited speakers. When I finished graduate school I had over 4,000 cards. Later, appointed to the University of Maryland faculty, I was often the only person who had complete notes on a visiting speaker when a review was needed. I was not a very good companion at these meetings; I was too busy.

For most of us who don't have perfect memories, paying attention, by itself without practice, results in very little learning. For study time to result in better grades, kids need to get busy—rewriting notes to replace shorthand and turning brief comments into complete sentences that will make sense after class is over and test time is near.

Even when reading is the assignment, active behavior will yield better results. "Never turn a page without writing down something" is a good rule to get material to stick.

3. Separation shock: The first day back at school

Ashley is 12. Brad is 13. Both started middle school this year. Both are worried and stressed with the new school and their parents try to help as much as they can.

Their mother told me, "Middle school is scary for them, but it should be a great stage of childhood. I hope they are enjoying it more than they seem to. The junk on TV and some of their friends can make them pretty upset."

Even if the first day back to school has not yet arrived, some attention now will pay dividends later—especially if your teenager is starting a new school.

Visit the new school with your teen beforehand—if only to walk around the outside. This will help ease your teen's first-time jitters, even if he or she has been there at other times.

Also, do some early shopping for school supplies. You may not yet know all the special items teachers will require, but buying some supplies now will start your son or daughter looking forward and it will reduce last minute, hectic shopping.

On these outings, bring up the school bus times, lunch situations, and after-school arrangements so that first-day misunderstandings and surprises can be avoided. After my first day in my Chicago high school, I just started walking home as my older brother had done on many occasions. Mom found me after a short, frantic search.

The first days of middle school can be especially lonely for sons and daughters. Three months ago they had one main teacher, familiar long-time classmates and a simple schedule. Now they have several teachers, classmates from many schools, and a variable class schedule. It may be the biggest culture shock in their life so far. Yet parent involvement both at school and at home seems to taper off in middle school—just when it's needed most.

As the kids encounter the new school, you may feel that you've lost your influence over them. The kids may try to give you that impression, but as every teacher, counselor and minister knows, you have an effect, even when the kids react with, "You don't know anything about it" and "It's not the same nowadays."

Parents can also help their new middle schooler when time management becomes a problem. It was probably not a challenge before, but now larger schoolwork projects require realistic planning and work. Short-term goals can help your student organize big school projects and fend off procrastination, "Just write down the sources you need for your paper, then take your snack break."

Homework will more likely be finished and in good form when done first—before the fun activities. Kids often want the reverse—after-school snack, TV, check the computer, and then, if there's time left, the homework.

Just your recognition of these problems will help relieve the loneliness of middle school. Stay handy and ready to listen.

Most of the tragic stories of kids gone wrong at this stage begin with a surprise—a surprise to the parents that the kids even had a problem. But as the review goes on, it turns out

Middle school may be the biggest culture shock in their life so far.

Most of the tragic stories of kids gone wrong at this stage begin with a surprise – a surprise to the parents that the kids even had a problem. there were signals: frustration with a troublesome subject, a bad attitude learned from new classmates, fear of being embarrassed in class, or bullying by others that went unreported.

On that first school morning, it's tempting to be a last-minute critic with too many "don't's" and "watch out for's" intended to ensure your teenager will do everything right. But the first morning rush is a bad time to undermine confidence and inflate worries. Your student will be especially thin-skinned, defensive, and easily embarrassed on that first morning.

Day one is a good time for a compliment, optimism, and a show of confidence. If we parents are to keep up with how the first days go in middle or high school, we will have to consciously slow the pace of conversation so the kids will follow our lead and make more sense.

Remember conversation makes a bad competitive sport. If you try to "one up" every remark, your student will harden his defensive style early and real information about his school fears now and his experiences later on will be scarce.

In the everyday rush to jobs, shopping, and school buses, take the time to go slow and to hear about what's going on. Watch for your chances to listen and attend these moments. They can help you keep up.

4. Give your middle schooler extra help

Change comes fast after fifth grade. Brad and Ashley have new responsibilities for doing homework and scheduling their time. Less than a year ago they were the oldest ones in their grade school. Suddenly they are the youngest ones at the new school, have many teachers, and they worry about getting along.

Their daily world is filled with school and friends and yet, through the internet, CDs, radio, and TV, Ashley and Brad are learning about a bigger world of action, love, money, and world terrorists.

To help with such a confusion of ideas and values, a parent needs to understand what priorities their teen might have at any moment. For instance, when going off to school, their biggest fear is likely to be that they'll be embarrassed. They're wondering: "Do I look OK? Am I cool? Am I liked?"

Here's a good time for, "You look great. I like the way you are." It is not a good time for, "You still look too sloppy. Wear something else. You had better start acting differently. (You are just not good enough)."

Brad or Ashley can feel vulnerable on the morning school bus if the parting words from Mom or Dad have been negative. Their friends are likely to detect the feeling and may use it as a chance to say something "cool." This usually means something critical. One great disadvantage of middle school are those 11- to 13-year-old friends. That could stress even the most level-headed person. Parents can balance the impact of young and selfish friends by providing the positive support school friends seldom give.

Brad and Ashley can feel self-conscious with friends or even with loving relatives. "Do I look good (my body is so funny)? What should I say (people never understand what I mean; they might laugh at me)? How should I react to a compliment (they may think I'm conceited or not cool) or a criticism (they may think I'm not tough)?"

Parents will need all their listening skills for these hectic years: Paying attention to their teen's concerns; resisting the temptation to offer advice or suggestions too often; being more empathetic and less critical; and, above all, keeping the pace of conversation slow enough so both sides have time to think.

In the everyday rush to jobs, shopping, and school buses, it's easy to miss your chance to hear what's going on. Watch for it and use it.

Compliments on their abilities and good social perception can give them confidence. From that will come the strength to face the next challenges of school with a better perception of themselves and a better self-respect.

> **Parents can balance the impact of young and selfish friends by providing the positive support school friends seldom give.**

5. Should students be paid?

"Capital Gains" is an experimental program that gave away $137,000 to 3,300 middle school students in the District of Columbia last year. The Washington Post reported that the students liked the money-for-effort program and their schoolwork is improving.

The program works like this. After 30 classes in a two-week period, students earn $2 for each additional prompt class attendance and $2 for model behavior in class. Each day that all homework is completed, they earn an additional $2.

Of course, money is a good incentive for adults and it keeps the economy running—at least it did until recently. But many parents think it doesn't seem quite right for school kids. Even some students are annoyed by the assumption that they had to be paid to take school seriously.

Other rewards ought to work as well, such as parental encouragement for their teen's growing competence, gratifying applications of school lessons to practical problems at home, and the self-satisfaction of progress toward a productive and useful life.

If the kids in the program can't remain enthusiastic about school unless they're paid, their parents need to put in time on encouraging them before the money dries up. If we know anything about government experiments it's that the money always dries up.

In school districts not so moneyed, we parents need to pay attention to what is going on in school and pony up the time, interest and encouragement so kids will know the value of their learning.

These days, classes and learning continue throughout life. Picking up efficient habits early can be an advantage for years to come. The best homework practice will come from talking to others about the work, drilling important concepts, rewriting notes and important material, and drawing new diagrams or tables that organize facts differently.

The practice habit is hard to maintain because we like to do things we do well and we shun activities that seem uninteresting. So practice of school work requires real creativity on the part of parents. Could your daughter use her math to keep track of the family checking account? Receive a fee for doing so? Could your son handle the grocery list? Take the money and do the shopping?

Will they make costly mistakes? Yes. But can they stay interested without your interest, praise and patience? Probably not.

6. "Mom, I can't go to school today."

Getting your teenager off to school can be a chore and an aggravation if he resists with frequent reasons for not going. Some students will snatch at any excuse: "It's too cold...it's too hot...it's too boring or too much work, and of course the ever popular "Mom, I don't feel good." Keep up on the details of your teen's school situation with good listening skills; even your son may not know why he doesn't want to go.

Damon: "Man, that school is such a drag!"

Mom: "Went pretty slow today, I guess" (Mom just uses different words for "drag"; this is reflective and less likely to stop the conversation than, "You need to try harder!")

Damon: "You bet."

Mom: "What's the worst part?" (Here's a good "it" question. It starts with "what," instead of "Why are YOU so bored?"

Damon: "I don't know. I guess it's the whole thing."

Mom: "What's the best part?" (Good question that may help Mom help her son. Better than: "There must be something wrong [with you]!" That would be threatening.)

Damon: "I like seeing everybody, but my new English class is so hard."

Mom: (Now armed with a tip on the focus of the problem) "Let's look at your assignment in English."

The complaint about school boredom is familiar to most parents. Mom put the "quick-fix" suggestion on hold and waited for Damon to tell her his reasons. Because Mom allowed her son to direct the topic by asking questions and responding reflectively, information flowed to Mom instead of from her as advice.

When the conversation is about school, listen for clues to problems. School counselors say there are six common reasons for truancy:

1. To avoid scary situations: bus, school room, tests or teacher.

2. To avoid uncomfortable social situations: bullies, teasers, or a perceived hostile teacher.

3. To get attention at home: Mom (or Dad) provide more personal attention at home during complaints.

4. To stay home for entertainment (TV, computer games, play).

5. To avoid possible embarrassment of going back after previous absences.

6. To avoid the inconvenience and effort of getting up to go. Having clothes ready to wear would help, keeping materials ready for school, or keeping up on homework.

How can a parent help with these problems?

1. Keep listening so you are up to date on school activities and problems.

2. Watch those late-nights. Often a teen demanding to stay up for late-night TV is the same one demanding to miss school the next day. A teenager short on rest is more easily aggravated by a test, a teacher's correction, or a teasing student. It's the same problem a tired adult might have. Allowing late-nights may mean a whole day of trouble, an absence, or at least a big argument in the morning.

3. Keep an eye on the morning drill for getting to school. School buses usually won't wait and it's easy to make trouble for yourself by procrastinating too long in the morning.

> Keep up on the details of your teen's school situation with good listening skills; even your son may not know why he doesn't want to go.

4. Build support for school and school activities. Praise learning, respect it, make it useful to your teen, now. Let him: balance the checkbook, do some cooking, figure out your next trip on the map, explain TV news about science, art, or government.

5. Volunteer. Volunteer in order to get a first hand look at the activities and atmosphere in school. Volunteer to help make the school more attractive for your teenager.

When an absence is unavoidable, try these suggestions to keep it from becoming a habit:

1. **Limit entertainment for just staying home** (TV, computer games, etc.).

2. **Check all excuses with a call to the school** ("The buses aren't running today." "We're supposed to get out early anyway.") Your teen may not have the right information. Even the favorite, "I'm sick," may be suspicious if it always seems to come up on school mornings, complaints are vague, and improvement in the late morning is miraculous. Also, if your teen is responsible enough to be left alone, be suspicious if he seems anxious to get you off to work: "I'll be all right—just go!"

3. **Don't allow other activities to take priority over school:** "I need to stay home to get ready for the soccer trip, practice my school play lines, catch up on old school work."

4. **If you are suspicious but must leave your teen by himself now and then, come home at irregular times occasionally.**

7. How can you keep them motivated?

Why do so many teens drop out of high school? It's easy to blame the schools, but the problem also requires help from home. A teenager's eye may become fixed on an attitude that does not promote learning and separates school work from "real life" at home.

Kids, faced with daily school demands, often define intelligence as the ability to learn things quickly and easily. Learning by effort signifies lack of ability to a childish mind. So says author Allison Zmuda in her book, *Transforming Schools: Creating a Culture of Continuous Improvement*. This distinction between easy and hard learning can produce cynical low-performing students. They may believe their problems are the school's fault for making things difficult. Even a successful student may shy away from challenging tasks and embrace routine assignments which he finds more comfortable, says Zmuda.

Dr. D. Betsy McCoach developed the Social Attitude Assessment Survey that measured self-concept, self-motivation and attitude toward school in hundreds of students. These factors account for more of the variance in school grades than even innate academic ability, Dr. McCoach says. Crucial self-concepts develop at home.

Keep school connected to life at home. A teen's interest in school and motivation to make the effort to learn is a habit that starts at home. Given a chance, kids may choose only the orderly and comfortable lessons at school and shun confusing and challenging homework they must do on their own. If grades are not working out, students may put the blame on themselves for not being smart enough, or they may conclude that homework is irrelevant and disconnected from real life outside of school.

Show your kids that difficult problems are an enjoyable challenge and are to be expected. Being able to solve them is more related to effort than to intelligence. Parents need to show the connection.

Parents can help in three ways. First, they can model good learning habits, ask questions about school work and pose hard problems for their kids to struggle with.

Second, parents can show the relevance of school through the daily news and the daily paper. Where is Somalia? What was the history of France's involvement in Vietnam? Also Mom and Dad can give their budding student tasks that are relevant to his or her math (preparing the monthly checks from bills for Mom or Dad to sign and updating the check book), and, for her government and social studies: where is Burma and why is help so difficult to give there when we can provide help easily to New Orleans?

> Parents need to be interested in, and praise, their teenager's school work. How are they to remain interested if Mom and Dad show no interest?

Third, parents need to be interested in, and praise, their teenager's school work. How are they to remain interested if Mom and Dad show no interest?

How hard can it be to do an experiment about how the color of light affects plant growth. For what treat will your dog learn best? What stock would be best to buy? How would you know?

How far away is your teenager's school? Not in miles but in connectedness to life at home. The relevance of specific lessons is not the most important part. Mom's and Dad's attitude and example of the usefulness of the subjects are the priorities. That model is right in front of their kids every day.

CHAPTER 18

"Who am I at school?"

1. Who is gifted?

Soccer and basketball coaches are not the only adults putting kids to the test and seeking the stars. The schools are forever testing our teens, looking for the "gifted." They do it because they have special programs for special kids. And some of us want "trophy children." But how would a parent recognize, and how should a parent react to, their teenager's "gifts?"

Who were the geniuses of the past? Einstein, for sure, even though his genius wasn't detected until he was nearly an adult. Many people would include Mozart who was writing operas at the age of three. But neither the musical genius of Mozart or Michael Jackson guaranteed a long and happy life.

We might include others in math and theoretical physics, as well as additional nominations from the list of classical composers. No doubt these people were born with something special. Einstein even left his brain to science so they could try to figure out what it was—they have offered no conclusions.

Schools usually limit definitions of "gifted" to areas they teach and evaluate—math, science, language-related talents such as seen in spelling bee winners, and sometimes music.

Other gifts, such as social skills, artistic ability, and common sense, are not so easily evaluated. It may even seem silly and arbitrary to think of the "County

Common Sense Champion" or the "Personality State Champion." But these other talents need to be recognized so that a parent's expectations can keep pace. Business professionals tell us that the strengths which lead to success are more likely to be perseverance, hard work and social skills—not academic trophies.

I know a fifth grader who represented all his county grade schoolers at the national spelling bee in Washington D.C. We don't know if his spelling talents mean he could learn other languages at an astounding rate, but we know that multilingual applicants will be prized by businesses of the future. If we wait too long to teach languages to him, he will not be able to learn another language without an accent.

Is it enough to be proud of his accomplishment and continue his schooling with no foreign language training until high school? Should we take the wide view of "gifted" and let him at least sample challenging language training now? How many seeds of unrecognized genius wither because they did not fall on fertile ground?

Parents are often aggravated by their talented teenager's failure to carry through and use his unusual blessings. Why would he come up short on effort when he has the gift? The answer, sometimes, may be that procrastination has set in because of fear of failure, particularly if failure is defined by himself or his parents as anything less than perfect.

My grandson is a good example of this situation. Completed history assignments ride in his backpack weeks after they were due. What's going on? He says they are "not quite right." So he's a perfectionist who is flunking history.

Keep a modest reaction if a coach or teacher says your teenager is gifted. If he turns into a perfectionist, he may avoid the risks of trying new activities and expressing new ideas. Don't be misled by society's narrow views of gifts and talent. Look for and encourage all your son's or daughter's gifts.

> Business professionals tell us that the strengths which lead to success are more likely to be perseverance, hard work and social skills – not academic trophies.

2. Mixed blessings

Concerning the lighter side of early development, take Alex, now 16. He spent his babyhood thumbing through magazines while his fellow one-year-olds played with simple toys. By the time he was three, he would correct his mother if she skipped reading a line in a story by placing her finger on the missed phrase.

Alex has hyperlexia, a condition opposite to the learning disorder, dyslexia. He has a very advanced ability to identify individual sounds while reading, and he also has an advanced ability to manipulate those sounds in his head. But he has trouble understanding what he reads and he was delayed in learning to speak.

He now speaks in a normal fashion but uses the cadence of reading out loud and he avoids interjections such as "like" that many youngsters his age use incessantly.

But Alex is running for his student council and may win because he is a fearless public speaker. Alex seems about normal in any category outside of his language ability.

Helpful parents deserve daily credit for encouraging all competencies beyond what a scientific test might discover. They can help in all cases by watching for chances to bolster confidence and by avoiding the straight diet of advice, quick fixes, and focus on shortcomings that hit vulnerable spots.

"Practice what you want to become" is a good rule for teenagers. "Model what you want your children to practice" is a good rule for parents.

3. Which teens are at risk for trouble?

How can you know which kids will get into trouble? The nightly news might give you the impression that low income and poor family structure are the primary causes of dangerous and destructive paths.

But the long-term Adolescent Health Study shows that the kids most likely to get into self-destructive activities such as drinking, drugs, or crime are kids who do poorly in school.

The study has been following 10,000 students since 1994 when they were 12 to 17 years old. It is finding all the familiar problems you would suspect. At first, one in ten reported weekly drinking, and the amount of sexual behavior was alarming. One in five seventh and eighth graders had explored sexual activities and two out of three high school juniors and seniors were sexually experienced.

After problems with school, the second best predictor of these bad habits was the amount of unsupervised time a teenager had. This influence showed up in drug use, violent behavior, and sex. "Among all the factors that can be associated with teenage sex, the big one was opportunity," Dr. Robert Blum, the director of the study, said.

We seem to have adjusted to a daily routine that says, "Get teens up before it's light; get them to school by 7:45 ready or not; and let them out by 2:00." To do what?

Teens on the early morning schedule. Even a large proportion of adults have trouble being bright morning people. This goes double for teenagers going through the growth and hormone years.

Since after-school time is such a factor in risky and violent behaviors, maybe we should reorganize high school schedules. When classes begin at 7:45, teens go home at 2:30 to an empty house and three hours of unsupervised time before parents get home from work.

Bus drivers and others who have built their schedules around dropping the kids off early would find this a troublesome change. Sports practices would be disrupted by a later schedule, and part-time jobs would be more difficult to arrange, but what is our priority? Six dollars an hour or fewer teenage pregnancies? What sense is there in going to math class at 7:45 a.m. in a sleepy haze and going to football practice at your afternoon peak? It should be math at your peak and sports when they can be worked in.

Other studies investigating the sources of school violence show that almost half of all students are concerned about pressure for school grades. The stress builds with the morning rush followed by the cascade of short classes.

If a good education for our kids is our goal, it's time to get started. Let's plan to change their daily schedule to give them the best chance to learn and to practice safe habits.

4. Bullies, victims and hiding out in school

Every school day this year 160,000 students will stay home because of bullies, the U. S. Department of Justice estimates. Also, 100,000 students will bring guns to school, 6,500 teachers will be threatened and 250 teachers will be attacked.

> Since after-school time is such a factor in risky and violent behaviors, maybe we should reorganize high school schedules.

Bullies often justify their aggression by saying they were provoked and the victims deserved mistreatment because they didn't comply with the bully's demands. Bullies like to dominate others and think they should always get what they want.

Girl bullies may use more subtle tactics than their more violent brothers such as insults and ridicule, but the terror they inflict can still be intense. So victims avoid unsupervised areas, playgrounds, restrooms, and the lunchroom to keep from being the repeated targets.

Victims of bullies can be passive or provocative. Passive victims are often alone, anxious, sometimes weaker, and may cry easily. Provocative victims can bring trouble on themselves because they tease and irritate others and don't know when to back off. When they get an unwanted reaction, they sometimes fight back, but usually ineffectually.

What can a parent or teacher do? The single most effective deterrent to bullying is an adult authority. We parents and teachers should intervene. We can do it with a no-nonsense style, as a problem solver and as a third person who smoothes things over.

In the cafeteria, Caitlyn, who is 14 and has been the subject of many bullying complaints, shakes her fist at Marea and says, "You'd better give me that extra quarter you have left over from your lunch."

Ms. Anderson, the social studies teacher, overhears and says, "Caitlyn, that doesn't go here. Come to my room for the rest of your lunch time—we need to talk." (The no-nonsense and prompt action approach.)

Preventative school policies hold bullies responsible for their behavior. Staff may feel uncomfortable confronting bully behavior and may ignore it. Or they may feel isolated and unsupported when it comes to intervening in the lunch room, hallways, or on the playground. The power balance needs to shift—the pendulum needs to swing away from power for bullies and back to the school staff.

"No-Bullying Rules" and school policies that encourage students to speak out and to get adult help when needed should be supported by parents. Our goal should be to protect the victims and to help the bully replace negative behaviors with skills that involve treating others kindly.

This problem requires a statement right from the top. School superintendents should assure principals, and principals should assure teachers that they will be vigorously supported in their efforts to stop bullying in the school and on the playgrounds.

One excellent source for help is *Bully-Proofing Your School: A Comprehensive Approach for Elementary Schools*, published by Sopris West, 4093 Specialty Place, Longmont, Colorado, 80504 or, sopriswest.com. This book describes effective long-range programs for schools and parents and it provides useful handouts, exercises, and needed strategies.

> Every school day this year 160,000 students will stay home because of bullies, the U.S. Department of Justice estimates.

The West Middle School of Detroit, Michigan, began its anti-bullying program by prominently displaying school posters with anti-bullying messages such as "Friends aren't friends if they put you down" and "Your silence means your approval." The school also has a "bully box" for students to anonymously report incidents. "No-Bullying Rules" and these school policies encourage students to speak out and to get adult help when needed, and they should be supported by parents of bullies and victims alike.

The Detroit program alerts parents to watch their students for telltale habits:

> The single most effective deterrent to bullying is an adult authority.

• Making excuses for not wanting to go to school.

• Increased fear of school situations such as riding the bus, going out at recess or using the restroom.

• Missing personal items or needing extra school supplies or money.

• Extra trips to the school nurse, unexplained bruises or torn clothing.

Until parents take up that awareness, kids will be hiding out in school and losing out on their education while they try to stay out of harm's way. "If I don't go to the bathroom (gym, school bus, recess, or lunch room), I can avoid Billy (or Beth) Bully for another day."

Teachers and principals deserve your support. And many teenagers need special practice learning how to talk firm, walk tall, look a tormentor in the eye and say loudly, "Back off!" As city police often tell us, some people need to practice how to avoid looking and acting like a victim.

Also the bullies need help. They, too, are missing out on their education while their attention is on confronting, fighting, and abusing.

They will soon be out of school with minimal social skills and the mistaken notion that abusing others is acceptable. They need redirection. Many of our community problems will come from these misdirected students if their behavior at school is tolerated.

Let's help them now while they are in school and teachers and staff have an influence.

The person who brings the problem to our attention is often denounced as a "tattletale." One reason tattletales annoy us is that the help requested is not easy or comfortable. In some cases, it's dangerous. The bully may retaliate or the bully's parents may object to our interference.

Our freedom and safety exist only because most people will not tolerate behavior that endangers others. If we saw thugs beating up someone, we'd yell

> As city police often tell us, some people need to practice how to avoid looking and acting like a victim.

for help or call the police. We wouldn't expect the police to say the victim should "solve his own problem." And we would not expect to be ridiculed as a "tattletale."

Bullies at school are a local example of a weakening of the majority's will to protect the individual. Tattletales are not admired and neither are bullies. But school polices should encourage students to object when one of their own is bullied by another. And teachers should support reasonable requests for help. Tattletales are not always wrong.

The internet site, CharacterCounts.org, suggests this pledge for schools: "Anti-bully Pledge: We will not bully other students. We will help others who are being bullied by speaking out and getting adult help. We will use extra efforts to include students in activities in our school."

School psychologist Izzy Kalman offers direct help for the kids with a free online manual, *How to Stop Being Teased and Bullied Without Really Trying*. His new website, www.bullies2buddies.com also has a free manual and advice for adults.

The rewards for teasing and bullying are in the reactions of the victim, says Kalman. He makes specific suggestions about how a teen should react or not react.

The bullies of today will be the community problems of tomorrow. From their ranks will come the next generation of child abuse, spousal abuse, road rage, and "life rage".

5. Magical thinking and mental habits

The signers of the Declaration of Independence knew the value of both education and hard work. It was clear to them that effort and learning in school would be rewarded in work and life.

Today, many students believe they might "make it" even to enormous financial success just by luck, or by skill in sports, or by knowing the right people. It's a possibility promoted by TV news and game shows.

So without incentives to focus attention on the learning at hand, many students become victims of magical thinking about success, and they develop unrealistic views of how "luck" will carry them through.

We adults also become victims of magical thinking. That's why we now approve of lotteries and other gambling, but our grandparents wisely, I think, did not.

We sometimes engage in magical thinking not only about a financial windfall, but also about our students: "The ones with the 'right stuff' will always do well." "The kids will work harder at school if parents take a harder (more punitive) line or if the teachers enforce more strict (more punitive) rules."

Faced with a student's failure and rebellion, a parent is tempted to criticize and punish. But the solution is on the positive side—with incentives, praise and respect expressed in concrete ways that raise self-esteem and confidence.

Some may object that gushing with praise is the wrong solution, but the danger for most of us is not in overdoing it, but in doing it at all. Encouragement and parental support involve a commitment of time and attention.

But schools are crowded, teachers are very busy and our culture is inclined to provide little compensation for the essential activities of attending school and learning.

Representatives in Congress with their large salaries and teachers on the line with their modest ones should pause before objecting to the notion of rewarding students. It may be the most important part of the teaching and the parenting job. Few of us work for nothing.

I know it seems like a lot of trouble and we wish all students would work just for the love of it and learn just for the love of learning, but most will not. We are a goal-oriented species with ambitions that can go astray. We need daily course corrections through positive feedback.

> **We adults also become victims of magical thinking. That's why we now approve of lotteries and other gambling, but our grandparents wisely, I think, did not.**

If a student behaves badly in school, we often say it is his fault—he is rebellious, aggressive, too distracted, or not very smart. A recent study focused on the ways we explain children's problems in school. School psychologists listed the following causes of school problems:

1. The material was not appropriate,
2. The teacher was not doing a good job of teaching,
3. The organization of the school was wrong,
4. The parents of the student were not supportive,
5. Something about the student was amiss—motivation, low ability, or emotional disturbance.

When teachers were asked to think back about the students they had taught, they attributed 85 percent of the problems to No. 5, the students themselves. This is partly true, of course, but it attributes the problem to the factor that is least changeable.

Both parents and teens can engage in the faulty mental habit of blaming a person's basic personality. This can get in the way of resolving the problems. Attention to the daily frequent successes with encouragements and compliments produces the best long-term progress. Knowing the pitfalls of blaming the teen's personality can clear the way to a better attitude and a better solution. Here are a few versions of faulty blaming habits that sometimes afflict both parents and teenagers.

1. Oversimplification. We are all inclined to simplify to keep order in our mind where some disorder is inherent, but the habit is destructive.

"All those teachers are mean."

"Well, if you would just try a little harder, I'm sure things would get better."

You can see that oversimplification can be both a parent's and a teen's problem. A good step forward in this conversation would be to ask a specific question, "What would show your teachers your good side?" Of course, this question won't get a direct and constructive answer, but it will turn the topic toward a more specific direction than "trying harder."

2. Absolutes. We prefer absolutes. Gray areas and contradictions are too hard to handle while an absolute demand seems more likely to get results.

Faced with an absolute demand, "I want all your homework done before supper, not a bit left or no TV later," a teenager may react with his own no-room-for-argument tactic, "Either you love me or you don't. If you loved me, you would let me do it when I want to, so I guess you don't love me."

Mom could make better progress here by setting a reachable goal, "If you have the writing part done before supper, you can do the math after your program." This suggestion won't stop the arguing, but it is more likely to reach a solution.

3. I'll make them sorry. "I just won't do her stupid project; that will fix her."

"Mark, giving up won't hurt your teacher; it will only prolong the problem and it will lower your grade." Mark dreams of his power over the teacher, but Mom has to help him be realistic.

4. Everyone is watching me. "My hair looks terrible. And everyone will notice this shirt is crummy and faded."

"Lamont, your hair is fine and your shirt is fine, too." Mom could do better here by giving Lamont a broader view: "Lamont, what were Althea and Larry wearing last Tuesday?"

"Mom, how would I know?"

"People don't pay much attention, do they? The same goes for Althea and Larry."

We all want the best for our children and that's why we are tempted to point out the shortfalls, but it's the example you put in front of them—even the mental habit you show—that has the most impact. A discussion of all sides of the problem will produce the most useful conclusion.

6. Yearning to be told

When my daughter Pam was 14, she asked if she could go to an older friend's high school party after the next football game. Luckily I was distracted with yard work at the time and said her mother and I would talk about it. I asked Pam a few questions and heard that most of the kids would be older, but she didn't know much more about it.

Later we found out that her friend's parents would be out of town, and on other occasions they had supplied beer for parties since the kids were too young to buy it themselves.

We said no. Pam complained, said we never let her do anything, promised she wouldn't drink any beer, but we still said no. She made quite a production out of calling her friend, she complained about her old-fashioned parents and said she couldn't go.

Years later she told me that many times she was afraid of some of those "friends" and had hoped we would say no. That way she didn't have to think of herself as a wuss and could blame us for having to back out.

She now has a 14-year-old of her own who recently asked if he could have beer at his birthday party. Of course she said no. He whined that his friends said they had beer on their birthday. She said that because the argument lasted less than three minutes, she wondered if the strategy from her own childhood was being repeated by her son.

The struggles between teenagers and parents may not always have clear motives. Even in the mind of the teen, impulses and good intentions may conflict. Sometimes parents have to help by setting down a strict rule.

Whether you are on your own or in a partnership, other parents can create a sounding board for your concerns and provide the assurance that others have problems similar to yours.

A few calls or an announcement in a church newsletter will produce other parents who are willing to take an evening a month for a parent coffee (see page 313 for more).

CHAPTER 19

How to do better on tests

"I can't do this stupid stuff. I'm going to watch TV."

"Wait a minute. You have your test tomorrow, what's the problem?"

"It's about math sets."

"Oh. Well, you just have to keep at it."

When it comes to schoolwork, parents can feel inadequate to the task because lessons and subjects change from one generation to the next. But school is such an important part of teenager happiness that trouble with schoolwork and school grades can invade a kid's disposition from morning to bedtime.

Long-established principles can help your teen do well no matter what the topic on the test. The tips in the next section will help you help him keep his grades up.

1. Students who "have trouble with tests"

Learning to look ahead seems to elude almost all kids until they reach their late twenties. They figure that if only they could get through the next test, demands for all tests would be over. But there's always another test, and learning good ways to handle them will bring great rewards for years to come, especially with the current emphasis on tests. Now it's not only the students that are tested, but the results are also used to evaluate the teachers and the schools.

In 2005, New York State gave its children and teens about 3.5 million tests at a cost of $6.5 million, says the New York Times. States with less population will do less. West Virginians, for example, will give about 350,000 tests to their students at about the same expense rate.

The movement of "high-stakes" testing central to the "No Child Left Behind" legislation has stimulated research by teachers' unions skeptical of the results of increased testing. These studies show that while performance on the new tests improves each year, performance on other independent tests does not increase and in a few states that performance has gone down.

As the tests become cornerstones in public education, teachers are tempted to teach to the test. If this becomes teaching students to parrot particular answers, it is not a good goal for schooling.

Audrey Amreim, senior author of Arizona State University's national study of the high-stakes testing, says, "In theory, high-stakes tests should work, because they advance the notions of high standards and accountability. But students are being trained so narrowly because of it, they are having a hard time branching out and understanding general problem-solving."

"The most perverse problem with high-stakes tests," said Eva Baker, director of the National Center for Research on Student Testing, "is that they become a substitute for the curriculum instead of simply a measure of it."

Whatever the faults of the tests, they are likely to be with us a long time. How can you help your student do his best on them?

Good test strategies are no substitute for preparation and practice, but after studying hard and using the good homework habits described in this chapter, your student's approach to testing can make a difference. Instead of just a weak attempt to motivate your teen with, "Just study hard and you'll do fine," suggest these strategies.

Strategy 1: On objective tests answer all questions. In school and even later in job-hunting, the tests are usually objective. The answers are worked out in advance using a multiple choice or true-false format. When taking these tests, students need first of all to understand that they should avoid leaving any question unanswered. Although wild guessing is a waste of valuable time and some teachers use a formula that penalizes guessing, these procedures only penalize random, wild guessing. Most students can reject some of the options before they reach the point of confusion and for them, guessing is definitely in their best interest.

Strategy 2: Read carefully. In studies where students were interviewed immediately after the test, their explanations about items they answered wrong showed that 15 percent of wrong answers resulted from misunderstanding the item: "Oh, it asked which of the following was not true, I didn't see the 'not.'" Fifteen percent can easily make a letter grade difference.

Strategy 3: Check the question. Before moving on to the next item, the student should re-read the question one more time to be sure that the selection is actually the answer to the particular question in the first part of the item. Very often wrong choices are, in themselves, correct, but not the answer to the question.

Strategy 4: Keep a moderate pace, you probably have plenty of time. Many students feel rushed by multiple choice tests and feel that they can't take time to read carefully and eliminate the obvious wrong choices (50 items in 50 minutes! That's one every minute!). A good exercise to ease this panic is for Mom or Dad to time their student while he takes a practice test or an old test that needs review.

Usually the experience will show him that he has plenty of time for careful reading and for eliminating wrong answers before making each choice. Practice tests also motivate your student to go over good answers, review the important material, and calm his anxiety because the test format becomes familiar territory.

Strategy 5: On essay tests, two answers can be better than one. The first answer can be in outline form and the second can be the complete essay answer. The student's first answer can be done quickly in the student's own words and shorthand. For example, in response to the question, "What was important about the Gettysburg Address?" the student might jot down, "Lincoln, at graveyard: during Civil War; trying to unite the country; said country must try hard to finish the war; for equality and people to run government; give quote."

Now, looking at the first answer, the student is likely to make the second answer complete and in good form. Also, as the student is writing the final answer, new points may come to mind to add to the final answer.

Also, remember neatness counts. The teacher is more likely to give a high score when the major points are easy to find. Studies show that even graders who say neatness doesn't count are more likely to give high scores to a neatly presented answer. If your student doesn't have an erasable-ink pen to avoid scratch-outs and arrows to the margins, buy one today.

2. Practice counts at home; your teenager's attitude counts at school

Teenagers, already preoccupied with worries about themselves, often find test time particularly threatening. Tests are a personal evaluation and you never know what to expect. The personal focus and the uncertainty can produce a bad case of the jitters.

This is a good place for the study exercise of "Make up the test!" If the student makes up the test he thinks the teacher will give, he will experience good practice with answers and review the important material. My students report that 50 percent of the real test turned out to be the same as their own practice test. They whizzed through that half and spent more time and effort on the surprises.

Learning and testing go on throughout life. Students often believe that if only they could get through school, the demands of studying would be over. Adults know that new learning tasks are always presenting themselves both on the job and at home. Many of the specifics of school lessons will be forgotten, but the means for finding and learning them again will prepare your teen for most challenges. Students with good learning habits and good testing habits will always have an easier and more enjoyable experience with each new opportunity in both their employment and home life.

Students can easily lose their motivation for schoolwork when dull moments set in. With so much competition for student time, how do you guide your student to make his best effort?

If you wanted to improve your tennis, you would probably arrange time to practice on the courts. If you wanted to learn a new guitar strum, you would practice it, of course. When it comes to schoolwork don't let your student forget how much practice counts.

As your student gains new skills from school each day, he should be encouraged to use them at home. Sometimes that requires real creativity by parents.

Encourage practice in study sessions. Students often try to study by doing the practice in their minds while sitting and staring at a book or homework sheet. This is not real practice.

Most of us don't have the kind of memory that retains a great deal from just looking; it's the <u>doing</u> that will be remembered. Successful work shows up in grades if the student uses active practice; not just staring at pages, but reading aloud. Not just "trying to remember," but talking to others about the work, drilling important concepts, rewriting notes and important material, and drawing new diagrams or tables that organize facts differently—preferably on cards. For each page of reading the student should take some notes. "Never turn a page without writing something," is a good study rule.

When practice has become a habit, the next concern is student attitude. Often students don't believe their attitude shows and they discount its effect on their teachers. But counselors often coach students to improve their classroom habits as well as their practice habits. Here's some pointers on improving the classroom situation.

1. When there is a choice, your student should sit in a seat as close to the front as possible and keep good eye contact with the teacher during presentations—just as you would practice good listening skills in a private situation.

2. A continual banter of unnecessary questions will do no good, but good questions help learning <u>and</u> teaching. Einstein's mother used to ask him when he

> Encourage practice in study sessions.

came home from school, "Did you ask any good questions today?" If you try to ask good questions in class, you have reasons to follow the teacher's presentations more closely and are more likely to learn.

3. Your student should occasionally talk to the teacher about the class with a question or comparison to some aspect of other subjects or experiences.

Some people may object to the contrived nature of these suggestions, but many teens have the mistaken notion that the classroom is, or should be, a place where only completely passive learning takes place.

The fact is that a classroom is a social situation where exchanges are a part of the learning and an active, assertive role is necessary. The exchanges may not influence the teacher's grading, but your teenager's relationship with his teacher will improve active learning, and that will improve grades!

3. How can your teenager make the grade?

School days can make a teenager and his parents dread the daily struggle, "Do I hafta do my homework?"

Assignments that require memorizing can be particularly boring and hard to keep going.

Greg: I just can't keep the states straight. We're supposed to know them by Friday!

Dad: What are they going to ask you about them?

Greg: We have to point them out on a blank map with no words or anything.

Dad: Do you have a map?

Greg: I have the one in this book and I've been studying it a lot, but I don't remember much.

Dad: How do you do the "studying" part?

Greg: Well, I look at the states and try to remember which ones go where.

Dad: Greg, I think you need to go through a drill in a situation like the one you're going to have next Friday. How about

> Leaving a student on a chair, even one in front of a computer, will not produce much learning by itself.

tracing that map so we can have one that's blank like the one you'll see on Friday. Then we'll make a few copies when we go shopping today.

Greg: OK, then I could practice by filling in the names on the copies we make.

Greg has been trying to practice in his mind ("I've been studying it a lot"), but sitting and staring at a book or homework sheet is not real practice—performance of a behavior—and Greg has not made much progress.

To make homework time successful, Dad first asks Greg what he is doing. Most students who are falling behind are not doing anything. When they study, they stare at things—notes or books—but they don't DO anything.

What specifics do you remember from your own school days? Spelling? Math and vocabulary you still use (do things with)? But I'll bet you remember little of social studies, geography, history, or math you have never used.

Computer programs from school or at home can be very helpful, especially if the drills are similar to the other schoolwork and to the tests that will evaluate progress. But for most teenagers the novelty of working the screen wears off, and adult encouragements and real life applications are needed to keep interest up. It's the same support from parents and teachers that homework and lessons have always required. Leaving a student on a chair, even one in front of a computer, will not produce much learning by itself. So plan to continue regular contributions to the computer learning in the form of home projects and specific encouragements.

With a computer, the student learns to press the right buttons on his mouse and keyboard to answer the questions, and his performance will be best there and less perfect on paper and pencil tests and in verbal drills. We adults are amazed that learning the names of the states on a computer doesn't result in a correct answer on every test paper after that. Here's another place you can contribute: make up some tests. Quizzes and drills with pencil and paper will give your teenager practice in expressing the answers as required later when no keyboard is around.

CHAPTER 20

Keeping their activities on target

February's short days or May's long ones can put a teenager into school doldrums. Parents also may start to run out of enthusiasm for school activities that would pump up a teenager who is running out of steam. Here are some notions that can encourage your teen's sagging attitude.

1. Support the creative projects

Creativity requires a lot of confidence. That's why most parents instinctively tolerate "mistakes" when teenagers investigate a new challenge.

But during the long parenting days of the teenage years, errors may be harder to tolerate and parents might be tempted to criticize, correct or take over altogether just to get the jobs done. Dads in particular can have a hard time in allowing practice.

Dad tolerated a half-hour of mistakes and spills to finally hear Keith say, "OK, Dad, I'm putting my cake in the oven!"

"Great. What temperature?"

"350 degrees. I'm setting it now."

"Keith, why don't you wait a few minutes for the oven to warm up. Then the temperature will be right the whole time."

"Oh. That's why it says 'preheat' in the recipe?"

"Right. This is going to be a great supper!"

Skills your teens learn now will be a source of pride today and useful throughout their lives. The self-respect gained from their new skills and the appreciation for these activities from others is also important to happiness.

Dads can learn to tolerate the inconvenience of allowing their daughters and sons to make mistakes as they improve with practice, if they view this practice as a sign of growing up. Give responsibility gradually, now.

As the kids try new activities, keep the praise and compliments handy even before success shines through. If something is worth doing, it's worth practicing, even if you do it poorly, until you learn to do it well.

As teenagers experience success or failure, their self-respect follows a roller coaster ride. Lacking Dad's experience with the ups and downs of life, a teen's mood changes can be much more extreme than those of us thicker-skinned adults.

As parents, our most helpful influence is the model we set of feeling good about ourselves. Share your highs concerning your own accomplishments and in some small way compliment your teens and preteens every day for their strengths and achievements. Encourage them to appreciate their own accomplishments and to concentrate on the strengths rather than the weaknesses of others.

> If something is worth doing, it's worth practicing, even if you do it poorly, until you learn to do it well.

2. The gender difference at school

Boys and girls have equal potential in many areas but the statistics just don't support the notion that gender makes no difference. Even with today's trends, women still avoid prison more, have fewer accidents, avoid trouble in school and perform better.

You can see the differences even in daily leisure activities. The usual day for a teenage boy differs from his sister's. Boys are more likely to watch TV (81 percent vs. 75 percent), play video games (40 percent vs. 18 percent). Boys are also five times more likely to watch sports programs than girls—not too surprising.

Why can't the boys cope better in school? The problem may have begun when high schools put preparation for college as the top priority. Too much concern about either gender going off to college may lead to less focus on school objectives concerning the practical life-survival skills.

Boys can be inspired by active projects in home improvement, financial management, small business management, mortgages, stock markets, computer management, applied science, and tracking diet and exercise. These projects encourage both boys and girls to be proud of their abilities right now and make them better prepared to be future citizens. Even abstract subjects can include practical projects.

School should help a student with his concerns now, at his present age. **"Someday you'll need this," is not enough.**

Many students need preparation for the critical jobs that keep the country's infrastructure together and don't require a college degree. Of 147 million jobs in 2005, only 32 million or 21 percent required a college degree. Moreover, the U.S. Bureau of Labor Statistics found that through the year 2005, one in three college graduates could not find college-level employment. Among those preparing for the professions, this number was one in two.

Of course a college education is about more than just getting a job. It's learning about all the possibilities and understanding the growth and achievements of the world's cultures. So the percentage of young men attracted to college has been growing even without a matching growth in employment demands—now the number of boys going off to college is up to almost 60 percent. The number getting college degrees has been steady at 25 percent.

For women the same statistics have grown faster and now exceed the men. Seventy percent of women go off to college and 29 percent graduate. We all have opinions about the balance of our school programs for both college and for life. But parents need to become involved through volunteering to understand what can be done.

In some states only 75 percent of our population has completed a high school education. It's easy to blame the schools for the other 25 percent, but

> Of 147 million jobs in 2005, only 32 million or 21 percent required a college degree.

the problem also requires help from home. A teenager's eye may become fixed on an attitude that does not promote learning and separates schoolwork from real life.

3. Why do boys do better later on?

Hilary Clinton did well in school—not unusual—and she's having a long and successful career—quite unusual. The "boy crisis," as Judith Warner of the New York Times calls it, is about statistics that show boys doing badly in school, dropping out in greater numbers than girls.

Yet among the boys who graduate, the success rate in careers later on is even better than their feminine competition who graduate. What happens?

This is a hard subject because we want everyone to have a fair chance. The topics of the early school years agree more with girls than boys so girls get a developmental head start.

There are exceptions, but generally girls develop social skills more rapidly, learn to please adults, teachers and parents, and surge ahead in school grades. The boys want to do things, do sports, do cars.

Even in college, school-performance is highest for girls. The gender gap is widest among African-Americans, only a little less between low-income white and Hispanic girls and boys. At higher family incomes, the American Council on Education says the gender and school-performance gap between the sexes becomes less and disappears altogether in the top 25 percent of family incomes.

Hilary Clinton's success in bucking the trend of career burnout is a tribute to her intelligence and perseverance, and I am sure to the models set before her. But Judith Warner concludes, "There's something more at work here [in gender differences] than relative levels of skill or laziness or drivenness or privilege, though all that clearly plays a role. From an early age, men seem quite clear about what expenditures of energy are worth their time. Like kids with ADD [attention deficit disorder], they're able to spend great amounts of attention and energy on things they find interesting, but show considerable signs of challenge when it comes to tasks they find boring or personally unprofitable."

Maybe there is a lesson to learn from the boys who blossom later. A girl's motivation to please everyone is an advantage in the school years and the broad focus means wider success. But when the graduations are over, juggling the added adult and family responsibilities may force a career woman to fumble some part of her daily agenda.

A boy's motivation to put the wrong priorities at the top and ignore the rest is a risk factor in the school years. He needs encouragement to tackle the hard tasks in school first. When school is over, however, boys more often keep their priorities straight and distribute their efforts narrowly.

4. Time, teachers and tutors

Future productivity will be in the hands of our children. That can make you worry when you see articles about students who are bored with education, kids with "output failure" (we used to call it "not doing your homework") and those far below reading and math levels needed for promising employment.

Dr. Mel Levine was praised in the Washington Post for his focus on student productivity problems. He is the author of *The Myth of Laziness*. He advocates encouraging small steps to build a teen's "working capacity." It's part of the answer but not one a harried teacher has time for.

The school systems are preoccupied with rushing to get everything done before the kids are 18. To accomplish this we use a schedule of school hours that has been essentially the same for over a century while the material to be learned has probably grown by a factor of 10.

Are there any relaxed classroom situations of more than 40 minutes? Some use a block system with daily schedule changes that create some classes, but the number of school hours remains short. So schools are in a bind and under pressure to move students up or out, even if it risks graduating some who read poorly or can't add three numbers. We have to pretend all students have finished yesterday's 40-minute assignments, and today we must rush ahead.

Most parents just don't want to hear that in order for students to learn more, students, parents and schools will have to take more time. Bus drivers would be inconvenienced, coaches of high school sports would feel pressed, we would need more teachers, and, of course, higher taxes.

Teens can learn by teaching. Teaching itself is a great learning tool. And one answer to the shortage of teacher time has been tutor programs. In one PTA program in Maryland, tutors were assigned to other (usually younger) students for crucial one-on-one time under teacher supervision. While the tutors practiced their skills, many young students gained helpful one-on-one time in math, science and other subjects. Each teacher supervised about 10 student-tutors which is a very efficient way to provide individual help to a large class. It was a winning situation for everyone.

Tutors don't have to be the best and brightest. In the Maryland program, tutors were even selected from the ranks of poor students, and they actually benefited the most. Tutors gained crucial motivation to learn when they had to teach the subject. Even many educators will admit that they didn't become fully comfortable with their subject until they started teaching it. If your students have siblings, tutoring doesn't have to be a school program. A few practice sessions between siblings is time well spent. Two people are learning in the tutor situation and both are learning more about the subject as well as practicing good social and language skills.

5. Making the most of a school conference

Our attitudes toward education have changed. Public Agenda, a research and policy organization in New York, reviewed 25 studies of parents, students and teachers over the last 10 years. While tests and grades remained important, parents and teachers now worry more about the violence and rowdiness of their students than they do about the school standards or accountability that draws the attention of politicians.

Also, a growing number of teachers feel that lack of parental involvement is a serious problem. Seventy-eight percent said too many parents don't know what's going on with their teen's education.

Should students run school conferences? Last year the Seattle public schools set out to do something about the sagging relationship between parents and schools. Instead of the usual conference between Mom and teacher or a rushed moment with

> We use a schedule of school hours that has been essentially the same for over a century while the material to be learned has probably grown by a factor of 10.

each of four or five teachers in middle or high schools, each student was invited to lead his conference by showing Mom and Dad his schoolwork and reporting on his progress.

Each student prepared a portfolio of daily work and his own assessment of his progress. Using the school's expectations for their progress, students could explain to their parents what they had been learning, how their work met general standards and what needed more effort. Conferences usually lasted between 15 and 30 minutes.

With the student's homeroom teacher as observer and facilitator, both social and schoolwork problems were discussed. Parents found this situation much more comfortable because the conversation was between parents and their student. They were not coming to school to hear teacher complaints but for their son's or daughter's report and to see the results of the work.

Parents could still ask for a traditional conferences or schedule a follow-up meeting with just the teacher. But most said the new conferences helped them understand how their student was comprehending assignments while giving each student a chance to spotlight his success.

The new system also puts the responsibility back on the teen when it comes to the quality of the daily work.

The number of conferences for each teacher was reduced because teachers need not have meetings with every parent of every student they see in all their daily classes. For the most part they only had conferences with parents and students who were in their homeroom.

The trend is spreading to other states including Oregon, Idaho, California and New York.

Replacing the traditional parent-teacher conference with a student-led conference is intended to increase parent involvement and student responsibility for what is going on and what is yet to be accomplished. Also, the student has to "get up in front" of his teacher and parent and make the presentation, a useful experience.

Last year parent attendance at Seattle school conferences was up from below 60 percent to over 85 percent with many more conferences attended by both parents. Mom and Dad both wanted to see their student perform. Maybe part of next summer's planning could include planning for the student as an active participant in the parent-teacher conference.

6. How can you help their school measure up?

The American Diploma Project's criticism of schools in the Washington Post generated a buzz of comments from both teachers and parents. Teachers were particularly miffed at the project's assertion that high school diplomas were merely "a certificate of attendance." And both parents and teachers thought the report's conclusion that diplomas have "lost their meaning" was narrow and one-sided.

The report laments students' low performance across the nation on tests in work-related areas such as math, science and English. But don't we hope for a lot more from our schools than high test grades in science, math, and English? We must keep our standards in the basics high, but there's more to school than test grades.

> Each student was invited to lead his conference by showing Mom and Dad his schoolwork and reporting on his progress.

What's wrong with using tests to measure school quality? Nothing, but, by itself, it does miss some important aspects. First, tests tend to measure only what is easy to measure, ignoring any complicated social goals both parents and teachers may have in mind. Second, once the scores are in, they tend to narrow faculty attention on the topics tested at the cost of other influences we hope the schools will have.

Learning social skills is at the top of my list. These skills may be even more important to getting and keeping a job than the math, science and technology that are so testable. A student's first job interview is likely to cover social skills and efficiency in addition to technical skills.

> Learning the basics of job skills includes learning to be reliable, prompt, courteous, honest and enthusiastic. To improve the employability of our students, these aspects of character are as important as test scores.

Tests are primarily for the basic academic skills, we don't test much about job searching and job success. If you get in trouble at work it's likely to be in getting along with fellow employees or mistreating a customer—not for fouling up the math of a customer's order. Learning the basics of job skills includes learning to be reliable, prompt, courteous, honest and enthusiastic. To improve the employability of our students, these aspects of character are as important as test scores.

Student teaching is a good way to practice social skills as well as subject content. Tutoring assignments benefit both the practiced students and the beginners they teach. Explaining what you know to someone who doesn't is a challenge we all need to practice.

Since the best learning is in the doing, cooperative school projects also help with teamwork, tolerance and cooperation.

If your son or daughter is headed off to college, test scores and grades count heavily. But as I have said to the college-bound I've known, "Your grades and scores on college entrance exams will get your application in the file drawer with all the other students with similar numbers. Now what will make your application stand out in that drawer? Activities, accomplishments, tutoring-teaching skills, and experiences in and outside of school, make the individual stand out.

The same goes for a whole school. What activities are available? What skills are practiced? The sports and club activities need parent support also. They will improve cooperative skills and develop a record of accomplishments that reflect broadening interests that will last a lifetime.

Of course, all parents want their children to be prepared, but they may not agree with the project's standards. Certain math courses for every student are specified along with specific written and speaking skills.

Nothing is said about all the other tasks we expect of the schools. In addition to preparation for the high-tech world, we want a focus on character and values, a low tolerance for bullying and violence, more tolerance for diversity, and zero tolerance for drugs. We also would add discipline concerning sexual harassment and encouragement for cooperative school projects. How is all of this going to be done?

Parents and local citizens are the most powerful help for school programs—if they want to be.

The PTA website (PTA.org) and FamilyEducation.com (of the Family Education Network) offer dozens of ideas on how parents can support and raise funds for school projects. Suggestions range from collecting ink jet cartridges for recycling to asking local businesses to donate raffle items for fun night.

Local businesses also help by supporting school initiatives. We all need to be sure they are recognized and appreciated and not merely called when our schools need more money.

One enterprising PTA arranged with deckgard.com (a supplier of stair barriers for kids) to provide a rebate to the school whenever a customer used a special PTA sales code. Very little work and no meetings, just income!

When my sister-in-law visited a New York suburban high school she noticed how bright and attractive the building and grounds were compared to her teenager's inner-city school. So she suggested to her home principal that a parent painting team could brighten up the halls with murals. She found 10 parents willing to help—two designers and eight helpers. But another obstacle was a rule that said a janitor had to be in the school whenever it was in use. To overcome this complication, she scheduled her crew to paint during Saturday basketball games when janitors were on the job.

The result was a brightly painted, attractive building for her student's education. Not bad for one parent with an idea.

In the early grades, most teachers welcome volunteers who can afford a half hour to read, to lead a discussion of homework or stay through a lunch period. Volunteers have a better view of what their student's school day is like.

Change has not always been welcome in our schools; it takes parents attending school sessions, speaking out, and asking concerned questions. Volunteer to help. Be there to become informed about the plans for your teen's years in school. We have to be sure our schools keep up.

> The result was a brightly painted, attractive building for her student's education. Not bad for one parent with an idea.

7. Taking school seriously

Keeping up on how your kids are doing at school takes effort, and many teens will resist their parents' prying questions. These procrastinators learned long ago that the more their parents know, the more likely they are to see the kids do the lessons.

Going over assignment books and through backpacks and folders with your student every week is a good idea. Even middle schoolers have long-term projects that need parent support just to stay on target.

Our kids have a lot of competition for the homework time. Mismanagement of time can make the biggest problem for a student more interested in TV and video games than schoolwork.

The Center for Disease Control reports that 38 percent of adolescents in grades nine through 12 watch more than three hours of television during the average school day. Only sleeping gets a larger amount of leisure time. Scheduling homework time into this routine will take some planning. Here's a place where a regular daily homework time can make homework a habit and give parents an opportunity to check their student's progress.

Often our kids will argue that since their grades are OK, no extra effort on schoolwork is needed. But we parents suspect that the grades exaggerate the

> College professors seem to have caved in almost entirely. C's now represent only 4 to 10 percent of college grades, D's and F's, 2 percent of all grades.

learning being accomplished. Grade inflation worries us because we think it shows that the kids are not required to learn as much as they could. They will slip by, knowing very little, but believing they can make it anyway.

Then comes graduation, and success after that will depend on the acquired knowledge and skills.

Grade inflation can result in a subtle attitude change. A teenager may come to believe in miracle grades produced by low standards instead of high accomplishment. If he's motivated to meet higher standards, he may come to believe in his own effort and develop an interest in the studies for their own sake. Then he will take pride in learning as well as grades and tests.

I have the feeling that grade inflation has not invaded grade schools and middle schools as much as it has high schools and colleges. College professors seem to have caved in almost entirely. C's now represent only 4 to 10 percent of college grades, D's and F's, 2 percent of all grades. Any college teacher will guess that most of those went to students who missed a lot of classes or never found the classroom at all. What is going on? Do we need another federal program titled, "No college student left behind?"

I was surprised to find that students don't drop out because they "flunk out." Of course they don't, if you give no flunking grades. Yet these teenage drop-outs slip into bad habits—working dead-end jobs, preoccupied with entertainment and relying on alcohol (or worse) for "fun."

Volunteer at your local schools to learn first hand what is being taught and what is being learned. Your interest and help will encourage the teachers and send a good message to your own students that you take their learning seriously.

CHAPTER 21

Building character

With all the stories of violence and general rowdyism of our young people in and out of school, you might wonder what happened to character building? For a definition, most of us would include honesty, reliability, respect and consideration of others. Some would add a sense of fairness, loyalty and citizenship.

1. How do you pass along character?

Just how to teach the specifics of character in a school or even a family is often a point of debate. Preaching doesn't seem to do it, and demanding doesn't work out well either. The kids seem to do best at copying their parents. In the long run, the model set before them leaves the most lasting impression, but television, videos and movies can all be used as starting points for discussions about what is right and wrong, good and bad.

These discussions could range from general philosophies of life to specific behaviors such as the "S.A.D." behaviors of sex, alcohol, and drugs. Parents will shape most of a child's character by sending answers about: What is expected? What is acceptable? What will make us proud? and asking questions ranging from, "What did you do last night?" to "What will make you happy?"

One mother recently wrote to say, "After a day out of school for not 'feeling well,' my son admitted he had exaggerated his 'illness' in order to stay home. I

> **The kids seem to do best at copying their parents.**

insisted on no TV or other entertainment for the next week, only homework to catch up. Later when I took sick leave as a 'mental health day' from work, my son, always alert to catch my mistakes, said, 'So it's OK for you but not for me.' Now what do I say?"

He did come forward to say he wasn't really sick. But Mom needs to point out the differences between missing work when a number of sick days are allowed and missing school when no specific sick days are allowed. Mom is on thin ice here but the discussion of what shows good character will be a productive one.

The standards set by parents to teach values such as honesty and respect for others will always be more perfect than the teenager trying to measure up to them or the parent trying to hold to them.

Excessive criticism and fault-finding will not build character. Your example, praise for progress, and respect when your teenager makes tough but right decisions are your best and most effective influences.

2. The subject that never came up

Questions of character will have to come up in order for these topics to be discussed. Who will start it off? Who will call a halt to the hectic family schedule and provide time and attention to allow a teenager to stop and consider the answers to questions of character?

A dog story. My howling beagle hound, Symphony, loved to chase rabbits, but she developed the character to stop and consider the task. She didn't just burrow through the weeds, tracking. Every 50 feet or so, she would stop and spring straight up above the weeds, her hound ears flaring like wings, spot her target, and land with her direction corrected.

I don't know where she learned the "pop up and take a look around" strategy. She didn't get to see other dogs trying their paw at the chase and she never talked things over with her parents. She just learned she had better get her head above the daily weeds now and then so she could know where she was going and what she was chasing.

Most dog owners are saddened, I suppose, to realize that their dog only learns the value of a few things and gets no answers to life's questions. The best Symphony could manage was an occasional flying leap for a better view.

If Symphony had been a child, she could have asked questions and could have learned about other goals and other directions. Kids learn the most from forming their questions and talking through their answers and yours. They will also watch others and develop their own opinions and values.

A teenager can miss out on learning life's options if competition for the family air-time doesn't make way for questions. The omission can produce other casualties in child-rearing—eroded values, and missed opportunities as well as stunted character development.

Good habits, routines, and attitudes cannot be established in sound bites. The media will have its influence, telling, but never listening, and always in a hurry to stay on schedule. Parents hold an advantage over the media here, if only they are willing to take it, because they can listen. They can allow the moments that will help their teenager develop good answers to questions of character.

Most of us feel a little uncomfortable posing the hard questions of honesty and character. But the question need not have a single answer or even a single answer that a parent should advocate. The main message here is that character questions are important even if the answer will always be debatable due to circumstances, timing, and who was involved.

In a court case awhile back, a judge asked a teen accused of mugging, "What did your parents teach you about treating others with respect?"

The teen said, "I don't think the subject ever came up."

> The media will have its influence, telling, but never listening, and always in a hurry to stay on schedule. Parents hold an advantage over the media here.

3. It's easier to lead a camel than to push him

Your third grade teacher's attitude will still be remembered at your 30th class reunion even though most of her lessons will have been forgotten. We'll retain the parts of her lessons that are still useful, but how she taught it and how we learned will stick and become a part of how we view ourselves and our successes.

We also absorb a lot of our own disposition from our parents and their philosophy of life. Even though we are sketchy on details of family moments, the impact of our parent's example is a major part of who we are. From teachers, parents and many others, we collect our experience and mold our character. The adults in our childhood and our teenage years become a permanent part of our makeup.

Although discipline is necessary when mistakes can't be tolerated, most child psychologists believe that 80 percent of a child's character grows from the example set by his parents. Schoolteachers at the first fall PTA often enjoy a game of matching parents to students. They use physical characteristics, but they also look for little mannerisms and parental attitudes to help them accurately play the matching game of who's who.

We sometimes hear parents tell their teenager, "Do as I say, not as I do." This attitude only provides both parent and teen with an excuse to avoid trying harder.

So when Brian was in trouble for fighting at school and did the same at home, his mother wrote to me for help. My first thought was that someone was showing him a bad example. I learned that Brian's dad wanted him to be tough and stand up for himself. Unfortunately, teenagers always seem to take our example further than we intended. So without the balance of the years of experience his father had, Brian took his dad's guidance about "courage" too far and was becoming a bully. Luckily for Brian and his future, his father took advice from Brian's teachers, changed his message somewhat and joined in coaching Brian's football team where he could be a more frequent help in molding Brian's social habits.

Brian's mother wrote recently and said Brian was still aggressive, but he had taken on his dad's habit of pumping up the other players when his team was behind.

Changes at school have been harder. Talks about confrontations at school have helped Brian try other ways to handle problems. He surprised his dad this fall by saying, "When Mike started bugging me again, I did what you do at football practice sometimes and asked him if he would like to try playing wide receiver if I threw him a few passes. At first the idea seemed to confuse him but then he said yes. He quit bugging me for a while."

We sometimes hear parents tell their teenager, "Do as I say, not as I do." This attitude only provides both parent and teen with an excuse to avoid trying.

During every moment you spend with your teen you are on stage. Your example plays the most important role in your teenager's growing up. Remember this old Arab saying: "It's easier to lead a camel than to push him."

4. Deflating peer pressure

Confidence and self-respect are the keys to resisting peer pressure. The test usually comes when parents are not around to provide a model, support, or direction.

Grandma's influence. "The kids wanted me to go with them to hang out in the mall today. They go around and laugh at people they think are weird," Jim said.

"You didn't go?" Mom said.

"Nah, it's dumb to go over there just to make a fool of yourself. I mean, what if Grandma saw me?"

Grandma has evidently let it be known that she thinks a lot of Jim and has high expectations. And Grandma listens and hears about what Jim has to say about the temptations of peers, without expressing a great deal of opinion.

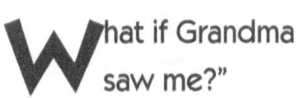

She supports his confidence in his own opinions. She takes time. She listens and encourages Jim's good attitudes. Without those positive experiences, it would be easier for Jim to say, "Who cares? I might as well goof off." He knows who cares.

With a poor perception of oneself, one "might as well"—hang out at the mall, eat junk food, and try out other risky behaviors. The National Academy of Sciences report concerning adolescent pregnancy concluded that "self-perception, that is, the sense of what and who one is, can be, and wants to be, is at the heart of the teenagers' sexual decision-making."

The art of countering peer influence. Like a contagious flu bug that takes advantage of the susceptible, peer pressure is most effective when the defenses are down. The temptations coming up for a growing teenager—smoking, alcohol, casual sex, and other risky behaviors—will be resisted best by kids who have self-respect and think they have a lot to lose. Where will they get that idea?

Lisa: "I'm taking my art project in today, want to see?"

Dad: "Yes, It looks like you put in a lot of work."

Lisa: "Mostly stuff I did at school."

Dad: "Really good, Lisa. You have an eye for the right colors."

And then at school: "Lisa, let's go bug Debra about those dumb shoes."

"Naw, it always ends in a fight and then we get into trouble, and I'll miss my best class, art."

Confidence-building is a hard parental job. Too many compliments and they become ineffective and resented. Specifics, "Nice of you to ask Aunt Donna if she wanted more potatoes," are better than vague compliments, "You were good at dinner."

Giving compliments has to be done without too much fanfare. Parents are tempted to add embellishments when they get no reaction. Silence doesn't necessarily mean there was no effect, and additions risk embarrassment. Since compliments are hard to handle, they are best left to marinate on their own.

Parents can't know what talents of their teens will blossom or what abilities will give them the self-satisfaction that keeps them on the

> Since compliments are hard to handle, they are best left to marinate on their own.

right track. You just have to provide as much encouragement as you can. It keeps most doors open and provides the best resistance when the peer pressure is on.

5. Resistance to peer pressure and LMS

Remember that supervisor who was always negative, always critical, and never satisfied? The critical evaluation could make you feel like doing less. The frequent zingers could also convince you that you are of less value.

A low self-perception decreases the chance of taking risks on good opportunities. Here's an example by a teacher where self-perception is given a boost and schoolwork improved as a result:

"What are you going to do for your social science project, Robert?"

"I don't know."

"When I mentioned making a newspaper from Civil War times yesterday, I noticed you were interested. How about that?"

"I couldn't do that. Nobody would help, and anyway, I'm no good at writing." "You have good ideas in your writing; I think you could, and I have some notes on the war that might help. Look them over and add your own ideas. I'm sure you know best what stories the students would like to read about."

Robert looked at the notes. Later, he added some ideas and showed them to two other students. His friends suggested ideas and a group project was planned.

This conversation turned out well because of a teacher who listened, modeled a positive attitude, made concrete suggestions that began with an easy request so that an opportunity for supporting success was likely. Robert started with a low opinion of himself and his own pessimism almost overwhelmed even a desire to try the first step. But the teacher's positive attitude and habit of listening and encouraging others had an influence. Without the model and some encouragement Robert would have gained little from the opportunities that came up.

Usually Robert is shy and hesitant around others and has little to say. While the problem is not large, he shows little initiative at home and resists performing the simplest task. Teachers believe he could do better academically but it is hard for him to get started and difficult for him to keep going.

His sister, Betsy, on the other hand is an outgoing person with many friends. She is helpful around the house and involved in several activities at school. She's always in a good mood and ready to try the next challenge.

The judgment of good or poor self-perception comes from an observation of behaviors. We would not have trouble picking out the Roberts and the Betsys in any classroom. It will come out most obviously when the peer pressure starts to build up or a new task is presented. Students who think well of themselves are more likely to stick up for themselves and make an effort to succeed.

How is good self-perception maintained? First of all, parents and teachers should keep in mind that self-perception is a constantly changing characteristic. The experiences of the moment influence the self-perception of the moment. I have used the term self-perception instead of self-concept or self-esteem because these other terms imply a permanent condition which is often not accurate when applied to young people. Self-perception is a changeable aspect of a teen, so the influence of a counselor, parent, or teacher can be surprisingly strong competition for peer pressure.

LMS (Listening, Modeling, and Supporting) can be powerful:

1. Listening time. There is no more impressive compliment than to find your listener taking time, looking at you, showing attention. With encouragement high and criticism low, the time spent will improve confidence.

2. Modeling. Dispositions of parent and teacher are the characteristics most often imitated. The tendency to express confidence in others and an optimistic view of projects creates a pleasant social environment, attracts others, and the positive person gets extra practice at social skills. The imitation creates a cycle and the disposition cycle can influence self-perception. Modeling a pleasant, positive disposition makes your home a nice place to live.

3. Support the successes and understand the rough spots. A teen's positive self-perception will come partly from knowing that there are others who feel and view things the way he or she does.

Recently I counseled 13-year-old Greg who said in many ways that he had a low opinion of himself. In our time together, Greg learned that many shared his difficulties and he was not alone. In a group session, he learned to express a liking for others instead of only worrying about being liked, and he practiced his own listening skills. Greg benefited from the experience and learned to apply his LMS lessons as well.

SKILL 5

◈

Coaching about time, money and happiness

CHAPTER 22
◆
Spending time

1. Teaching priorities

What is the top priority of most teenagers? Adults would put family, security and friends near the top, but most teenagers I know also assign high priorities to being liked, competent, and "cool."

As for the greatest fears, teens usually put fear of embarrassment, mistakes, and failure at the top of the list. Memories of our own teenage experiences include these same concerns—yearning to be liked and worried about embarrassment.

The next teen you encounter will probably have all these priorities and fears—all disguised or covered by an attitude that says everything is just fine. That teen needs you to confirm his or her competencies, likableness, and "coolness." Look for chances to ease the fear and bolster the confidence. Even though you may find plenty to fix and teach your teen, keep to the positive and resist the urge to work for perfection. Remember that criticisms, quick-fixes, and advice keep the focus on shortcomings. They press vulnerable buttons.

Admiration, compliments, and respect for them are always gratefully received and hit good buttons, even if your teen is too "cool" to acknowledge it. Encourage your teens to value themselves, and you will also help insulate them from the temptations to try dangerous "S.A.D." behaviors: sex, alcohol, and drugs.

> Memories of our own teenage experiences include these same concerns – yearning to be liked and worried about embarrassment.

2. Before we go on about the kids' time, have you prepared their future?

Many people think that a will is a waste of time until they are older because they have little money and could care less where it goes if they die unexpectedly. But there's more to consider than money.

The percentage of parents with minor children who have no will is nearly the same as the general population (74 percent). What would happen to your kids if you were suddenly gone? If one parent survives the other, the situation becomes less complicated, but for the growing population of single parents no will could be the worst thing you ever did to your kids.

Divorced parents with no will can create additional terrible problems for the children. A divorced mom may have full custody of her daughter, and Dad may have no interest. If mom dies with no provision in a will saying who should have custody over her daughter, a father who cares not at all could be assigned custody.

If you are divorced and don't have custody, you may think a will won't make a difference. But if you hope to leave money for your children's welfare or education you need a will to specify how the money is to be spent. Otherwise, your ex could spend your teen's inheritance as he or she wishes.

Examples are provided by Ellsworth T. Rundlett, an attorney who advises the useful website, www.gotawill.com. This site provides anyone who has web access with, "the ability to write his or her own will, in their own home, on their own computer, in their own timeframe and it's free."

Rundlett adds that parents often think that if their children are over 18 they don't need a will concerning custody. That's true, but if the parents suddenly die, an 18-year-old may not deal wisely with the money he inherits. A trust provision in a will could say how that money is to be managed and distributed to the "child."

Other websites on the net provide similar services. For example, www.nolo.com offers a Quicken software program called, "Willmaker." Freebusinessforms.com has a will kit with free software.

LegalZoom.com also offers a variety of legal services online. It was listed as "Useful site of the week" by U.S.A. Today. The site offers to prepare a personalized will at low cost.

> **If the parents suddenly die, an 18-year-old may not deal wisely with the money he inherits. A trust provision in a will could say how that money is to be managed and distributed to the "child."**

To protect the kids, start your will now.

3. Big projects and time management

Speaking of parent procrastination, the inability to consider long-term consequences is more typical of teenagers. What is happening now gets most of their attention. From homework assignments to brushing their teeth to healthy diets, kids tend to choose easy fun over short-term inconveniences. They ignore later results with magical thinking that says all will work out.

"When are you going to do your homework?"

"Later. I have plenty of time."

"Isn't your paper due tomorrow?"

"I'll have time before breakfast."

So it goes until at least their early twenties when they believe, "A couple of beers won't hurt my driving."

For the homework problem, one strategy is to encourage your balking student past the first step where procrastination is most likely to interfere.

"Write me a note about your plan for your English assignment, then you can go out." My mother used this angle to get me to put down my ideas for the paper. Usually, once I started this first step, I scribbled out most of the paper. If not, at least the next session was less aversive because I had a plan.

Most time-management problems are partly problems with priorities. If you allow TV time before homework time, you know the later part of the evening won't go well. Here's a place where Mom and Dad have to show some long-term foresight. Getting the priorities in the right order will go a long way toward a comfortable end to the evening.

One mother told me that on evenings hectic with homework she asked her teens, before dinner, to jot down on the refrigerator pad their hourly plans: 6 p.m.—relax, do what I want, set the table; 7 p.m.—math; 8 p.m.—watch my program; 9 p.m.—finish math then do my own stuff, read.

Sometimes the kids' dreams for the future are 20-20, "I want to be a doctor."

The shorter-term efforts required to get there are often missed, "So you really need to study that biology."

But the would-be doctor can be off the chart completely with, "Yeah, but first I'm gonna watch my programs."

This procrastinating can frustrate parents who easily preach what they have learned so well—the value of short-term efforts and practice. Now near middle age (from one side or the other), their own long-term goals may begin to wither and shrink (I just want to keep this job and pay the mortgage). Before the kids leave their own dream behind, parents can help their teenager stay on task.

Malea: "I'm already behind and we're still in September!"

Mom: "You've got to get organized."

Malea: "You sound like my teachers. There's just too much."

Mom: "Let's look at what you have to do."

Malea: "I don't wanna talk about it."

This familiar struggle can make parents want to weep. They know this is only round one of a whole year of panic projects and crisis deadlines.

The promotion to middle school or high school presents new demands. For students moving on, the days of one teacher are gone and assignments are increasing but the supervision is decreasing. The pressure is building to fit in study time, chore time, music lessons, dance, soccer, basketball, and social networking with all its technology..

What's a parent to do?

Faced with a large project, a student can become discouraged by the prospect of the whole job. Without a plan for each week this long view can bring on procrastination. Parents can help with this time management problem in four ways.

1. Get a weekly planner notebook and help your student develop a daily routine for what has to be done. Make sure there are breaks and flexible alternatives for conflicts and special events.

2. Make a place for study and homework. This should be free of TV and other distractions—including siblings.

3. Set aside at least one homework time during each week for Mom or Dad to give full attention to the homework schedule, the problems and the work itself. This is a good time for pointing out the usefulness of the subjects and also for highlighting your student's strengths and successes.

4. Limit all outside lessons, teams, Scouts, and sports to one or two. The pressure to join in also requires some selectivity in your teenager's schedule and in yours.

Scout and 4-H leaders and coaches of soccer, basketball, and ballet, good-hearted as they are, believe all children have time on their hands. They will tempt your son or daughter with a team shirt, or group pressure may take over ("Mom! All the kids are doing it!").

Without a limit, all the activities add up to four nights and three extra car pools as well as two extra shopping trips each week ("I need special shoes for soccer, ballet, bowling and tennis").

When the project takes more than one session. Another student temptation is to procrastinate starting schoolwork because the project cannot be done in a single effort. Kids have short-term views and a big project, paper or book that cannot be finished in the short term can be frustrating. Encourage your student to tell you about the first part of readings, not just after the end, or ask her to show you her progress at the halfway point.

We parents have the same problems and have learned that a weekly planning schedule that will get some of each project accomplished is the only way to avoid the procrastination, followed by the depression, followed by the panic.

If your student can develop a weekly schedule and have a quiet place to work, and you can keep up your weekly reviews, much of the panic and crisis deadlines can be avoided.

In fact, these time management skills may be more important than the work itself. Looking back on the school days, many parents believe it was the learning how to learn that has been the lasting benefit.

4. Summer games and looking ahead

Kids don't seem to be outside much these days. Their parents and grandparents remember long summer days of building secret hideouts, riding bikes, or running just for the heck of it. And there were always tennis balls, baseballs, and basketballs.

Now high tech is taking over. A computer more powerful than those on the Apollo Space Craft can be held in a teenager's hand. Unfortunately, it only offers games that are good for bad entertainment and usually lack any education.

In the 1950s, psychologist B.F. Skinner developed computer-like teaching machines as an answer to both entertainment needs and the problems in childhood education. The machines presented questions of gradually increasing difficulty and recorded the student's answers. In some programs, errors resulted in recycling to earlier questions to work out problems. Toys-R-Us still offers versions of these drills in arithmetic and language.

At first, Skinner's machines didn't work out well as either education or entertainment. The kids became bored with the questions and even when performance on the machines improved, the improvements didn't show up as well on schoolroom tests. Why not?

Feedback itself is not a durable reward and pressing buttons on a teaching machine or even those on a computer keyboard is not the same as working out an answer and expressing it in writing. You learn what you do, exactly what you do.

So here we are in the 2000s, and we have computers, called "games," that are mindless exercises the kids play when they're not watching TV. They're called "software" when they're intended to be educational.

Teaching machines, as Skinner called them, have been successful not as the answer to all education problems, but as an efficient addition to lessons and drills. Still the biggest factor in school success this fall will be a parent's attention, encouragement and example.

Some parent groups meet regularly to talk over their teens' situation at school and plan a sharing of after-school supervision. Parent groups (see page 329) can have healthy effects and relieve the loneliness a parent can feel if things start to go wrong. Parents also gain strength from these talks and from agreements to enforce standards for TV and computer time and other activities.

Remember that talk about drugs and other adventurous and dangerous activities are favorite topics for most healthy teenagers. They need this free conversation as a way of exploring these risky topics without actually taking a risk.

Many parents say their kids will occasionally exaggerate for effect. But those same parents will go into orbit when the conversation explores risky topics. Parents and other adults around your teen should not react too emotionally to just talk. Save dramatic reactions for a time when the concrete evidence concerning temptations and risky behaviors is in.

5. Gifts of Time

"You were always such a good kid," Lorien's mom said. "What motivated you?"

"Lots of people motivated me. Uncle Larry was always explaining his projects to me, and I felt a little more important because he took the time."

"And Aunt Eileen would take me to lunch now and then and ask how everything was going. She even took me to soccer when you couldn't and to the fair every summer."

The Aunt Eileens and Uncle Larrys in Lorien's life gave gifts of time. They added to Lorien's sense that other people cared about what she did and what she thought. And they gave her the benefit of the thoughts, ideas, and interest of other adults.

Lorien saved birthday cards that said, "Good for one Saturday lunch and a downtown outing with Aunt Eileen," or "Redeemable for one homework kibitz session with Uncle Larry." These were more memorable than money or another plastic gizmo.

Lorien's mom asked Eileen why she didn't take both teens on these outings and give Mom a little time off. Eileen said, "I'd be glad to do that another time, but this outing is for one-on-one with Lorien."

In another family I know, Uncle Dan took an old piece of leather and, with a soldering tool, he burned a treasure map in its worn surface. Then he asked his nephew, "You're always reading about treasure, Eric, what do you make of this?"

Ten-year-old Eric knew his uncle well and suspected that the treasure map was not an old one. But he had learned to go along with Uncle Dan, "Could be a mystery, I bet I can figure it out."

Together they went over the details of the map and Eric gradually figured out the map's hints and markers planted in the neighborhood by Uncle Dan. Following the map, they found a "treasure box" filled with "gems" (old costume jewelry) and an adventure book about treasures Eric had wanted for a long time.

Uncle Dan's effort to arrange clues that fit the map and led to concealed treasure sent a message to Eric that he was worth the consideration. It was another "gift of time" from the extended family to a boy in need of a reason to think that others, beyond his parents, cared.

Aunts and uncles giving time need to remember that kids may not always seem properly grateful. What may seem like a major effort to Aunt Eileen may be just a ride to McDonald's from Lorien's point of view. And Uncle Dan's efforts may seem to be only marks on old leather in Eric's view. Kids may be slow with gratitude and aunts and uncles will need to be patient. In the long term, those gifts will bring dividends.

Gifts of time help children value themselves as they realize others value them. Put a museum, zoo, or special lunch in your next birthday card to a teen in your greater family. Or give some time for no special reason, it will be even more appreciated—maybe on a school holiday Mom and Dad can't cover.

CHAPTER 23

Spending money

1. Teaching about money

Less than 15 percent of our children receive any school lessons about money management, yet they deal with more money than we ever saw in our childhood. Chicago's Teenage Research Unlimited estimates U.S. teenagers spend $175 billion each year without much thought. That's up 38 percent since 1997, and it's enough to bankroll the war.

Even preschoolers begin to form early attitudes about the value of money. My first parenting lesson on this topic came when my daughter asked for a candy bar at our local convenience store. I said yes and I knew she was forming a bad attitude when she picked up the candy and walked toward the door, leaving me to clean up the details. I called her back and asked her to find out how much her candy was. Then I gave her money to pay for it and asked her to count the change. She might as well start learning the economics of shopping and using her arithmetic as well.

Middle school children can be willing students on this subject because they are more inclined to listen than their high school brothers and sisters. Help your young teens create a budget and stick to it each month.

Share financial information with your children as you can. How does the stock market work? What is compound interest? Teach the basics of a checking account and debit and credit cards – including the bills they produce.

Teenagers can be particularly dependent and irresponsible about money. With no concept of living expenses, they may think their parents have a huge amount of money.

Having the kids watch and do arithmetic while you pay monthly bills is a good dose of reality. After high school, they will be bombarded with pre-approved credit card offers. They need to know more about the bills and the possible debt problems easy plastic spending can produce.

My daughter had a high school friend who decided to drop out and get married. Her boyfriend had a job at a fast food franchise. "He makes a lot of money," she said.

Another teenager I interviewed had been arrested for drunk driving. When I asked what insurance he had he said he didn't know. "How much does it cost?" I asked.

"I don't know, Mom said it's a lot." That makes two problems, he doesn't know and he doesn't pay. Don't ride with anyone who doesn't pay at least part of his own car expenses and insurance.

Encourage the kids to stay within their monthly budget. For example, how about matching any amount they deposit in a savings account? Give your children a chance to see savings grow instead of taking up bad habits and bad debts with plastic cards.

Chicago's Teenage Research Unlimited estimates U.S. teenagers spend $175 billion each year without much thought. That's up 38 percent since 1997, and it's enough to bankroll the war.

Whether you're teaching sports, school skills or money management the same principles apply – consistent encouragement, follow-through, patience and practice.

2. Home rules and money

A Mom e-mailed me and said, "My 15-year-old daughter is skipping class and drinking. I have a no-tolerance attitude for alcohol because of drinking problems in our family, and I have been fined over $400 in court because my daughter skipped school. What can I do?"

I asked who paid the $400? She said, "I did. I told you she's only 15."

"Did you pay all of it?" I asked. She said she did.

I didn't ask where the money for drinking came from, I'm sure it came from Mom or from friends with bad intentions. As they told us in the Nixon era, follow the money to find the culprit.

When you hear such a terrible-teen story you might wonder where the kids get the idea that school doesn't count and that expenses for bad habits don't count either.

How do the rules for 10-year-olds change, now that a few more years have gone by? In our next exchange of e-mails I asked Mom what her no-tolerance for drinking meant for her daughter. Mom said she sat her daughter down for a "good talking to." Maybe Mom told her to grow up but nothing is likely to change without specifics of what growing up means.

Now would be a good time for Mom's 15-year-old to learn about money management and responsibility. Yes, more freedom in curfews and entertainment, but no longer a teenager's free ride either. Yes, more decisions for herself about food and clothes, but she will have to give up magical thinking that says mommy will pick up the tab for all the mistakes. She's too young to decide about school or alcohol and a "good talking to" won't stop a budding alcohol habit if money is still no problem.

Give your teen the hard facts of growing up as well as the freedom and opportunities. A free ride for an emerging adult is too dangerous.

3. Money arguments

When Thanksgiving is over, the Christmas season immediately begins. If you think that's too early, you haven't visited the mall lately. The kids start their countdown before Thanksgiving, and their lists would break the federal reserve, if the feds had a reserve.

The smart kids have given up on Santa Claus. They focus on a target closer to home and many don't take a break between Christmases. They expect a year-around money supply.

One recent letter to my column was from a Mom who asked if she should "limit" her 13-year-old daughter's allowance, so far not limited, as a consequence of being caught drunk in the car of a friend arrested for DUI. Another Mom wondered if she should ask her daughter to pay part of her upcoming insurance (she's 16) if she continued to refuse to read the driver's training book. Her daughter said she didn't need to read any book in order to drive.

Too much money. Most of us parents realize that unlimited free money is not in the best interest of our teens. While most of us keep a firm hand on the spending, statistics show most parents do not have a stated allowance for their kids. My parents did and I was required to put some of it in a savings account every week. Most of it accumulated there, but I had a winning whine and managed to withdraw some for an aquarium, a bike, and eventually even a used car. My pocket money was limited.

Too much pocket money leads to trouble. It attracts the attention of greedy people, but worse than that, it starts bad habits. Teachers have noticed a trend to bad behavior related to money. For example, surveys of teachers, quoted by US News and World Report, show the changes in teacher worries from 1940 to 1990.

For 1940, the number one problem was talking out of turn, followed by chewing gum, making noise, running in the halls, cutting in line, dress-code violations, and number seven was littering.

By 1990, number one was drug abuse followed by alcohol abuse, pregnancy, suicide, rape, robbery, and number seven was assault instead of littering. The 1940 list is about daily behaviors; the 1990 list is about addictions, unrestrained impulses and money.

Not all of this is related to the money available to kids, but the top two, drugs and alcohol are, especially in families where parents don't keep an eye on the money flow.

Even teenage robbery and assault can be related to parents too willing to bail out their kids when they cause trouble. One shoplifting "child" I counseled said, "Mom and Dad will always help me out, what's your problem?"

One trend I see in these lists is that teachers have been burdened with responsibilities that belong to parents. Teachers with only 30 hours a week of a child's life cannot monitor and correct the bad habits extra money and lack of parental attention can cause.

> Too much pocket money leads to trouble. It attracts the attention of greedy people, but worse than that, it starts bad habits.

Parents, with the other 138 hours, need to take a hard look at their child's developing attitude toward money and be sure that spending habits include responsibility.

4. More about money matters

Yes, money does matter, and most preschoolers only beg for it when they think it's necessary, grade schoolers will hoard it but don't know the price of groceries—even the ice cream they like—and most teenage mall-shoppers cannot come close to guessing the balance on the card they are handing to yet another sales person.

With so little education, it is not surprising so many get money matters all wrong when they become adults.

Larry Winget teaches tough lessons on Big Spenders, a TV program about young adults who have gone off the deep end of debt. Spending hundreds more a month than they earn and shopping impulsively, they regularly beg their parents and friends to bail them out.

One big spender had talked Mom and Dad into a new equity loan on their house in order to pay off her maxed-out credit cards ($43,000) only to charge the balances right back up to max leaving no change in the situation except that her parents had another mortgage to pay.

I was prepared for this little lesson because I heard a mother at the food store ask her 12-year-old son, "Is the $3.39 cereal box size really a saving over the $2 size?" I could almost see smoke rising from his ears as he wrote numbers on the back of Mom's shopping list to divide the quantities written on the packages by the prices. Great question.

Share financial information with your children and teenagers as you can and teach the basics of a checking account and debit and credit cards – including the monthly statements and the bills they produce.

When one mom asked her son to sit down with her on bill-paying day he said, "Mom, I don't want to know about that, it'll just stress me out." Yes, but it's a stress we all need to learn to endure.

Having the kids watch and do arithmetic while you pay monthly bills is a good dose of reality. After high school, they will be bombarded with pre-approved credit card offers. They need to know more about the bills and the possible debt that easy plastic spending can produce.

Of course the young ones don't pay for clothes, food, etc. But as they grow, they need to know what things cost—before high school when reckless spending can get started. For middle schoolers, start with a simple budget about their allowance, then add the "off budget" items they don't pay for: clothes, food, etc.

CHAPTER 24

Pursuing happiness

Our kids are forever following the latest news about their celebrities and their millions. It's easy to conclude that success and money would surely lead to lifelong happiness. But as the later biographies come rolling out we learn success and money just didn't do it.

The great and near-great often trip over their own egos on their way to the good life or they dabble in drugs or alcohol, and then they can't give up these sticky habits.

1. I bet you can't make me happy.

Every child/teen has a view of what will make him happy. "Mom, I just have to have that toy! It was on TV, everybody's got one." For older ones, substitute cell phone for toy.

Every parent will recognize this routine. There's just one more thing and then...there's just one more thing.

The routine changes as the kids grow up. First it's toys and things, then quickly it's the money to buy the things. Even we adults believe at times that if we could just buy the right lottery ticket, everything would be fine.

This Grandpa has noticed that if you watch TV even a little, you would think that all you have to do to win a million dollars is guess the right answer on a TV quiz show.

A teenager may think: "If I could just win on that program, I could have everything and never have to go to school again."

Media stories about the winners give the false impression that winning a fortune is much more likely than being hit by lightning. This leads to Little League players who dream of fame and fortune and college football players who hope for big bucks with the pros—against all odds. Parents need to counter this misleading hype that implies that hard work and learning are only compromises for those unlucky enough to fail at the big score.

This might be a good time to set our teenage dreamers straight on the notion of quick money and long-term happiness. The notion that happiness is about what you "have" and not about what you "do" is a common confusion among teenagers.

Gambling is the next common step for a teenager turning 20 who is reluctant to leave his dreams beside life's road. If luck in sports didn't do it, maybe, he thinks, "I could win on the slots or at the races."

Speeches by politicians and sermons by ministers could take a page from preachers of the past who said gambling is wrong because it erodes the character, burdens the poor and diminishes the values and motivation of our children.

Without our wise advice from experience, many students will quit school or at least quit trying and become cynical while hoping, against all odds, to hit the jackpot later on. Others will just lose motivation not only for school but for any other hard work, such as getting along with other people.

Lottery tickets on the coffee table or taped to the refrigerator, misdirect a teenager's dreams of deserved success to notions that happiness is just luck.

But the faces at the Charles Town slots or the Las Vegas gambling (gaming is such a weasel word) tables are not the happy ones you see on TV. They are grim. They reflect the forlorn hope of making back losses, not the dream of easy riches.

> **P**arents need to counter this misleading hype that implies that hard work and learning are only compromises for those unlucky enough to fail at the big score.

When the first theory of happiness (winning enough "stuff" will do it) fails to produce results, a growing-up person may move on to: "If only Mr. (or Ms.) Right would come along, he (she) could make me happy."

Without our wise advice from experience, many students will quit school or at least quit trying and become cynical while hoping, against all odds, to hit a jackpot later on.

Grandpa or Grandma could point out from experience that even Mr. or Ms. Right was not perfect and often came up short on the "providing happiness" scale.

Perhaps we can then guide our children on to the third theory of happiness—that happiness is in the doing of life, not in collecting stuff. It comes from satisfaction with yourself and what you are doing. Parents can help by keeping the kids busy learning about and developing their own abilities.

A parent and teenager conversation that takes inventory of a teen's successes and strengths can help with the do-it-yourself job of happiness. "You really understand these computers. Your mom and I need you around just to keep us out of trouble!"

As a grandparent, my responsibility is to encourage my grandchild's interest in activities and goals that provide productivity and satisfaction in life.

We can all help by interpreting movies, news, and gambling ads, pointing out the value of self-respect, self-accomplishment, and self-improvement. Gambling hype should not be allowed to eclipse the role of self in the pursuit of happiness.

2. Picking a partner

Child-rearing lasts long into the 20s as every experienced parent knows. A concerned mother wrote to ask about her 20-year-old daughter's romance-turned-serious. She said, "My daughter's boyfriend is 26; she's only 20 and wants to marry him. Am I wrong to deny permission? I think she's too young and he's too old."

Twenty is young but not outrageous. Six years difference is a lot at this age, but I think other questions would help this would-be bride more.

For example, how does he treat her? The answer should be "wonderful" because this habit is not going to get better after the wedding.

Is he interested in her life, helpful and understanding or uninterested in her activities and sarcastic and critical?

How does he feel the domestic chores should be shared? Has he learned any? One woman told me she was so pleased when her husband did dishes the first week. After their honeymoon, she was disappointed because he never touched another dish.

What presumptions does he make of her abilities and her desires? Is he thinking of her choices as well as his plans for the future?

How does he talk about and treat women? How do his friends talk about women? Many young adults talk of "getting a wife" or "getting a man." A healthier attitude would be "joining a partner." What jokes are funny? We all know jokes reflect the more serious attitude, as well.

When a man of 26 proposes to a 20-year-old, what does he think of her future? Is her future important or does he only expect her to be there on the long winter nights? If that is the case, has he thought of what she would want during the day?

Contrary to the way it happens in the movies, we parents know that living happily ever after requires work. Will the person you choose try when disagreements come up or changes have to be made?

For example, what about moving decisions? If one spouse has a job opportunity far away, who should agree to leave family, friends, church and community behind? Will he try to separate her from family and friends?

How do the couple's views of neatness and cleanliness match? A view of his current situation is a good indicator of that.

What about other habits? Bad

> Is he interested in her life, helpful and understanding, or uninterested in her activities and sarcastic and critical?

habits not only show self-abuse, they also abuse others who must breathe their smoke, overlook their eating habits, both quality and quantity, nurse their illnesses and tolerate their mood changes.

If the answers here are good, maybe marrying a man six years your senior is better than marrying wrong. If the answers are discouraging, no age gap is right.

And one last question about habits: Are his verbal habits generally upbeat or negative? Does he or she look for credits more than she looks for blame? If grumpy criticism is her style and finding fault is easy, the hours can be long between compliments. As with children, "I love you" is not much without "I like you."

> If the answers here are good, maybe marrying a man six years your senior is better than marrying wrong.

3. Growing up mid-season

Mid-season, that is, the teenage years, begins at about age 10 in the United States. The hormones blossom early and puberty seems to come on overnight. The change is magnified by too much "adult" experience—second-hand, of course—from movies, TV talk shows, CD's, and peers with too much information and misinformation.

An overload of information about sex and drugs, and cynical attitudes about people, school, and the future are in abundance by the time a middle school student heads for high school.

The teenage years ending. The teenage stage ends when the young adults develop the self-confidence of a grown-up and show considerate and thoughtful behavior even when near their parents. Without some confidence-building from parents along the way, this adult stage can be delayed until our "teenager" passes 30!

How can parents hang on to a little sanity and still help their child-almost-adult survive the upcoming critical decade? The first step begins with an understanding that the greatest need of a teen is to be liked. Not just by peers, but by family also.

A parent can help by watching for chances to bolster confidence and avoiding a straight diet of advice, quick fixes, and a focus on shortcomings that hit vulnerable spots.

It's easy to forget the compliments because teens, like many of us, don't handle compliments well and feel an obligation to brush off any positive remark. So parents may think this kind of effort has no effect.

But parents who find the best in their teens instead of the faults establish confidence and self-esteem even though their teens may not show their appreciation until they are in their twenties—or later.

You may be getting tired of this theme of stressing the positive. But the danger is not that you will overdo it. The danger by far is that it will not be done enough. The attitude your teen comes to expect and the messages you hope to get across also make up the style and atmosphere of the family.

Fear of embarrassment keeps many teens from practicing new skills. When you were a teenager, did you allow yourself to try out all your abilities and risk the embarrassment in front of classmates?

The fear continues at home too. So while you are bolstering your teens' confidence, be careful to avoid embarrassing them.

"Practice what you want to become" is a good rule. If our practice attempts are ignored and the focus is on our mistakes, the effort to take a chance will become a risky business. Intimidation can produce a young person with nothing to do. Keep the pessimism low and the encouragement high.

The family goals are to raise a teen to become a competent adult, to have all the family members *enjoy* the family, and to remain close friends when the job is done. We look ahead to times when we can relate to our sons and daughters as equal adults, sympathizing with each other and supporting each other. Start the model now.

4. Happiness revisited

Most teenagers think they know what's going on out there in the real

> **The first step begins with understanding that the greatest need of a teen is to be liked. Not just by peers, but by family also.**

world from their electronic connections. TV and internet executives may not always get it right, but they know how to get the attention of the kids.

Real life doesn't measure up to the adventure, money and excitement on TV, so kids dream about what course corrections they should make now. Perhaps they should leave school and get a job. Perhaps there is a dream situation in music out in California. Maybe success as a sports star would open all the doors. Or is there more to learn in school?

When it comes to teaching morality, social skills and attitude toward life, our track record is spotty at best. Our record of teaching the practical side of life also falls short. When it comes to everyday life—working, making money and spending it, credit cards, interest rates, health care and mortgages—most kids get little help from parents or school, they know almost nothing and blunder into costly mistakes well into their 30s.

We don't want next May's graduates to face all these stresses now, but once they graduate, we will insist that they do.

About half of the student population will drop out before graduation. They are a more aggravated group, impatient with the system and anxious to find a job and get on with life.

Steve: "I'm going to get a job so I can buy the things I want."

Mom: "What do you want?"

Steve: "That cool cell phone and a few other things. And then I want to save for a car."

Mom: "So you're getting a job after school?"

Steve: "Mom. I want real money. I'm quitting school."

Steve needs a course in home budgets. If his school doesn't offer it then Mom or Dad should make room for it. They should include the cost of cell phones and computer connections but don't forget the essentials—food, rent, clothes, credit card rates, car payments and insurance.

Most kids don't know what their health care plan is much less what it costs. Interest rates on mortgages and credit cards are also not part of the plan when they are thinking about "making it on my own."

The circumstances of high school have changed. Four years of high school that sufficed in the 1950s no longer cover the events of our fast-paced world, but we cling to the notion that four years will do it—even with 50 years of new advances in every field. We even shorten the days of the senior year as if the kids have learned enough.

But they have not learned enough. That's why many parents still have 30-year-olds at home. Who will tell them about the many ways to a successful career before they pass up opportunities and shut doors by becoming too impatient and cutting education short? To live well in our society, education must be lifelong.

Now is the time to teach your kids the broad facts of life and happiness.

CHAPTER 25

◆

Now that high school is ending

1. When will it be over?

The father of a new baby was lamenting to me about another night of lost sleep and said, "It must be nice when they're 18 and no trouble any more."

I didn't have the heart to tell him about the teen-rearing challenges of the early and late 20s and 30s. They'll catch him on his blind side soon enough.

The temptation for kids to delay adulthood is in part an example of a self-delusional game of "If I don't learn it, I won't have to do it." I remember dodging my mom's attempts to teach me how to iron my own clothes thinking, "As soon as I learn it, I'll get the job." I thought it was in my interests to ignore the necessary training and goof off.

So the not-so-young-anymore will avoid calling the bank to get their account straight, looking for a job, gassing the car (even when it is your money) or remembering a family gathering—much less getting a card or gift.

Child-rearing seems to go on forever. Even parents of kids out on their own are surprised by a return visit of "just for a while and have you got a couple extra bucks?"

Parenting during the late teens and twenties may be a bigger job than the

We don't want next May's graduates to face all these stresses now, but once they graduate, we will insist that they do.

early years. Parents need to provide advice and a good example about management of time, money, habits and relationships.

Sometimes we mistakenly start the freedoms before the responsibilities, letting our kids use credit cards without paying the bills or giving them driving privileges without any costs.

In habits and relationships, training is mostly by example, opportunity to make mistakes and a lot of talking–not only with your teen but with other parents who might have information about what's going on that has slipped by you.

2. Use allowances wisely

Teenagers who are becoming capable of living on their own need practice at home. The first practice is needed in money management; if they make money they will want to spend it. The temptation is to push savings as a means of controlling (limiting) the teen's power. But the best learning will come from sharing the expenses so he learns the costs and the priorities.

The old, "While-you-live-in-this-house…" can make everyone feel more competitive. It sounds like you are threatening to divorce your teenager. Include a gradually growing request for sharing the financial aspects of the family, it is more likely to teach the habits needed and provide a measure of equality among family members.

Learning with less frequent pay-offs. For most adults, concrete rewards come after long intervals. Only occasionally does someone say how attractive your clothes or home furnishings are. But adults have learned to expect benefit sometime in the future. We are comfortable with the convenience of the order we maintain.

But young people are only starting to learn about the convenience and satisfaction that comes from taking responsibilities in the family, from preparing meals and helping with chores to taking care of their clothes and rooms. In the earlier teens, concrete rewards must come more frequently than for adults, and social praise will need to be given more obviously and more frequently.

As the end of high school approaches, a teen's role in the family should not stay the same as when he was ten. A system that allows payoffs for individual behaviors shouldn't be used to bribe teens to get work done, but his contribution to family routine and domestic necessities should be recognized and compensated. In this sense, family life is an economy in which there's an exchange for activities on the part of members and their compensation for those activities. Psychologists call this exchange system a token economy because in many early programs based on the concept, tokens were used to represent the payoff. The traditional idea of an allowance is one kind of token economy system, using money for tokens.

> As the end of high school approaches, a teen's role in the family should not stay the same as when he was ten.

But an allowance system usually doesn't have strict rules. In some families there may be no rules at all and allowance may be given freely every week. Consequently, a young teen's approach is to time his or her request for allowance according to the moods of his or her parents. Chores and other domestic activities are done only after nagging and coercion, and without much incentive from the allowance system. The young person may even feel a little degraded by the situation because it seems it is not his effort or worth that makes him deserving, just the momentary generosity of his parents.

As the weeks progress, tallies on the weekly allowance chart become more numerous and a teen starts saving for shopping. If he behaves badly, it's tempting to use fines or subtract from his allowance. If so, parents take away some of the confidence that the system will be reliable in the future. Fines undermine confidence in the economy by establishing a policy that says the government can make money worthless any time it wishes. Consider having the teen make amends or use other alternatives to punishments mentioned earlier, instead of using the allowance in a negative way.

Once the allowance is established, promotions can be added. The most important of these are promotions based on performance. This procedure allows for duties on the chart to be changed, improved, and modified as performance improves. If the teen performs well on some chores, she/he might be promoted to a better set of duties. Promotions are an important addition to any token economy; they represent improvements in expectation and respect from the parent for improved capabilities. If no promotions occur, then to some extent, that system fails to do its job, because the teens are not growing up to new responsibilities.

For example, one mother and I developed an allowance program providing an incentive for her son's chores. After the system was applied for several weeks, the son complained that some of the things he was required to do were "kid's stuff." Taking out wastebaskets and garbage sacks were particularly unpleasant tasks for him. Because of his attitude, a great deal of nagging, procrastination, and general unpleasantness was going on. A new procedure provided that if he successfully performed the task for fifteen straight days, without coercion from his mother, he would be promoted to a new task, washing the car. The chart would be changed and the job of removing wastebaskets would be given to his younger brother. The older son looked forward eagerly to this possible change of events because he liked doing anything with the car; the younger son welcomed an additional task because he had fewer opportunities than his brother to perform duties in the routine.

> The young person may even feel a little degraded by the situation because it seems it is not his effort or worth that makes him deserving, but the momentary generosity of his parents.

It might seem that all this concern for explicit rules about money or tokens and how the children get their share is too detailed and too mechanical. However, teens will be given their share of family income by some means or other, so they might as well learn habits they will need to know.

Will your teen's satisfaction from learning be enough? At times children are fascinated with learning new ideas and responsibilities. Love of learning may be a motivation, but many chores are drudgery and not inherently fascinating. Such chores can become satisfying when parents use concrete incentives as well as social approval to help a teen gain useful know-how and habits.

An exercise about being useful and becoming independent. Make a list of responsibilities adults should have and the ages when you believe these responsibilities should be assumed. Remember to get down to the specifics as in the sample below. Make your list long and complete. For example:

RESPONSIBILITY	AGE
Room picked up	4?
Bed making	6?
Selecting clothes to wear	7?
Bath frequency	8?
Cooking meals, with help in selecting and planning	9?
Homework with no parent nagging	10?
Bedtime	11?
Diet, what to eat of what is served, without nagging	11?
Saving and spending money with explanation	11?
Cooking meals without help in selecting foods, etc	12?
Saving and spending money no explanation necessary	12?
Buying clothes	12?
Doing all of his or her own laundry	12?
Deciding on music lessons	13?
Choosing summer camp, job, or other time-off activities	13?
No limit on evening hours:	
Before 10 with explanation	12?
Before 12 with explanation	16?
Limit only weekday hours	17?
Limit only for convenience of family members	18?
No explanation necessary	18?

3. Graduation, what's the big deal?

Is graduation an important event for your child or teenager? Some would say the high school diploma is the highlight of education, but I think the end of high school is too late for sending the message that school success is important. Show support while the work is still in progress.

Chicago only had two graduations when I was growing up – grade school and high school. These days almost every adult knows someone who is graduating from something, grade school, middle school, high school or college. Even many pre-schools have a ceremony.

Whether you are the parent or just one of the extended family, you should go. Not so that years later they will remember that you attended, as you remember who attended your own, but to provide the encouragement the kids need for the next step.

They may not thank you for the attention, they are so distracted. They may not even recognize their own feelings about it, "Don't worry about graduation. It's no big deal." But in their plans for celebration you can see that it is a big deal.

Even if it's "only grade school" or "only middle school," I would argue that your presence is all the more important. For almost half the students who make it all the way to high school graduation, it is the end of the effort—too late for more help.

I don't know how many parents, grandparents, aunts, and uncles provide extra incentive by attending grade school and middle school graduation. If such statistics were available, I bet that on the average, family attendance helped many students who would otherwise have dropped out.

The future options of your children shrink with each decision to study less, avoid hard subjects or to give up going beyond high school because high school was hard. Keep the encouragement up at grade school and middle school graduations.

It's tempting to relax your interest as the teens go through high school and beyond. But as the choices become more voluntary, you need to be even more supportive of what you know is the right direction. Magical thinking is a tempting trap for high school seniors especially if no one seems to care.

Without amazing luck most high school athletes have been left behind because the college scouts took the better student who was more likely to stay the course in college. The truth is, short-sighted kids make decisions that open or close long-term opportunities. They need these ceremonial moments to keep up their long-term direction while their focus is still wandering.

Graduation counts with teachers, too. The schools need the support also. Every teacher, principal, and political leader is aware, at least unconsciously, of the importance of parent attendance at the different school events. Make sure graduation keeps its priority over basketball and football in the minds of these leaders. Your teen's school, his next school, and your county system need to know you are concerned, and you expect fine schools and appreciate fine results.

> They need these ceremonial moments to keep up their long-term direction while their focus is wandering.

They need these ceremonial moments to keep up their long-term direction while their focus is still wandering.

CHAPTER 26

Planning college or something else

1. What do you want to do five years from Tuesday?

Asking a student, "What do you want to be?" may get a dreamy answer where, "What do you want to do?" may be more helpful. Better to be even more specific, "What would you want to do five years from Tuesday?"

To relieve the pressure, your student may snatch at an answer, even if he or she has little information about it. Parents can accidentally add to the pressure for a career answer when the fact is that any answer is probably temporary with much learning and training for other options still ahead.

Most of us parents had little information about the variety of opportunities. We took advantage of what came our way or we followed the expectations of our parents. Even today, most job and career information for young people comes from family and friends. The media often influences the selection as well (something magic will come along, look at what happens on TV!). Your average college freshman who thinks he knows all about the jobs out there can only name about 20 college majors out of the hundred or so available at most state schools.

Some churches and PTAs hold community potluck suppers where teens are invited to listen to adults describe their jobs and how they got them. Usually half a dozen adults volunteer to tell their stories and each is assigned

> Your average college freshman who thinks he knows all about the jobs out there can only name about 20 college majors out of the hundred or so available at most state schools.

to a table for one course of the supper. Students move to a different table for appetizers, salad, main course, and dessert. Other adults with similar occupations join a table-leader for the whole meal. With two or three adults and different students joining them for each course, a wider view of job possibilities can emerge.

It's often an eye opener to the kids when adults describe the variety of jobs they go off to every day and the work and training required. This can lead to realistic discoveries of what is attractive and what sounds like drudgery. Yet parents shouldn't expect dramatic announcements after such an evening supper. The experience may take years for its influence to appear.

When possible, take your son or daughter along for a day at work with you. It's an excellent way to stimulate stirring discussions about careers.

Good advice may sink in from career stories that are likely to be stories about changes. The stories will suggest good strategies such as: Spread out your options by expanding your education. Show up and take advantage of all training. Pick your jobs carefully—money isn't everything. Plan your summers to help you learn.

Most of us parents have a story of coincidence, timing, accident and convenience that steered us to our current job. But the outcome is too important for just selected stories of coincidence and hearsay from relatives and friends.

We all wonder about the possibilities left behind. The question deserves some parental planning to help your son or daughter explore the alternatives. It's a long way from graduation to retirement.

2. College visits this summer?

Whether your teen is a high school sophomore or junior, now is the time to excite his or her appetite for more learning after high school in a college or other training program.

Why go to college if you don't know what you want to do? Over 90 percent of college freshmen will change their intended major, and 50 percent will change at least twice. So don't put off college visits because no main field of study has popped up on the horizon. College can offer, first of all, a way to learn about yourself and how your own special talents fit the undiscovered possibilities.

A picture may be worth a thousand words, but a visit is worth a thousand pictures. Fifteen-year-olds don't have much foresight and you may think there's plenty of time, but your sophomore's summer and the next summer are the only chances to see colleges close up before applications are due.

Even if your high school student has no idea about his or her future, don't put off career-finding visits until next year.

Your daughter particularly needs your support for college and other visits. She is 50 percent more likely to finish college than her brother and she's in the majority of students in law school, medical school, and graduate school.

Your son or daughter needs first-hand information in order to get excited. Your budding college student should interrupt his or her computer game-time now to visit web sites of likely colleges. Collegesource.org is a good place to start collecting notes.

Have your student make up a chart to use for web visits as well as campus visits. In addition to school size, expenses, and distance, the chart should include a place for ratings of dorms, sports, majors, financial aid, competitiveness and size of classes. Over the next two years it will be easy to forget details.

Encourage your student to call ahead to set things up because visiting to "just look around" is likely to meet with a lot of closed offices. Suggest that your student call the college admissions office. He or she can simply tell them of his interest in scheduling a tour of the campus that includes a talk

> Your sophomore's summer and the next summer are the only chances to see colleges close up before applications are due.

Next spring, a second visit to the colleges your prospective college student has already visited is not unreasonable.

with an admissions person, a visit to a dorm, and a chance to speak to someone about financial aid programs.

Your student might also ask about meeting with students in interesting majors. If the admissions office can't help with that one, you or your teen may know someone you could look up during your visit.

Colleges are all different. The rumors and TV-news cover only football teams, basketball finals and homecoming queens. They only touch on fascinating research projects if they mention academics at all.

As with cars, you will want information from more sources than just the ones selling the product. Friends, teachers, and others who have "been there and done that" can be a big help. For a balanced view talk to several.

Next spring, a second visit to the colleges your prospective college student has already visited is not unreasonable. His or her top-rated school was probably one you visited at the very first. With some practice at visiting colleges this summer, your prospective freshman will probably have different questions she wishes she had asked in your first visits.

If your teenager will be a senior next year, what she does in the summer between her junior and senior year may make a critical difference on job or college applications next winter. My next door neighbor spent her summer working on a survey of bears in Wyoming before applying to major in biology at her top choice college that fall.

3. Financing College

Rumors and stories about college expenses can be a worrisome burden for both parents and their college-bound son or daughter. And while it is true that the tuition bills alone at some schools are over $25,000 a year, most are less and some are below $2,000. Actually, fewer than one percent of all students in the U.S. pay as much as $25,000.

Of course, tuition costs do not include living expenses, travel back and forth, books, etc. But on the other hand, they also leave out financial aid, scholarships, work-study programs (college-financed campus jobs), and grants.

Half of all high school graduates go on to college, and two-thirds of them receive some kind of financial aid from the college they select, the state, or federal programs. Close to six million students have some kind of help.

Many parents will suffer unnecessary expense at their son or daughter's college of choice ("Mom, it would be so neat to live in Boston!"), when a less expensive compromise for the first year or so would allow time for a career search and more growing up.

I would offer this advice to a student college bound. In the first stages of searching, include colleges that may seem out of your price range. The expenses may be less than you think. Also, the financial aid office of the college you select may be able to develop a package of grants, loans and scholarships that will bring the cost of even expensive schools down to an affordable level.

But also keep the more local and less expensive schools on your list. The smaller schools are not necessarily limiting; Shepherd College in West Virginia offers 70 programs of study.

If your college of choice seems too expensive, investigate the resources. Many financial programs are "need-based," meaning that your family income and expenses must be submitted to determine if you are eligible. But many others are non-need-based programs where your family finances have nothing to do with your eligibility.

Your local library or bookstore will have the latest reference books on college financing. New sources of information include: *Paterson's Get a Jump! The Financial Aid Answer Book; Money Management for College Students* by Larry Burkett ; *College Costs and Financial Aid Handbook* by The College Board and Financing College by Kiplinger Books. Also review *Barron's Complete College Financing Guide*, which walks you through the forms and questions with tips on how to answer them. Also check out *Barron's Complete College Financing Guide* by Marguerite Dennis. This book presents many of the financial and informational forms and walks you through the questions with tips on how to fill them out. Another useful book is *College Check Mate: Innovative Tuition Plans That Make You a Winner* by Ann Schimke, Octameron Associates, Alexandria, VA. This book provides a list of financial programs by colleges across America.

And look into the *College Costs and Financial Aid Handbook* by the College Entrance Examination Board, New York, which provides details of costs at individual schools and by programs. It also separates need-based and non-need-based programs. You may be surprised to find that many need-based programs have a liberal interpretation of financial need that would include your situation.

> Many parents will suffer unnecessary expense at their son or daughter's college of choice. ("Mom, it would be so neat to live in Boston!")

Ask your high school guidance counselor for other resources. And take advantage of the College Answering Service toll-free line 1-800-891-4599. Then explore the website, salliemae.com, and other sites for each of the schools on your list.

4. College applications

You would think that grades, test scores and class rank would just about cover the important points of a college application. But those numbers will only put the application in a file drawer of others with almost identical academic records. Past activities and recommendations as well as writing style on the application, can make it stand out.

With some exceptions, application deadlines occur in January and February. A good rule for a high school senior is: Make your selections by Thanksgiving and finish applications for next fall by Christmas.

The people reviewing your application will have a large pile of folders to go through and yours will probably be in the middle. Make the high points easy to find.

Word processors and online applications make the task easier, but a senior with her keyboard is tempted to keep her answers to herself. If parents and teachers review the application, they can help with editing and keeping the style consistent and attractive.

Requests for recommendations will need to be done this fall also. Your son or daughter should be clear in their request as to why they are asking a certain person. Perhaps that person would give his impression of the student's science project or comment on a community effort for which your student volunteered. Make sure they know you hope for their comments on special projects. Recommendations from persons unrelated to your student's academic or community activities are usually less helpful.

The Best College for You is a magazine that lists costs, admission standards, location, and other particulars of 1,220 colleges. *The Best 371 Colleges, 2010* by Princeton Review is another good reference. Be sure to get the latest editions of these and other sources in your library.

Next, bring up the internet information on colleges. One address to visit is http://www.collegenet.com. This website includes the chance to create an "Applyweb" account at the site to store your data for applications.

Your daughter particularly needs your support for college prep. Our future depends on her having an excellent education.

> Make your selections by Thanksgiving and finish applications for next fall by Christmas.

5. The market

Unfortunately, there are just enough basketball, soccer, and rock stars to keep the dream of success without work alive for millions of students. The temptation is to wait for magic to strike rather than make plans for training and work.

Most parents hope to see a clear direction in their high school graduate's career planning. But there are very few sons or daughters who take an unwavering track from high school to a life-long occupation. "What do you want to be when you grow up?" is often a hard question even for a 60-year-old.

Parents need to be especially supportive of students who don't select a college path. Their teens should know that an enjoyable and rewarding work life as well as job security will depend on additional training and lifelong learning. College, of course, is just one avenue to a great career, but it is one that pays. According to the U.S. Bureau of Labor Statistics, the unemployment rate for high school dropouts is twice as high as for high school graduates and four times higher than for persons with a bachelor's degree or higher. Annual salaries at age 25 average from less than $20,000 for high school graduates to over $30,000 for college graduates (2005 data).

High school graduates may put off the college decision for a year. The "year-gap," as counselors call it, may be worthwhile for the student who needs time to discover the motivation for specific training. Students can mature with a work experience and will get more from college as a result. Students who delay college should focus part of their effort on correcting shortcomings in their college applications. This could include selecting a job experience that will enhance their application or taking a part-time course load that will improve their college chances.

6. College is going to be a SNAP

Surveys show that poor decisions about work, night life, and money are the major causes for not carrying through on training. Poor attendance in classes remains the best predictor of dropping out of courses whether in college or other training programs.

So the best advice for your continuing student can be remembered by the letters in "SNAP." **The "S" stands for "Show up."** Comedian Woody Allen once said, "Eighty percent of life is just showing up.

The second letter is a reminder to take Notes on readings as well as in the class. Most students forget this handy tip and take very few notes even in class. They seem to think they can remember everything all semester just by listening. And most students think they can remember reading assignments from now to finals by just "reading it over." Not so. Class and reading notes will help your student keep track of progress and make review time easier also. I never had a student flunk who could show me reading and study notes.

The "A" in SNAP stands for "Active studying." Most students study by staring at books and papers, but study time can be put to better use by making lists of important people, ideas, and concepts that become a part of their course notes. They should always have their pen busy during study time. This practice makes for better learning that shows up in test grades. A note for every page is a good rule.

The last letter of SNAP stands for "Planning." For students just out of high school and often on their own for the first time, managing their time, without teacher or parent to tell them what to do and when to do it, can be a real challenge. Encourage your son or daughter to keep a weekly calendar of plans and priorities to see that the work gets done.

High school graduation may seem like a promise of new freedom, but it's also a time for getting the extra training to turn dreams into success. Parents can help by supplying the training tips of SNAP: Show up, take Notes, study Actively, and Plan your time.

7. Tricks to college

It seems odd that only ten percent of college dropouts have failing grades, yet 30 to 50 percent of freshmen never make it to a degree. Small colleges do a little better and large universities do a little worse.

The most common dropout factor is housing too far away from college, followed by bad habits, and bad time and money management.

1. Living far from campus means a long commute, parking problems and then a long drive to work. If college life is limited to a job, classes and a car that looks like a trashed office, then dropping the classes will be easy. Without the campus life of activities selected from dozens of on-campus groups, campus jobs, campus research and social life, you only have classes to quit.

2. Bad habits may come as a surprise dropout factor. You would think young college students would have the best record in maintaining their health but they rank near the bottom.

Once Mom and Dad are not around, kids are even more reckless with their diets, their exercise and their self-care. Skipping meals, sleep, or exercise makes getting sick more likely. Overdoses of salt, fat, sugar, and caffeine make them sleep poorly and feel tired and depressed.

Speaking of reckless, traffic accidents remain the biggest killer for this late teen group—even the ones in college. Drinking is the most common factor in these accidents.

Drinking also has an added danger for college women. Fifty percent of women sexually assaulted on campus have been drinking at the time—making themselves more vulnerable—at least in the eye of the predator. And women in the college-age-and-pregnant group report they had been drinking at the time of the dream-ending mistake.

3. Bad management of time and money is a college danger because it's just as easy to squander your time on entertainment, partying and computer games as on the more familiar time-robbers of drugs and alcohol.

Money is the other side of the management problem. A freshman's mailbox is filled with credit card offers that should be ignored. Ask your student to stay with a budget. Many families are in debt after their teen goes to college not because the college expenses were so high, but because of frivolous credit card rampages.

4. Proud parents can inadvertently encourage isolation from college activities by approving of too many hours at a part-time job that becomes a convenient distracter from important assignments. After parents get past the worry of their son or daughter getting into college, they start to worry about whether their student can stay the course and get through college.

One parent told me proudly, "Fred is wonderful. He's taking 18 credits, works 20 hours a week, and reads to the blind on Saturdays." Fred burned out and dropped out in his second year.

Another mother told me her son had skipped my psychology course "once or twice" because he didn't have time. Checking the record, I discovered he had attended only the first three classes and then cut the next two weeks. He said he had to work instead. It's time for a more honest conversation between Mom and her son.

How about an "off-to-college" shower? Have friends and relatives over for a send off to college. Each guest might bring a small gift representing their thoughts on, "When I was in college, I had a little…travel kit organizer for toiletries…a pack of erasable-ink pens…a

It's just as easy to squander your time on entertainment, partying and computer games as on the more familiar time-robbers of drugs and alcohol.

phone card. It was the best help." My sister-in-law gave my daughter a $10 roll of quarters for the laundry—not a four-year supply, but a very thoughtful gift.

This special send-off party lets your budding college student know others are supporting the effort. Invite all the relatives and friends. Ask each guest to write a little advice on their greeting card or in a guest book, "The best thing I did in school was…have a good breakfast, use my breaks from classes for study time, join the computer club, travel or bike club." Gifts can be small. It's the show of support and well wishes that will help keep your student on the right track.

8. Raising the next generation—up

The cockroach is a survivor as we all know. It reproduces and replicates itself in each new generation. It survives well but it is not improved, so the number of centuries it will continue is not a very interesting question.

The monkey takes more care of its offspring, but it does not raise them up. So again the number of generations of monkeys is only important to the monkeys.

Human beings rise above other animals when parents of one generation nurture and encourage the next generation to a standard even higher than their own. We should try to provide examples of a higher character and better (not necessarily more) productivity.

We parents stand close and directly in front of our teenagers nearly every day. What example will we set for the next generation of educators and parents?

How will we measure up as models and how will our teens measure up as parents?

How will we measure up as models and how will our teens measure up as parents?

The answer, of course, is in the time we have for them and the practice they are allowed. Our local paper described a 13-year-old boy's first successful hunting experience with his dad and grandfather; and our adult community education program includes Saturday classes on "Mom and Me - Crafts," a creative experience in the possibilities of parents and teens working together. These are only two small examples of parents getting close to their kids where experiences improve a teen's abilities and his or her character and self-respect.

All families can develop activities that include everyone. In one family I know, everyone played soccer and encouraged each other's successes on the field. In another, everyone volunteered to ring the bell for the Salvation Army at Christmas. The buzz of conversation about their different experiences with people created common ground as well as valuable social practice. Sports, arts, crafts, community activities—all are excellent training grounds for learning skills, self-respect, and how to get along with others.

How our country, our culture, and our children survive the new century depends on how well we do the child- and teen-rearing at home and at school. Possibly our kids will only carry our way of life a little further by merely drawing on the last life of the planet, browsing, as other species have always done, on what the planet has left to offer.

Or will our example lead them in a better direction with more care for our planet and a better prospect for happiness as the next turn of the century comes around?

Epilogue

Start a parent group to keep yourself up to date as your teenager grows

Child-rearing rapidly turns into adult-rearing as parents of teenagers face the paradox of keeping control while also giving it away.

Is it time for a change? That's the nagging question faced daily by the parents of fast-growing kids. Since challenges in parenting are often first-time experiences, even parents with many children are surprised at what the next one demands, and most of us realize we treated our later kids more liberally than the first one.

Other adults in your family or extended family can be a help or a hindrance when your teen develops adult abilities. We are in tough parenting times because of all the sources of information and influence our kids encounter. Relatives, spouses and even ex-spouses can add balance if they stay on your side.

Another great help when teen-rearing problems pile up can be a parent support group. Whether you are on your own or in a partnership, other parents can create a sounding board for your concerns and provide the assurance that others have problems similar to yours. Even a reluctant spouse will develop new ideas and attitudes from a discussion group.

As your son or daughter encounters the teenage years, support from other parents can strengthen your stand against heroes of violence in movies, parties with alcohol, and other perils and temptations coming up. A few calls or an announcement in a PTA or church newsletter will produce other parents who are willing to take an evening a month for a parent coffee.

It's not necessary to agree on rules and strategies or to stand together on common issues. The group can mainly provide a place to discuss what's going on and get a new perspective from someone else.

Agreement on parental strategies is <u>not</u> a requirement. The opportunity to think through common problems is what's important. People in your support group see your child less often than you do, so they may see gradual changes taking place between 10 and 20 that are easy to miss. We often think of our teenagers as about the same when changes are actually taking place every week and month! The parent support group can help a mom or dad who, when not recognizing growth, continue old limits on responsibilities and opportunities. Timely changes would strengthen their son or daughter's always-fragile self-worth.

Since school is such a large part of your teenager's life, parents with teens in the same school can always learn more about what's going on at school from each other in the discussion group.

At the first get-together of the group, you might want to discuss ground rules and come to an understanding, if not an agreement, on how the conversation should be limited. For example, you might agree that everything said in the group is confidential (no repeating stories back home).

Suggested topics to get things started might be: handling meal-time problems, balancing homework, TV, and computer entertainment, dealing with character problems such as lying, and getting the kids involved in civic, church or community activities. Another discussion might center around how each parent handles the sometimes conflicting roles of parent and friend.

Keep the group small enough to allow a single conversation among all the parents.

Teamwork is basic to football, basketball, and soccer, and it is just as important in parenting. **Your kids will probably grumble when you talk to other parents, but whether you are on your own or in a partnership, keeping up with other parents can be a great help.** They provide the assurance that others have problems similar to yours, and that can give you strength.

"Mom, Carter is having an all-nighter, can I go?"

"You mean a "sleep-over?""

"Yeah, a 'sleep-over,' whatever. Gosh, you're so old-fashioned!"

"Just your friends? What are you going to do?"

"We're going to watch a movie with, ah, some other people and then we're going to do an all-nighter."

Mom translates "other people" and says, "And how many are going to be there just for the movie?"

"I don't know, Mom, why are you being so picky?"

"Well, let me phone Carter's mom and then we'll see."

"Mom!"

Carter's mom is probably dealing with the same pressures and will welcome the chance to sort out the party ground rules and limits with another parent. Both parents will find the negotiations with their own sons easier knowing they are not alone.

Parents can lose influence just by neglecting their child's expanding areas of interest. A teen's complaint of "nothing to do" may mean it's time to make changes that will strengthen a son's self-worth. One fast way to alienate a member from a group (or family) is by not allowing him to contribute when he's ready!

Threatened by his perceived "worthlessness," he will cast around for a way to show off—what will he find? Even though he may complain, Mom or Dad's suggestions of chores give him a measure of self-respect and some skills he can use all his life.

These growing stages are good times to do parental teamwork. Experience counts and one short cut to experience comes through hearing the good advice of other parents.

It's easy to be cynical about the progress when you review the surveys: school dropout rates remain near 50 percent and over 40 percent of teens list pressure in school as their biggest worry. Twenty percent continue to be bullied in school and 4 percent have missed school because of it in the last 30 days.

The same percentages show up when teens are surveyed about thoughts of suicide, problems with drugs and alcohol, weapons at school, and many other problems.

As child-rearing becomes adult-rearing, parents can be enlightened by conversation with other experienced parents.

INDEX

A
active practice, advantages of, 240-1
addiction in teenagers, signs of, 185
Adele Faber, co-author of *Siblings without Rivalry*, 77
ADHD, 178, 213
adolescent fears, 30
Adolescent Health Study, 227
after-school programs, 176
age of responsibilities, 297
aggression, 229-32
alcohol addiction, 183-5
alcohol consumption
    and driving accidents, 54
    and pregnancy, 199
Alex gets unconditional positive regard, 42
Alex Rosen and his advanced abilities, 227
allergies, 144
all-stop method for tantrums, 85
allowances, 294-6
amends, 103
American Academy of Pediatrics, 154
American Diploma Project
    and poor schools reports, 252
American Family Res. Council, on bedroom TV, 204
American Heart Association annual meeting report of short-term diet effects, 138
American Heart Association's CPR course, 146
Amrein, Audrey, studies of school testing, 238
Amy and the 'no earrings' school rule, 75
Anorexia, 133
Anthony and his math problems, 27
Archives of Pediatrics and Adolescent Med., 136
artificial flavors and hyperactivity, 118
Ashley, 214
Aunt Eileen, 95
aunts and uncles chiming in, 98

B
B.F. Skinner, 274
bad behavior lists of, 1
bad habits, 130
bad language, 112, 192
bad movies, 151
Bar Mitzvah ceremony, 122
basic three, 131
beagle hound, Symphony, and her task, 258-9
bedtime, 138
bedwetting, 140
bee sting emergency, 144
behavioral smile, 110
Ben's waiting room behavior, 41
Betsy helps out at home, 264
bill of rights for parents, 65
birth circumstances and health of babies, 179
birth order and genetic factors, 78
biting, 91-2
blackmail, 67
blame
    placing the, 81
    and blaming habit, 234
Bluff-and-Huff game, 103
Bob and lying to hus teacher, 72
body language, 3
boredom, 221-2
boy and girl attitudes toward education, 20, 246
boy crisis, 248
Brad, 214
Brent at Dad's work, 49
Brian, fighting, 260
bulimia, 133
bullies, 229
bullies need help, 231
bully-proofing, 130
bullying, problems that lead to, 234
Bureau of Justice studies of crime and graduation, 121
business professionals, skills they look for, 226

C
caffeine intake, 171-2
Cambridge Center for Behavioral Studies, iii
camel, easier to lead than push, 260
Capital Gains, experimental program, 218
career planning, 307-8
Carlos' father and discipline style, 123-4
Catch 'em being good, 19
cautions in conversation with teens, 7
celebrities, happiness of, 285
Center for Disease Control reports of the
    "twin epidemics", 161
    and depression, 181
    and TV habits, 255
Center for Health statistics, 133
Center for Science in the Public Interest
    and study of food stuffs and behavior, 118
character, 257-8
character building, 50, 258-9

Character Counts, website of, 71
  and bully pledge, 232
Caroline, 62
Chicago's Teenage Research Unlimited teen spending, 279
Child and Family Welfare Association of Australia alcohol abuse study, 205
childhood depressions, 176
childhood obesity, 133
choking, 145
chores, 141-2
classroom habits and grades, 241
Clinton, Hilary, on school and careers, 248
Club Mom, 10
coach, qualities of, 212
coaching Brian's bullying, 260
Cody's mood changes, 89
Colorado Adoption Project study of language abilities, 78
competition with our children, 73
compliments
  and nature of, 265
  danger of withholding, 210
compliments, importance of, 51
compulsive behaviors, 166
computer companions and game addictions, 149
computer programs for schoolwork, 243
confidence-building, 265
confrontation as entertainment, 18
control, where you have it, 134
conversation as a competitive sport, 4
conversation strategies, 13
CPR (Cardio-Pulmonary Resuscitation), 146
creativity and confidence, 212
curfews, 54, 197

D

Dad, Dan still waiting for, 46
Dads overlook the good, 41
Dad's parenting style, 126
Dad's war stories, 47
Dajon's tantrums and diet, 117
Damon, 236
Darnell's comments on pollution, 30
dating, 197
December tantrums, 84
Department of Health and Human Services asked to emphasize diet, 118
depression, 89, 106, 180
diabetes and exercise, 80

diet, 119, 171
Diller, Lawrence H., Running on Ritalin, 178
disagreements between spouses, 126
discipline, parenting styles of, 123
disposition, 279
disrespect, reasons for, 83
divorced parents and wills, 270
Dodd, Christopher (D-Conn.)
  calls for restrictions, 53
dog training in the army, 211
Donna's fear of pollution. 30
Do-what-I-say-or-I'll-throw a fit, 68
drinking, and surveys of children, 227
drinking and driving, 186
driving, understanding of, 9
drugs, 171
  after school, 176
  and money, 177
drunk drivers and who pays, 280
Duncan's summer homework, 97
Dylan learning to be useful, 148

E

earrings and school rules, 75
Easy Child, 143
eating, 131-2
Ehrlich, Dr. Peter, Morgantown Hospital, 108
Eileen, 64
Eisenberg and research on mealtime effects, 135
Elaine Mazlish, co-author, *Siblings without Rivalry*, 77
embarrassing questions about sex, 28
emergency basics, 144
erasable-ink pen, 240
Eric, 95, 276
Erik and his ideas about girls, 120
escalation, danger of during tantrums, 85
essay tests, strategies for, 239
evil and terrorists as conversation topics, 33
exercise by teenagers, 160
expectations and gender differences, 118
extended family, 12
eye contact, 5

F

family circumstances and genetics, 78
Family discussions, 16
Family First Aid's report on teenage pregnancy, 203
family meals together, 134-5

family notes to sort out problems, 84
father's rating, 49
fear causes lying, 69
fear strategies, 32
fears, 30
federal labor statistics report on working parents, 93
Feingold, Benjamin, and study of hyperactive children, 118
fidgeting, 164
Fight Crime: Invest in Kids of California survey of juvenile crime, 176
fits, 83
food additives, 172
  in U.S. and Europe, 172
food allergies, 187
food intake study, Pediatricians Research Group, 159
food intolerances, 173
food serving, 134
friendship, 210

G

games, 58
games of sibling rivalry, 76
gay, thinking about being, 201
gender differences, 21, 121, 245
gender gap, 121
gender prejudice, 119
geniuses, 225
get tough punishment approach, 101
gifted in school, 225
good leader, importance of, 58
good questions, 241
good self-perception, 264
grade inflation, 256
graduation, 298
graduation rates of boys and girls, 21
Grandma and her influence, 261
Greg and homework behavior, 244, 265
ground rules for parental cooperation, 127
Guthrie and Horton, 9

H

happiness, 285
high school schedules
  and troublesome behaviors, 228-9
Hilary Clinton, reasons for her success, 248
Holford, Patrick, study of hyperactive children, 117

homework, 242-3
Huesmann studies of school-age children and TV, 155
human beings above other animals in parenting, 311
Hurley, Ben, and exercise and insulin sensitivity, 79
"hurry up" strategy, 63
hyperactive kids study, Institute of Child Health, 117
hyperlexia as opposite of dyslexia, 227

I

I gotcha!, 60
I'll bet you can't make me happy, 59, 90, 285
I'm not responsible, you are guilty for my mistakes, 60
incentives, 114
If you really loved me, you would serve me, 60
ignoring, 104
imitation, 106
  power of, 108
Imus and remarks about women, 120
influence and parents fading i., 215
inherited characteristics, 78
inside blame, 26

J

Jamar and my problem and your problem, 60
Japanese schools, 101
Jeff and parenting shortcuts, 19
  and allergies, 173
Jeffrey choking, 145
Jeremy, 74
Jerry Seinfeld and his replica boyhood bicycle, 162
Jim in games of sibling rivalry, 76
Joey, talking fast during request, 23
Jose and Dad's discipline, 126

K

Kaiser Family Foundation, 156
Karah and morning prorastination, 88
keeping a daily record of chores, 143
Kennedy, 51
Kevin's Mom abuse, 94
kindergarten, first day shock, 209

L

Lafcadio Hearn, journalist, 47
Larry's fear of meteors, 30
Laskowsk, Edward, and parent-child exercise, 80
laundry, college student caring for, 155
Levine, Dr. Mel, The Myth of Laziness, 249
Liking Clifton, 40
Liking Tyler, 39
liking your kids, 39
Linus-comforter, 165
Lisa and her art class, 262
listening, 10
LMS, listen, model, support, 263-4
logical consequence, 103
Lorien's time for relatives, 275
low self-perception and risk taking, 262
lying game, 69

M

magical thinking, 232, 271, 281
make amends, 103
Mark staying at friend's house, 8
Mark's nagging, 8
Marvin Boris, and diet before medications, 118
Mayo Clinic's Children's Health Center Tv Study, 162
McCoach, Betsy's Social Attitude Assesment Survey, 221
McMorris, Dr. Mark S., about allergies, 144
mealtime, 135
mealtime talk, 22. 136
media violence, 154
Mediacsope's National Television study, 157
medications, 171
mental habits, 232, -3
messages about alcolol, 184
middle school, 216
mistakes, 66
misunderstood defense, dangers of, 86
mixed blessings, 227
mixed messages, 11
modeling, 264
Mom abuse, 94
Allen's example, 95
Mom and Dad disagreeing, 62
money
    teaching about, 279
    home rules about, 280
money arguments, 281
money management, 282-4

monkeys and parental development, 311-12
moody child, 89
mopey child, 89
morning procrastination, 87
morning send-off, 44
Ms. Anderson, teacher handling bully, 230
multiple choice tests, 238-9
my problem is your problem, 60

N

nagging, 84
nagging for a loophole, 61
nagging games, 60
National Academy of Sciences report on pregnancies, 262
National Drug Use & Health reports, 109
National Institute of Alcohol Abuse study of death in teenagers, 205
National Institutes of Health reports
    allergic diseases, 171
    sports injuries, 191
National Safe Kids Campaign shows summer is most dangerous, 191
National Victims Center's study on abused women, 53
negative reinforcement, 113
negotiations of parenthood, 67
negotiating, 111
Newsweek survey of parental goals, 71
no-bullying rules, 230
Nutrition Action newsletter on health and exercise in children, 80

O

obesity in children and teens, 159
objective tests, strategies for, 238-9
one shots, 103
one shots as punishment, 102
one ups, 16
one-upmanship, 16
Oregon Counseling Organization list of depression synptoms, 181
outside blame, 26
overindulging is not loving, 91
oversimplification, 234

P

parent abuse, 90
sources of, 94

parent disagreements, 126
child's view, 95
parent power, 105
parent rights, list of, 66
parent support group, 313
parenting principles, 125
parenting shortcuts, 15
parenting styles, 124
parents efficiency mode, 18
parents help with time management, 271
partner, selection of, 287
paying attention, 213
peer pressure, 261-4
PG movies, 152
physical reactions, as signals in conversation, 1
piano practice and video games, 148
pizza experiment, 173
Pogo, 55
positive reinforcemnt, 113
power, parent use of, 86-8
    imitation of, 105
Power Struggle Mode, 86
practice, allowing p., 142
practice tests advantages of, 238-40
pregnancy, 198
    frequency of, 203
preschoolers and caffeine, 172
President Clinton on gun violence, 52
principles in parent games, 74, 125
priorities changing as the children grow, 75
    teaching priorities, 269
procrastination, 216
prompt decisions advantages of, 85
psychological leash, 42
PTA website, 254
Public Agenda, studies of parents and students, 109
punishment
    alternatives to, 102, 116
    modeling of, 51

R

reading errors in testing, 239
referees are fun, 59
reflective statements, 6
relatives role of, 95
response cost, 138
rewards, 112
    and bridery, 143
rhythmic habits, 163
risk-taker has to feel safe, 212

R-rated movies, 152
Rundlett, Ellsworth, gotawill.com, 270

S

SAD, seasonal affective syndrome, 175
S.A.D. behaviors, sex, alcohol and drugs, 183
safety imitation, 107
school absence, suggestions for handling, 220
school bus, dealing with trouble on, 102
school conference, making the most of, 250
school skills, 241
school volunteers, importance of, 22
schoolwork, 237
Seasonal Affective Syndrome, 175
second child and competition, 76
Seinfeld, Jerry and his bicycle, 162
self-perception, 263
self-respect, 263
separation shock, 209, 214
setting TV limits, 150
sex, 202
    talking about, 28
sex differences, 120
sexism, strange effects of, 122
sexual behavior and surveys of children, 245
sexually transmitted diseases, 201
shortcut parenting, 15
Siblings Without Rivalry
    about brothers getting along, 77
sleeping, 138-40
smoking, 188
son's threats, 113
Southern Regional Education Board school
    study, 20
spank-'em-don't-pay-'em attitude, 114
spoiled child, 112
sports fanatics, 167
spouses, 95
stages of happiness, 285-7
statistics about young drivers, 54
Steve
    in sibling rivalry, 76
    leaving school, 291
stubbornness, 85
study sessions
    approaches to, 242-7
supermarket incident, 107
Symphony, the dog, 258

T

table manners, 135
tantrums, 82
tattletales, 231
teacher who listened, 263-4
teacher's attitude, influence of, 240
teaching machines, 274
teen's biggest concern, 27
teenage crime peaks in the afternoon, 94
Teenage Pregnancy Prevention Month, 198
teenager bashing, 52
teenagers imitate, 108
teenagers taking things personally, 6
teens of alcoholics, 109
temptations, and bad habits, 271
tennis-game conversations, 18
terrorism in conversation, 35,114
test taking stratigies, 223-42
testing, testing, are you still my friend?, 75
tests, 237
time and its gifts, 275
time management, 271
time on computers and video games, 156
time out, 104
time poverty, 35
Todd's chair kicking, 163
tomatoes as behavior disruptor, 172
toys and happiness, 287
trainers, good army t., 211
Tremblay, Dr. Richard, about baby health, 179
tutors, students as, 250
TV
    and its effect on depression, 89
    and prime time, 70
    staying up too late for, 219
TV's view of sex, 28

U

Uncle Dan and his treasure map, 276
U. S. Department of Justice
    estimates of bullies effects, 245
U.S. Department of Agriculture study soft
    drink intakes, 171
U.S. Department of Agriculture's Center for
    Nutrition and study of teenagers' eating
    habits, 137
unconditional positive regard, 43
University of Minnesota Medical School study
    of family meals, 144

V

values, 258, 259
video game privacy, 153
violence in movies, 154
volunteer, parents should see school as, 224

W

Warner, John (R-Va.)
    calls for restrictions, 53
Warner, Judith
    of New York TImes coined "boy crisis",
    248
Washington Post, report on drivers, 54
what happens next?, 148
white rat in fidgeting experiment, 164
Winget, Larry, an lessons about money, 283
worries, 32
Wright, Dr. Gloria, about men who suffer, iv

Y

Yes, but.., game of, 61

Z

Zack, not going to school, 208
Zmuda, Allison, her suggestions for
    transforming schools, 222

www.ingramcontent.com/pod-product-compliance
Lightning Source LLC
LaVergne TN
LVHW091529060526
838200LV00036B/539